My Commonplace Book

MY
COMMONPLACE
BOOK

Mary Stocks

PETER DAVIES : LONDON

To my great grand-daughter Rebecca;
who, if she ever reads it, will think it
all rather odd.

© 1970 by Mary Stocks
First published 1970
Reprinted 1970 (twice), 1971

432 15750 6

*Permission has been given by George Allen
& Unwin Ltd to reproduce the personal letter
from the late Gilbert Murray to the late
Professor J. L. Stocks, appearing on page 104*

Reproduced and Printed in Great Britain by
Redwood Press Limited, Trowbridge & London

Contents

Contents

Illustrations

Prologue

SHOULD I, IN THE YEARS that remain to me, become notably delinquent, I shall only have myself to blame. No psychologically trained probation officer will be able to explain my anti-social behaviour by reference to parental dissension or domestic insecurity during early years. I enjoyed a very happy childhood in a secure home environment. My parents were devoted to one another and to me, and I was devoted to them. Since then I have suffered no major frustrations; nor was I ever crossed in love. The only man I wanted to marry wanted to marry me, and did. My opportunities have always exceeded my abilities, my good fortune has always exceeded my deserts. My eventual accession to the Peerage was due to personal publicity incidentally conferred on me late in life by the Light Programme of the B.B.C. Anything that I may have done for other people has been immeasurably exceeded by what other people, especially members of my own family, have done for me. The only experience that I would have liked but have not had, is the experience of growing old with my husband.

All this would suggest the emergence of an inexpressibly banal autobiography. There are, however, reasons why an uninteresting personality may be tempted by an importunate publisher to embark on such an enterprise. These are encounters with interesting people, participation in interesting events, and a favourable position from which to observe such events taking place. Such is my own operative temptation—at any rate the best I can think of. The events are not spectacular but their final outcome is, for they cover the evolution of British society from extreme class privilege to comparative equalitarian opportunity, and from Victorian convention to the "permissive society".

For observing these events I have two good qualifications. One is more than seven decades of stored memories. The other is a mind conditioned by educational advantages against a stimulating family background. In this last I was vastly more fortunate than the great mass of my less-privileged fellow-citizens, who happened to be born, as I was, in the year 1891, Queen Victoria being then on the throne and sovereign of a world-wide Empire at the zenith of its power.

6th February, 1970   MARY STOCKS

I

The Age of Security

I WAS BORN IN 1891, the eldest of three children of Roland Danvers Brinton, M.D., newly established as a single-handed general practitioner at 8 Queen's Gate Terrace. This practice was in South Kensington, a middle-class residential area of tall five-storey terrace houses in single-family occupation, built to reflect the class pattern of the eighties. Osbert Lancaster has classified its architecture as "Kensington Italianate". These houses were furnished with basements in which the servants lived and worked, and top storeys where they slept. There was a bell-pull on each side of our front door. One was marked "Visitors", the other "Servants". Today their place has been taken by rows of electric bells indicating multiple occupation. Our house boasted no telephone and was lit by gas.

Behind the terraces ran mewses containing stables for the horses and carriages of the more wealthy terrace dwellers, with living quarters for their coachmen. My father was not, however, a carriage owner. He visited his patients on foot assisted by hansom cabs. His work consisted almost entirely of home visits. He was, however, available to patients at 11 a.m. in his consulting room, the word "surgery" being applicable to a different class of practice. By eleven o'clock, therefore, the dining-room next door to the consulting room would have to be cleared for the few patients who might be required to wait. These were supplied with the *Morning Post*, *Punch*, and the *Navy List*. My father was at a loss to understand why any waiting patient should not find this last volume enthralling. He had himself wished to enter the Navy, but for various reasons had been constrained to follow his father's profession of medicine. He was therefore determined that his son should do what he himself would have liked to do. My younger brother, Ralph, thus became a naval cadet at the age of twelve. He was, however, a born artist, and it was not until after retirement from active service in the First World War, that he was able to embark on a career, beginning with architecture, which eventually brought him considerable fame as an art director of films. As things turned out the Navy was a fortunate choice because my brother belonged to the age group, which, driven by genuine patriotism, poured helter-skelter into the graveyard of the Western front at the call of Kitchener's army.

From the constraint imposed on my brother it must not be inferred that my father was either austere or autocratic. He was neither. He just could not imagine that any male person could prefer art to a naval command. Indeed his own aesthetic interests were limited. He loved Gilbert and Sullivan, "The Arcadians" and Tolstoy's *War and Peace*. When Bernard Shaw broke into our lives, he mistrusted the man as a socialist, a teetotaller, and a vegetarian, until he was taken to see *The Doctor's Dilemma* which fascinated him. All the medical types with which my father was familiar came gloriously to life, he could put a name to all of them. How *could* Shaw have known so unerringly what they were like? I don't know whether my father ever considered that question. I have certainly never been able to answer it.

But to return to the nineties: In such a house, in such a neighbourhood, my first memories came alive. At that time I became conscious of parents who welcomed my appearance—as later they welcomed that of my brother Ralph and my much younger and very beautiful sister Joanna. In fact, including Sarah our nurse, I was conscious of having three devoted parents.

Life was orderly, comfortable, and supremely secure. It was lived on a cushion of domestic service. Ours consisted of a parlourmaid, housemaid, and cook. If any of these left us, others were readily available at moderate wages. How moderate, may be gathered from the fact that when a bachelor uncle who was also a medical practitioner, engaged a cook at £30 a year, the act was regarded by his family as a bachelor extravagance. A cook of that quality would, they said, let him in for more expense by demanding a kitchenmaid. Sarah, thank heaven, never left us (see Plate 2*b*) except to minister to a later generation of the family. Her own family became distant figures to her. Our family was her family. On this domestic harmony outside events impinged scarcely at all.

I think my first memory was of being carried upstairs by my father—my second, of being carried, perched on his shoulder, into Queen's Gate to see a crowd dispersing after the opening by Queen Victoria of the Imperial Institute. And cursed be those who seventy years later demolished it to make more room for the banausic sprawl of the Imperial College of Science and Technology.

I can more vividly remember rising early, in 1897, to get to a cousin's house in Grosvenor Place before crowds blocked Knightsbridge, in order to see the procession which took Queen Victoria to her Diamond Jubilee celebration in St Paul's Cathedral. I well remember the long wait on the balcony of No. 3 Grosvenor Place before that procession emerged from Constitution Arch.

Even more vividly can I remember the Battle of Omdurman— all the more so, because my father's handsome and dashing first cousin, Jack Brinton, participated, or so I was told and I believe he really did, in the charge of the 21st Lancers, which was a feature of that famous engagement. Pasted on our nursery wall was a picture of it: the thin red line of British infantry in the foreground, firing steadily at a seething mob of scimitar-waving Sudanese natives in the centre, while the 21st Lancers charged in a cloud of dust on the extreme right.

The curious thing is that my next conscious memory of external events, as consciousness became more articulate, raised the same imperial problem, but sowed a seed of doubt. At the age of eight I was scarcely aware of the events which precipitated the Boer War, or of the manner in which it was waged. But for some reason I announced that I was pro-Boer. Perhaps the consciousness that a great imperial power was in action against troops of un-uniformed farmers defending their homesteads, was associated in my mind with a David–Goliath confrontation. Perhaps it represented the first stirrings of a lifelong addiction to the support of minorities. But there it was. Nor did it prevent me from contemplating with pleasure the row of coloured portraits of British Generals, beginning with Sir Redvers Buller and ending with the appealing figure of Lord Roberts, affectionately known as "Bobs", which supplanted Omdurman on our nursery walls. Nor did it prevent me from accepting the public image of President Kruger as an old savage who had been known (or so it was said) to cure an attack of toothache by gouging out the offending tooth with his own jack-knife. This was regarded as a thing that no civilized man should do. Today we should regard it as a commendable and courageous response to the injunction Do it Yourself.

But such outside events were passing shadows. The centre of existence was 8 Queen's Gate Terrace; its life conditioned by a sufficient income from a medical general practice plus incidental benefactions from a rich maternal grandfather. Its clientele would look meagre compared with the list of a National Health Service practitioner today. But it was a paying clientele, and in so far as it was not, the fees of those who could pay enabled my father to extend much free service to those who could not. This he did with great liberality because he was that sort of man. Night calls were infrequent compared with the demands of a working-class National Health Service practice today, so that deputising services were unnecessary. Nor would my father have been content to consign his patients to any doctor not of his own choosing. For an annual holiday a trusted locum would be mobilized, or the co-operation of one or other of the competing but friendly and trusted well-known colleagues within easy reach.

Under such leisurely conditions doctor–patient relationships could develop happily, and in fact they did. One rich, kind, unoccupied lonely maiden lady called Miss Nix, living in Belgravia, adopted us as a family and we regarded her as part of ours. Among other benefits for which I owe her a debt of gratitude was an annual excursion to the Drury Lane pantomime, which left an undying memory of Dan Leno in a variety of female parts. There were also many drives round Hyde Park in her Victoria, with two horses to pull us and two uniformed and cockaded men on the box: one to drive and one to open and shut the carriage door and adjust the carriage rug. It was on these drives that one became familiar with the little black crouching figure of the Queen, indulging in the same open-air exercise but with two men standing at the back of her carriage in addition to the two on the box. But if Miss Nix added adventure to our lives I think that we added adventure to hers by introducing her to the pleasure of public transport. She had never been in a bus. Up on to the top of a bus we persuaded her to go, where from the front seat she could look down on the straining horses or even talk to the driver on his high driving seat,

[4]

whose head was so near those of his passengers. Miss Nix was enchanted with the experience, though I do not think that she ever indulged in it alone.

In the period of which I am writing individual attention by a family doctor was enjoyed only by that minority of the population able to pay for it. And the sick members of that minority would be cherished in their own homes by resident trained nurses, with their own doctor in continuous contact with the patient and a consultant within call. It was thus that my brother was operated on for appendicitis.

Meanwhile, the great mass of the population received no such attention. They depended either on voluntary hospital out-patient departments, or, with luck, a free bed in a general ward where incidentally they provided valuable teaching material, or the workhouse infirmary—or alternatively on the ministrations of such practitioners as Bernard Shaw's Dr Schutzmacher, whose surgery door bore the inscription "Advice and medicine sixpence. Cure guaranteed."

Even in birth, rich and poor were divided. For the rich, a doctor and resident "monthly nurse" and a comforting whiff of chloroform at the last stage. For the poor, a doubtfully trained midwife and the unmitigated pains of childbirth.

Despite the advances we have made since that time, if we intend to generate a comparable standard of medical care and responsible doctor–patient relationship for the entire population of Great Britain, rich and poor, we must reconsider the present conditions under which general practitioners work. Early memories of the advantages to the few of a class-conditioned system of medical care have made it easier to appreciate the achievements of the new order which are considerable, while recognizing its defects which are lamentable, and dreaming of its potentialities, which are encouraging.

There was, it then seemed, another race of human beings with different forms of behaviour, different needs, different habits of speech, different kinds of clothes. They were the working classes, many of whom were poor and must be helped. They did not visit foreign countries except for permanent settlement as emigrants or temporarily as personal servants with their masters and mistresses. Miss Nix, for example, when she went to San Remo to visit relatives, would take her maid, James, who was a friend to all of us but would not have dreamed of addressing us by our Christian names. It is noteworthy that when, about this time Miss Beatrice Potter, later to become Mrs Sidney Webb, wished to stay with a working-class family in order to study their way of life, she had to adopt an elaborate disguise in the manner of an infidel European explorer sojourning among Eastern nomads in order to observe their habits and customs.

From the ranks of this lesser breed came the friendly domestic servants who cooked and served one's food, made one's bed, emptied one's slops and cleaned one's rooms. From their ranks, from a tailor's shop in Bury St Edmunds, came the beloved Sarah who put me to bed, got me up, brushed my hair, mended my stockings and saw to it that I washed my neck thoroughly every evening in the bathroom. Some of these things in due course I learned to do for myself, but never until well on in adult life was I required to make my bed, cook my food, or clean my room. Yet in spite of intimate and friendly relationships which developed with children's nurses, and indeed with other domestic employees, that "other nation", to use Disraeli's phrase, remained another nation, the whole pattern of its life being quite different.

It was not only domestically and medically that the pattern was quite different for that "other nation". Educationally it was quite different. For us, the accepted conventional pattern for boys was a preparatory boarding school from the age of eight or nine; after that (apart from naval cadets) a public school leading to Oxford or Cambridge, or a professional training leading to a salaried job capable of supporting a family able to enjoy the same educational advantages. Thus did our educational system (or absence of system) perpetuate inequality of income.

For the wage-earners, there was rarely any opportunity for secondary or higher education, though the Balfour Education Act of 1902 opened new vistas. There were the Board Schools, at long last free and compulsory, to the age of thirteen, and thereafter wage-earning or apprenticeship. The educational class barrier could indeed be climbed by exceptional boys with exceptional good fortune. Sir Ernest Barker climbed it with the aid of grammar school and university scholarships. Or its initial frustrations could be made good later by individual enterprise in a competitive free-price economy. "Since time whereof no memory is"—certainly since the Industrial Revolution of the eighteenth century—exceptional individuals have been able to amass fortunes, establish businesses and found dynasties, starting from the gutter, the bench, or the sixth standard of a board school. But when they jumped the barrier in this way they did not kick it down, they landed on the other side and on the other side they and their offspring remained.

There was, for instance, my father's uncle by marriage: W. H. Smith. According to W. S. Gilbert he started life as an office boy and "polished up the handle of the big front door" so "carefullee" as to become eventually "Ruler of the Queen's Navee". His life story as recorded in *H.M.S. Pinafore* represents operatic licence and does him less than justice; but it is certain that Great-Uncle Henry achieved considerable wealth and Cabinet rank from small beginnings, and left behind him a dynasty of Viscounts as well as a notable chain of retail shops. And other contemporaries achieved comparable eminence from even smaller beginnings. It could be done; but by so few as not to disturb the structure of the social system through which they had climbed against the obstacles which discouraged and hampered the many.

Such was the pattern of education for boys of the privileged class into which I was born. For girls it was a different pattern. It was not considered necessary to exile them to boarding schools, though some were indeed so exiled. My mother, for example, went to a boarding school at Fontainebleau which has been immortalized in a very remarkable novel called *Olivia* by Olivia.* It was in fact written by Madame Bussy, a member of the Strachey family, who in old age recalled her memory of the school. Her story takes dramatic liberties with the facts, but the atmosphere of the school, its personalities and their tensions, are as my mother and others of her contemporaries remember them. It was the kind of school to which Chamberlains, Roosevelts, and Stracheys sent their daughters. And when it was moved from Fontainebleau to Wimbledon, members of my own generation followed their mothers and aunts and continued to study French literature under its inspiring but intimidating headmistress, Marie Souvestre. Her name appears in so many published diaries and autobiographies that it need not play any further part in mine. I was, when young, secretly disturbed by the fear that I might be consigned to her care. I never was.

* Hogarth Press, 1949.

Only my brother, being a boy, had to be forced into the accepted pattern of male education. He was despatched at the age of nine to a preparatory boarding-school at Rottingdean, and I well remember the periodic scenes of distress as the beginning of term approached. The distress manifested by him provoked answering distress for my mother, and should he also now show signs of delinquency, which he has happily not yet done, I feel sure that a probation officer trained in psychology would find scope for expert explanation to a sympathetic magistrate. A generation later my own son was subjected to the same treatment but without comparable distress. This may be due either to a less austere scholastic régime, or to the fact that he and I have less sensitive natures.

For us girls, home life and a day school were normal procedures. And the Girls' Public Day School Trust provided excellent educational opportunities. In some cases the now almost extinct race of resident governess might provide an alternative. In my own case, St Paul's Girls' School, which opened in 1904, was the solution. But at the end of school life it was counted as no disgrace for a girl to pursue no profession, do no systematic work, and "come out" as a young adult female available for invitations to dances or proposals of marriage. In due course I "came out"; but for reasons later to be elaborated, I was an unco-operative and reluctant debutante.

Here again, as with male education, the pattern, though distinct, was subject to deviations by exceptional girls, which became increasingly obvious as I passed through my second decade. Women doctors were ceasing to be eccentric pioneers. There were back doors, such as the factories department of the Home Office, for entry by women into the Civil Service. Academically minded girls with co-operative parents envisaged university entrance; the women who had taught at their day schools were themselves graduates—or in the case of Oxford and Cambridge, graduates in learning but not in name. Two of my female cousins went to Cambridge and afterwards became doctors.

Such opportunities were open to me had I been academically minded. Alas, my chief aim at St Paul's was to get away from it as soon as my parents allowed; and a failure to pass Higher Certificate at the appropriate age enabled me to leave on my seventeenth birthday. I carried away with me a gardening prize, since devotion to gardening had offered a means of avoiding games, a capacity for concentrating, under discipline, on subjects which did not interest me, and a profound respect for headmistresses. Miss Frances Gray, the first headmistress of St Paul's, though dumpy in stature and academically undistinguished, was a figure of such dignity, and an embodiment of such high ideals, as to fix in my mind the pattern of what all headmistresses should be. To be sent to her room for admonition, which happened to me twice, was an experience one would wish to forget without being able to do so. To have my essay on Pontius Pilate read aloud by her in class because she thought it good, as happened once to me, was an experience one would cherish.

All this carries my chronicle far beyond those early years when life centred on the nursery at Queen's Gate Terrace, with Sarah presiding over up-getting and bed-going. I inhabit it in memory when the incandescent gaslight over the fireplace has been lit, the red curtains drawn, and nursery tea spread on the table. Into the nursery would come, from time to time, familiar sounds from the outside world. The muffin man's bell on Sunday afternoons and on Monday evenings, the German band which played year after year in the same places in the same streets; or more often, the shrill whistle of someone calling for a cab: one blast for a four-wheeler, two blasts for a hansom. And between tea and supper there would be reading aloud by my mother downstairs in the drawing-room— or painting or some form of craftsmanship for which she had considerable talent. It was thus that I had my first introduction to Scott and Dickens, later to Jane Austen and Charlotte Brontë. At a later date these hours were destined to be befouled by homework.

Outside Queen's Gate Terrace, Kensington Gardens was our playground. It seemed to me enormous, and with Hyde Park added to it, illimitable. Today certain obscene architectural excrescences, such as the Hilton, the Lancaster, and the tower block of Knightsbridge Barracks—with doubtless more to come—break its skylines and diminish its sense of spaciousness. Between the wars one was afraid to love the beautiful features of London too much, because always there was the thought: they may be bombed. As indeed many of them were. Today, while the old fear remains, a new and more immediate fear takes its place. Do not love them too much: they may be "developed". As indeed many of them have been.

[9]

But in those far off days of the eighteen nineties I was conscious of no fear of anything. Only as the new century opened out did I become conscious of something disturbing: a realization that all was not well with the position of women, and that outside the charmed circle of Queen's Gate Terrace, all was not well with the social system in which we were able to live so comfortably.

2

External Family Contacts

LIFE AT QUEEN'S GATE TERRACE was lived on a conventional pattern, but it was not lived in isolation because my parents were part of an enormous and accessible family circle. There were uncles and aunts, great uncles and great aunts, first cousins, second cousins, first cousins once removed, and grandparents.

My mother's side of the family was the more closely knit because it was strongly centered upon my grandparents, Sir Alexander and Lady Rendel who lived at 44 Lancaster Gate, later at 23 Russell Square, and during the summer months at Rickettswood, near Charlwood in Surrey. On my father's side there were Brintons and Danverses in great numbers, since my Brinton grandmother was a Miss Danvers, one of a bevy of sisters, all but one of whom married and produced cousins, as also did one Danvers brother. Among the sisters, was great Aunt Emily, the widow of W. H. Smith, who lived in an enormous house at the corner of Belgrave Square (it is now part of the German Embassy), served by a very gentle spinster niece-companion and a considerable domestic staff, both male and female. W. H. Smith, I have been told, refused a title, saying that he was a "simple man". His widow accepted a Viscountcy in her own right as a posthumous honour to him. This did not of course entitle her to a seat in the House of Lords as it would today, and this was perhaps fortunate: because though she was exceedingly handsome and would have been an ornament to that dignified chamber, she was not very bright.

Unfortunately both Brinton grandparents died before I was born; so there was, on my father's side, no centripetal force. For us, the nearest thing to it was three maiden aunts, Maud, Marion, and Edith, my father's sisters, who kept house together in London and were familiar visitors at Queen's Gate Terrace as well as at the house by the sea in Dorset which we acquired in 1900. They were gifted and witty women, Maud a competent pianist, Marion a trained nurse, and Edith (known to us as Aunt Tiddy) a talented artist. But according to the convention of the time, none was expected to earn her living, though all were capable of doing so. It was left to their brothers to achieve self-support, and to their father, a consultant of some note in his time, to amass before his untimely death a sufficient fortune to maintain his widow and provide his daughters with an unearned income large enough to ensure moderate comfort and the domestic service which ladies of their class would naturally expect.

As children we owed a lot to the Brinton aunts. They were devoted to us and spent much time entertaining us. They were original and imaginative story-tellers and rhymesters, and Aunt Tiddy's pictures were a continual source of pleasure.

Indeed the Brinton aunts must have been a considerable help to my mother in Dorset during summer holidays—though some of their domestic habits, as they arrived one after the other for a week or ten days, provoked occasional ribaldry. Unpacking and repacking of trunks was a serious, lengthy, and complicated business. Among other impedimenta one might find a hold-all containing two umbrellas (one for best and one for second best), and two parasols (one for best and one for second best). The best, according to the weather, would be used for churchgoing, since unlike my own family they were regular churchgoers. They were also Conservative in politics, and when the women's suffrage movement burst over us they stood obstinately aloof.

Among incidents which provoked ribaldry was an effort of Aunt Tiddy to preserve us from indelicacy. In Tennyson's poem, *The Revenge*, which was among those she read to us, occurs the line: "Bearing in her womb that which left her ill-content". Over the word "womb" Aunt Tiddy stuck a narrow strip of paper. My family still cherishes the tattered volume of Tennyson showing the marks from which the strip was surreptitiously removed by us to satisfy a curiosity very natural in the young. But none the less we loved the company of the Brinton aunts, and greeted their visits with rejoicing.

It was from the Rendels, grandparents, uncles, aunts, and

cousins, that deviation from conventional patterns came. From them, too, came outside contacts with an interesting variety of occupations and interests. There were, for instance, the Stracheys who lived at 69 Lancaster Gate, round the corner from the Rendel headquarters at No. 44.

In his recently published biography* of Lytton Strachey, Michael Holroyd leaves us with the impression of 69 Lancaster Gate as a tall, dark, dreary house in which the brilliant Lytton was incarcerated by fate under the stifling surveillance of too many women. My own early memory does not reflect this gloom. No. 69 may have been tall and dark but it was no taller and no darker than No. 44 which throbbed with Rendel vitality. Sir Richard Strachey, who presided over No. 69, had been a distinguished Indian administrator and had thus encountered my Rendel grandfather who, as a civil engineer, a builder of bridges and dams, left many traces of his work in India. Their respective families thus came into close and continuous contact when both settled in Lancaster Gate. To my grandfather's delight, his own eldest son James married Sir Richard's daughter Eleanor, an older member of Sir Richard's long family. Indeed four children of James and Eleanor were born before Lady Strachey had completed her own childbearing: with the result that her young son, James Strachey, was familiarly known among the young Rendels as "uncle baby".

Sir Richard Strachey was a remote and withdrawn figure to us, and I suspect at times to his own children. His much younger wife was not; though personally I always found her rather intimidating. She had considerable literary talent and a wide knowledge of literature, as indeed had all the Stracheys. She had a dignified Scottish ancestry, being a Miss Grant of Rothiemurchus, and she was exceedingly handsome. She was also a keen feminist and active participator in the campaign for women's suffrage. So too was her daughter Philippa (see Plate 2a), known to us as Pippa, whose contribution to the suffrage cause will be narrated at a later stage. Pippa, who died in 1968 at the age of 96, having outlived all her nine brothers and sisters, was the most charming, gay, unselfish, affectionate, energetic and humane of all the Stracheys. And so my Rendel uncle Herbert thought (see Plate 3) for he loved her exclusively and ardently for many years; but alas, she did not love him. In consequence, he long remained a bachelor: so long that

* *Lytton Strachey*, by Michael Holroyd (2 vols). Heinemann, 1967–8.

when in middle age he made a very happy marriage he had scarcely time in which to revel in his happiness.

Of the other Stracheys, all were intellectually able—one daughter, Dorothy, married a French artist, Simon Bussy, and translated many of the works of André Gide. Pernel became Principal of Newnham College. Marjorie wrote an excellent popular biography of Chopin. My grandfather admired all the Stracheys greatly, beginning with Lady Strachey herself. He was perhaps unduly appreciative of intellectual achievement and it is certain that his admiration for the Stracheys was a mild irritant to my grandmother: who was not intellectual at all but entirely feminine, beautiful and wholly charming. I think she regarded it as a reflection on her own family's superiority in every way over all other human beings. They were in many ways above the law; for I remember her saying to one of her daughters about to light a cigarette: "I don't approve of women smoking, but of course it's all right for you, dear."

The two elder sons of Sir Richard Strachey we scarcely knew at all. They went off to India in various capacities. The one always at home was Lytton whom we scarcely knew either. Not because he went off anywhere in any capacity, but because he appeared to be a weedy querulous recluse, incarcerated in a sitting-room of his own, provided by his family, in order that he might, free from interruption, cultivate the literary talent which he was believed to possess —and did indeed possess as his later career showed. During his twenties, and with nerve-racking mental labour-pains and many recuperative holidays, he did produce reviews for the *Spectator* of which his cousin St Loe Strachey, was editor. It has been suggested that bad health was responsible for his inertia and lack of early achievement, and this may indeed be true. But bad health begets self-absorption which in due course begets more bad health. This is apt in turn to beget lassitude, which uncharitable hale and hearty critics may describe as bone laziness. I fear that I do Lytton less than justice; and that is because I find it difficult to forgive a letter, included in his biography, in which he complains that his mother and Pippa, and indeed the whole household, are so absorbed in the organization of a great women's suffrage demonstration as to divert attention from himself.

Fortunately for him and his mother, the age of frustrated querulousness came to an end in 1918 with the publication of

Eminent Victorians, the first of three best-sellers which brought him a cloud-burst of literary fame, the enjoyment of much hospitality, and the achievement of financial self-support in a remarkably constituted household of his own. All of which is told at great length and intimate detail in his two-volume biography by Michael Holroyd. My own view, inherited from my mother who had romantic reasons of her own for cherishing it, is that Lytton was not a Strachey at all but, as his name suggests, a Lytton, called after ex-Viceroy Lytton who was a close friend and admirer of Lady Strachey.

Another family contact which brought colour and variety to the whole Rendel confraternity was the result of my mother's eldest sister Kate's marriage to Halsey Ricardo (see Plate 2a). He introduced into the lives of all the Rendels aesthetic interests which they might otherwise have lacked. Indeed from the moment of his advent he dominated and conditioned their taste.

Halsey Ricardo was a gifted if somewhat erratic architect, and was, through the years, employed by Rendels to build their houses and reconstruct their domestic interiors. I think his crowning achievement was a house built for Ernest Debenham in Addison Road in Kensington; by which time the Debenham business had produced a fortune which enabled Halsey Ricardo to spread his aesthetic wings without counting the cost. There it stands today, among the modest but spacious residences of that Kensington thoroughfare: a gleaming palace of peacock green and blue glazed brick, washed clean by every rainstorm, the external expression of an interior made glorious by de Morgan tiles, many of them of his own design. And may this monument to his rich and imaginative genius be spared from the depredations of the money-grubbing developers who have been busy of late in West London; because beautiful as it is, it cannot be very convenient to live in or very easy to turn into self-contained luxury flats.

Under Ricardian influence, Rendel households, our own included, became colourful with de Morgan tiles and pottery. To keep them company we all became patrons of Morris wallpapers, Morris cretonnes and Morris chairs. My own flat today reflects this aesthetic heritage, and few visitors to it leave without saying at some stage in the conversation: "Where did you get those lovely tiles?"

To me, as a child, Uncle Halsey Ricardo stood for something

more than an arbiter of Rendel taste. We spent much time with the Ricardos at weekends in Bedford Square and during holidays at Rickettswood. He was a devoted family man, and since most of his work was done at home he had plenty of time to spend with his children. He was a superb reader aloud and a stimulating talker. To him I owe my interest in the poetry of Browning, the music of Wagner, and the drama of seventeenth- and eighteenth-century English playwrights. The library at Rickettswood contained a complete edition of *Bell's British Theatre*, a row of little brown leather volumes which he read himself and encouraged me to read. They included for instance the original acting version of Gay's *Beggar's Opera*, which was therefore familiar to me long before its resurrection by Nigel Playfair in 1920. Alas, my grandfather, finding these volumes in current use, disliked the titles of many of the plays they contained, and drowned these cherished, and I suspect valuable, little books in a neighbouring weedy pond from which it was impossible to rescue them.

Another family connection, more remote because less London-centred, opened up a very different circle of cousins. One of my grandfather's sisters married the Wedgwood regnant of the famous pottery firm. The working centre of the Wedgwoods was of course in the Five Towns, and their family centre was a large house in the near-by village of Barlaston, where the Wedgwood factory is now situated. But Wedgwood cousins mingled with Rendels and they were a vital energetic breed.

The one I knew best was my mother's first cousin Josiah, who after an adventurous sojourn as a magistrate in South Africa, returned to England and settled in London as an active Liberal M.P. His niece Veronica Wedgwood has told the story of his life in her book, *The Last of the Radicals*,* and radical he certainly was: Liberal to begin with, and Labour to end with. He was one of those M.P.s—James Maxton was another—to whom the House of Commons, irrespective of party, will forgive everything: and perhaps they had much to forgive, for Jos Wedgwood was a born fighter. He married his first cousin, Ethel, the daughter of Fanny, another of my grandfather's sisters and the wife of Charles Bowen, an eminent judge, for whose intellect my grandfather had a profound respect. This respect did not extend to his own sister; and on one occasion, when someone traced a facial resemblance

* *The Last of the Radicals*, by C. V. Wedgwood. Cape, 1951.

between her and me, he remarked with some heat: "I won't have you say the child is like Fanny; Fanny's a fool." I fear she was.

Though Ethel indeed was a vital personality and certainly no fool, her marriage to Jos Wedgwood ended in separation. Rendel opinion was anti-Ethel; but I do not think that Jos could have been an easy husband. He was an impulsive, affectionate, emphatic, pugnacious, lovable creature who sought adventure "even in the cannon's mouth"—as did his erratic unsettled red-haired brother Felix. Jos survived the First World War in the Dardanelles. Felix failed to survive it on the Western Front. But I choose to believe, and indeed I do believe, that Felix really enjoyed the war during the time allowed him in which to do so.

Two other Wedgwood brothers had more serene and conventional, but perhaps more constructive, lives: Frank in charge of the family pottery firm, Ralph in charge of the Great Eastern Railway and much else. They sustained the Wedgwood vitality and ability as well as its pottery, and handed on these qualities to their children, among whom I proudly claim as a second cousin, one of our greatest living historians: Veronica Wedgwood, O.M.

Other outside Rendel contacts there were which diversified my youthful memories; and one of them brought tenuous contact with the theatre. This was the Nettleship family. Nettleship was an artist, popular in his time as a painter of animals, some of which appeared on Rendel walls. I have his eagle. My eldest daughter has his lion. What happened to Nettleship I do not know, except that he left his widow and three daughters ill-provided for.

Mrs Nettleship, whom I well remember, became a dressmaker and achieved fame as a theatrical dress designer. She made the famous beetle-wing dress immortalized by Sargent in his picture of Ellen Terry as Lady Macbeth—in fact one of her least sympathetic parts. My mother asserted, and in this she is to be believed, that she had helped Mrs Nettleship to sew on some of the beetle-wings which glorified that memorable garment, now at rest in the Ellen Terry museum at Smallhythe.

Unfortunately the tenuous connection between my mother and Mrs Nettleship's beetle-wing dress, and between Mrs Nettleship's dress and Ellen Terry, never brought me any nearer to that great and radiant actress than seeing her on the stage. I worshipped her from afar. I saw her as Portia in a Lyceum performance of *The Merchant of Venice* which must have represented the tail end of

[17]

the great Irving-Terry partnership. Later I saw her as Alice-sit-by-the-fire in Barrie's play of that name, as Lady Cicely Waynflete in Shaw's *Captain Brassbound's Conversion*, as Mistress Page in *The Merry Wives of Windsor*, as Hermione in *The Winter's Tale*, as Juliet's nurse, and as the tragic mother in a Stage Society performance of a Dutch play called *The Good Hope*—by which time her memory, though not her radiant charm, was beginning to fail.

For many years, indeed until her death in 1928, I continued to cherish a hope, which was, alas, never fulfilled, that I might some-day somehow encounter Ellen Terry in person off the stage. But memory of her continued to haunt me, and still does and so the news of her death in 1928 provoked me to write a sonnet.

Another and less tenuous contact with the theatre came from the Brinton connection. My father's paternal aunt, Mrs Baird, who lived in Oxford, had a daughter, Dorothea, who was in her day a notable actress. The story of her advent on the stage and her mar-riage to H. B. Irving has been told by her son, Laurence Irving, in his recently published book, *The Successors*,* which continues his excellent biography of his grandfather, Sir Henry Irving.

Dolly Baird, as she was known to the public, was a charming and very beautiful, if not a great, actress; and her marriage to H. B. Irving kept her on the stage long after her own interests had turned in another direction—this at any rate is my own specula-tion; her son might not agree. She was, in fact, an ardent philan-thropist, and in middle life became an active Poor Law Guardian in St Pancras where the Irvings lived. She was thus a friend and colleague of my aunt, Edith Rendel, who pursued the same thank-less, discouraging and time-consuming service to society. She was also a working pioneer in the embryonic maternity and child wel-fare movement, a voluntary enterprise which at an early stage achieved grant-aid from the Board of Education, since the Min-istry of Health was not then in being. Mrs H. B. Irving was instru-mental in founding the St Pancras School for Mothers, and it is recorded that when a cook employed at this pioneer centre com-plained of excessively exhausting work, she herself took over the job for a week, in order to ascertain at first hand whether the complaint was justified. I cannot, however, remember what her verdict was.

* Rupert Hart-Davis, 1967.

As a stage personality Dolly Baird achieved considerable fame at the very outset of her career, in the part of Trilby, the leading female character in a dramatized version of du Maurier's novel of that name. Those familiar with the novel will remember the significant part played by Trilby's bare feet. When Dolly Baird played Trilby with bare feet, it did not produce the same shock as Bernard Shaw's dramatic use of the word "bloody" spoken from the same stage many years later, but it was sufficiently arresting for the word "Trilby" to pass temporarily into current speech as associated with bare feet. I well remember Sarah's familiar injunction during the evening bath: "Now then, wash your trilbies."

I was born too late to remember this notable performance, though I well understood its aftermath in connection with bare feet. My first sight of Cousin Dolly Baird on the stage was in the first play, other than Drury Lane pantomimes, that I had ever seen. She played Helena in *A Midsummer Night's Dream* at Her Majesty's Theatre, with Beerbohm Tree as Bottom and Julia Neilson as Oberon. It was a thrilling experience to see a real play for the first time and an added thrill to stay up till 11 p.m. in order to do so. But the crowning thrill was to see on the stage someone who was a familiar figure in real life. Nowadays Helena is played, to my mind convincingly, with an element of comedy as a rather querulous blonde. Dolly played her straight, for the sympathy of the audience, and they loved her for herself.

It may be that these two contacts sparked off my life-long addiction to the theatre: but to someone living in London during the first decade of the century it was a stimulating era in which to be alive and theatre-conscious. Shaw broke over us, and Granville-Barker, and the Horniman repertory company from Manchester which gave us an annual London Season—as did also Lady Gregory's Irish Players from Dublin and Frank Benson's heroic touring Shakespeare company.

I did not know it at the time, but under the stimulus of Gilbert Murray and Robert Bridges, John Stocks of St John's College, Oxford, was also becoming theatre addicted; so that when, at the end of this decade, he and I joined forces, our mutual addiction became compulsive. We saw everything we could get to, in London, Oxford, and later in Manchester.

This excursion into the future, however, has led me far away, both in time and space, from the Rendel connection, to whose centripetal point at the turn of the century I will now revert. That it was a *connection* was observed by John Stocks in 1911, after his own inclusion in it, on becoming engaged to one of its very well-integrated members (see Plate 6). He accepted inclusion with pleasure and objective interest, not untinged with amusement. And being an academic, familiar with examination tests, he embodied his impression of the Rendels in an examination paper, which, he suggested, might serve as an entrance qualification for future prospective fiancés. The paper was well received by the family, which had indeed accepted its author with open arms, as a welcome recruit from the outside world. I reproduce the paper here in the belief that the chapter which follows may suggest answers to some of its questions.

FINAL HONOUR SCHOOL OF SOCIOLOGY

SPECIAL SUBJECT

History and Organization of the Rendel Connexion

1. Describe the rite of adoption, and account for its early importance in the Connection.
2. What other forms of adscititious membership were recognized? How did the status of these members differ from (a) that of members by birth, (b) of members by adoption, (c) of members by marriage? Account, so far as possible, for these differences.
3. To what extent has the introduction of the telephone modified the organization of the connection?
4. What traces are there in the religious, or semi-religious, practices of the connection of (a) ancestor-worship or (b) adoration of living members?
5. What is the proper sociological definition of a connection, as distinct from a clan or family or other similar social group? Illustrate from parallel cases, if you know any.
6. "Das Rendel überhaupt ist zwar ein Familienmensch, aber gar kein Politischer. Die ethisch-soziologische Entwicklung der Verbindung gibt die *Instantia Crusis* dieses Unterschieds." (Pfutzsch.) Examine this statement.

[20]

7. What machinery existed for the expression of the general will of the members? Examine the theory of "tacit expulsion".
8. Examine the status and duties of the domestic servant, and explain what qualifications were chiefly demanded. Give concrete illustrations.

3

The Rendel Connection

THE CENTRIPETAL FORCE OF the Rendel Connection was, of course, my grandparents, Sir Alexander and Lady Rendel, established first at 44 Lancaster Gate and later at 23 Russell Square in London; and during the summer months at Rickettswood, a large country house (see Plate 2a) standing in some 350 acres of garden, orchard, farm and woodland near Charlwood in Surrey. Reigate was its shopping centre, Horley its railway station.

From Horley my grandfather commuted during the summer months to his office in Great George Street, Westminster. He was an active senior partner in the civil engineering firm of Rendel & Robertson, later Rendel, Palmer and Tritton; indeed the firm still bears his name though there is now no Rendel partner, because it is a name great in the history of civil engineering. My grandfather remained actively connected with it, until a few days before his death at the age of 89, from a cold which turned to pneumonia. Fortunately for him there was no penicillin in those days, and no resuscitation. He swallowed his usual cascara pill, went to sleep and did not wake again.

His activities began when, as a young man, he worked under his father, James Meadows Rendel on the construction of Portland Harbour. James was a notable civil engineer whose achievements are duly recorded in the *Dictionary of National Biography*. My grandfather, who trained on the job, was left to complete Portland Harbour after his father's death, and his subsequent engineering achievements include the Royal Albert Dock, Leith Dock, as well as much important bridging, damming, and railway development in India, which brought him a knighthood.

His last achievement was the Sara Bridge across the Ganges—

[22]

now known as the Hardinge Bridge—which he designed but never saw. He was then over eighty.

Two of his brothers inherited the engineering genius: Hamilton Rendel, who was responsible for the machinery, though not of course the architecture, of the Tower Bridge, and George Rendel, a notable naval engineer who completed his career as managing director of the Armstrong works at Posilipo, near Naples.

These great-uncles were shadowy figures to me. I think I saw them only once; for Hamilton lived and worked in Newcastle, and George in Italy, and both died when I was very young. Hamilton died unmarried, the result of unrequited love for a member of Sir Andrew Noble's family. I have the very fine diamond ring which he gave my mother for a wedding present. But Great-Uncle George, who married twice, provided us with a family of cousins, of which the youngest and most distinguished member is Sir George Rendel, who rose through the Diplomatic Service to the position of British Ambassador in Brussels, and has told his own story in his autobiography: *The Sword and the Olive.**

Less shadowy was the third Rendel great-uncle, Stuart, who engaged in politics under the wing of Mr Gladstone, achieved a peerage, and lived till 1911. Where all his money came from I do not know; I have always supposed that most of it came through his appointment as managing-partner in the London office of the Armstrong engineering firm; but he certainly had a considerable amount of it. This enabled him to live on the grand scale in London and to buy and partially inhabit very many houses elsewhere. One of these, Hatchlands, was a superb stately home near Dorking. Another was the Château de Thorenc, near Cannes, where he once entertained Edward VII. Two houses, which he joined together, were on the sea-front at the Kemptown end of Brighton, and these he sometimes inhabited during the autumn months; for in those days there was a Brighton autumn season involving a mass migration of the Peerage to its sea air. These were by no means the only houses which Lord Rendel owned on the Brighton sea-front, but he could not himself occupy more than two.

It may seem as though I have dealt somewhat unsympathetically with Stuart, who was in his own way a shrewd and liberal-minded politician, and many Victorian memoirs contain references to his

* John Murray, 1957.

generous hospitality both in London and at Cannes. It was, however, noted by his Rendel family critics that such hospitality was
invariably directed to the upper strata of politics and society.
Perhaps we tended to see him through the eyes of his brother
Alexander, who greatly disliked him and towards the end of his
life refused to meet him at all. Writing to John Stocks, soon after
Stuart's death in 1913, I remarked on my grandfather's hard-
hearted references to a lately-deceased brother. "Last night at
dinner Grandfather was more flippant than I have ever known him.
He amused us all by telling us funny stories about 'poor old
Stuart' and shouting with laughter over them." A minor cause of
my grandfather's dislike was doubtless Stuart's attitude to property. He was every inch a Forsyte and a money-valuer.

But far more potent was my grandfather's disapproval of
Stuart's attitude to his own wife, my gentle, conventional and not
very intelligent Great-Aunt Nellie. That she was half afraid of him
I was once made aware by her ill-disguised terror when he arrived
unexpectedly from London and was about to enter a room, usually
occupied by himself, where she and I were playing chess. I think
he habitually snubbed her, and this my grandfather could not
tolerate.

My grandfather had become engaged to my grandmother when
she was fifteen and he scarcely older, and from then till the end of
his long life he remained deeply and exclusively in love with her.
She came of an adventurous family, having spent her earliest years
in New Zealand as the daughter of its first Governor, Captain
Hobson, R.N. But after marriage she was never allowed to do any
work at all. Her eight children were served by nurses, nursemaids,
and governesses. All business, such as the purchase and administration of Rickettswood, was done by her husband, and in due
course all housekeeping was done by an unmarried daughter, Aunt
Edith, of whom more will be told later. She grew old, prematurely
I think, for she seemed to me an old lady when in her early sixties.
She had charm and grace, and was always available to be at her
husband's side when he wanted her, or, when the time came, to
entertain her grandchildren. For my grandfather, a harsh or rude
word to her was unthinkable—it was thus, in his view, that men
should treat their wives. "With my body I thee worship, with all
my worldly goods I thee endow" was a promise made early in his
life and kept till the end of it.

But poor Great-Uncle Stuart, having married a wife who was beautiful, high-born, and I believe well endowed, was, I fear, bored by her intellectual shortcomings and deeply disappointed by her capacity for producing only daughters. One of these, the Hon. Maud, fulfilled part of his ambition by marrying the son of Mr Gladstone and becoming mistress of Hawarden; but he had hoped to found a dynasty of peers, and this was not to be.

Had Stuart Rendel's qualitative values been morally as well as socially and financially conditioned, he might also have gloried in the fact that among his daughters he produced a saint. This was Clare, the youngest, who remained unmarried and tended her parents during their lifetime. I do not think that she was intelligent by Rendel standards, nor was she systematically educated. But she was fundamentally wise, wholly selfless, and devoid of property sense. Having accepted the teaching of the Sermon on the Mount, she lived consistently in the light of it. And having decided that she could best serve her fellow mortals, or rather their children, by becoming a "masseuse", she had herself trained as one. We should now use the word "physiotherapist", and the training would require higher academic standards than Clare would have been able to achieve. So when her father died, leaving her the two Brighton houses suitably endowed for the sustenance of an unmarried lady living alone in upper-class comfort, Clare settled there and pursued her hospital rounds as a voluntary worker. She did not, however, live alone. To inhabit so large a double-fronted house for her own repose after a hard day's work would have been unthinkable. She therefore opened its doors to convalescent nurses, whom she considered were getting less than their fair share of public sympathy during the First World War.

Unfortunately, the endowment provided by her father was insufficient for such large-scale hospitality; but economic embarrassment was happily averted by her nephew Hal Goodhart-Rendel. By a series of financial reconstructions involving successive moves, he finally established her in a small semi-detached house with garden, behind the sea-front at Hove, in which, unencumbered by property she was serenely happy. It was still large enough for convalescent friends and relatives, but by ones and twos rather than by dozens. I have myself been cherished by Clare after an operation for acute appendicitis during the First World

War. Indeed sick Rendels, overworked nurses and superannuated domestic servants would naturally turn to her.

She died in 1958 and I attended her funeral in a small country church near Hatchlands. Later in the day I also attended a poetry reading at the Royal Society of Literature in London. Dame Peggy Ashcroft was advertised as the reader, but I did not know what she was going to read, and was pleased to find that she had chosen the Pompilia story from Browning's *The Ring and the Book*. Its concluding words are:

> Through such souls alone
> God stooping shows sufficient of His light
> For us i' the dark to rise by.

Blind chance (if indeed it *was* blind chance) had thus provided me with a wholly satisfying obituary for Clare Rendel.

So much for the Rendel great-uncles. I have already mentioned two of the three Rendel great-aunts, who lurked on the periphery of the Connection. There was, however, another great-aunt from the Hobson side who came close enough to be integrated into it. This was my grandmother's sister, Aunt Polly, who lived at Penlee House in Devonport until her death in 1908. Aunt Polly's life-story was a sad one. When the Hobson family returned from New Zealand, after Captain Hobson's untimely death in 1840, and settled in Devonport (which we always spoke of as Plymouth though administratively it was not), Aunt Polly was the unmarried daughter who remained at home with her widowed mother. I have been told that as a young woman Aunt Polly loved and was loved by a naval officer; but an over-cautious Victorian mother insisted on postponing their marriage and alas postponed it too long—and Aunt Polly's heart was broken.

Outwardly her life as a maiden-aunt and great-aunt seemed full and satisfying. She became a well-known and popular personality in her neighbourhood, occupying the large Penlee House, standing in its own garden with stables and outhouses, and served by a cook, a very ill-tempered but faithful house-parlourmaid called Ellen, a coachman and a gardener. As children we loved holidays there—indeed it was a favourite Rendel haunt. We loved Jesse, its white pony, driven by Aunt Polly in her governess-cart; we loved the daily journey to the Pier with its roller-skating rink and automatic machines, and the afternoon wagonette drives sometimes took us as far as Dartmoor, along roads impeded by turn-pikes. And from time to time there would be invitations to tea on ships in the Hamoaze river: where naval craft were in process of achieving their grey "new look".

Today, the Hoe is as beautiful as ever, but Plymouth itself is unrecognizable with its reconstructed middle and its pro-liferating suburbs, and alas, as a result of savage German bombing, no pier.

Aunt Polly was, as I remember her, always full of imaginative fun and devoted to her nephews and nieces. She was a faithful churchgoer and a patron of church bazaars, but well able to mock at her pompous and humourless rector, and at the silliest of his curates. I remember her delight when in the rector's presence at a church fête, one of them, taking part in a game of forfeits, received a smacking kiss from a young female parishioner. The rector was not amused. Aunt Polly was. In old age she developed an irrational mania for shopping. She would buy things that she did not want and could not use; and when my mother went to wind up Penlee House after her death, a gigantic clearance involved among other things the disposal of a quantity of unused and unusable photo-graphic material. A superb collection of unusual carpentering tools, however, provided much-needed equipment for a local technical school.

I have since reflected that had she lived a generation later her life might have been very different. Social service in local govern-ment or on the bench would have directed her natural qualities of wit, energy, and kindness into more responsible and satisfying channels than entertaining neighbours or cherishing curates. As it was, Aunt Polly was a well-integrated member of the Rendel Con-nection and a frequent visitor to its headquarters—as we were to hers.

The Connection was, of course, a three-tier structure—at its top level were the two grandparents and Aunt Polly. The second tier consisted of an incomparable maiden aunt, Edith (see Plate 4a), and two unmarried uncles, Harry and Herbert. Harry died sud-denly in 1903. But Herbert lived with his parents until he married in 1909. When he did, he brought his Scottish wife, Anne, right into the inmost heart of the Connection; and there is no doubt that of all his daughters and sons-in-law, Anne was the one my grand-father loved most. And not without good cause; because after the untimely death of Herbert she devoted herself to serving and cherishing him.

In addition to Herbert and Edith, the second tier consisted of three other married uncles, James, William and Arthur, and two married daughters and all their spouses, all of whom, with one exception, were happily integrated in the Connection. The one exception was Aunt Ruth, daughter of Kegan Paul of publishing fame, and the wife of William Rendel who died almost before I could remember him, of acute appendicitis diagnosed (not, however, by my father) as stone. Aunt Ruth, left a widow with three children, defied and continued to defy absorption in the Connection. I do not think the Rendels liked her, and they were not adept at disguising their feelings. But this may have been caused by her resolute determination to resist integration. She went her own way. It was not the case with her eldest daughter, Leila, who at an early stage became a resident at Rendel headquarters, either from natural sympathy or from force of circumstances. She was the eldest of the grandchildren and in due course, for reasons which will be related later, she became one of the two most distinguished.

Such was the second tier of the Rendel Connection. With the exception of Aunt Ruth they all lived in London: Bedford Square, Melbury Road, Queen's Gate Terrace, Norfolk Crescent, Gordon Square. Weekly "at home days", maintained on Mondays, Tuesdays and Fridays by Rendels, Ricardos and Brintons and arranged not to coincide, as well as my grandmother's "at home day" on Wednesdays, together with Sunday suppers at headquarters, produced much cross-visiting, so that they all knew what all the others were doing and where they were. Rickettswood was an ever-open holiday home. During the summer months attendance at family meals at Rickettswood would run into double figures. (See Plate 3.) I cannot remember any member of the family being refused weekend or longer accommodation on the ground that there wasn't room. It may have happened, but I do not remember it. Nor, at the time, was I conscious of the burden which the housekeeping of Rickettswood must have imposed on Aunt Edith. Pressure was doubtless lightened in 1900 when my parents acquired a house at West Bay, Bridport, which we inhabited during the summer holidays, with many Rendel visitors. Later, Halsey Ricardo built his own country house at Graffam, which lightened

Ricardo pressure, and later still Uncle Arthur Rendel retired from general practice and set up house in the middle of Dartmoor.

It was Uncle Arthur who brought one of the most colourful second-tier members into the Connection. This was Aunt Elsie, daughter of Colonel Blair, whose family came of a dynasty of Scottish lairds. She was tall, slightly deaf and strikingly handsome. Her dress was unconventional, her conversation far more so. She was deeply religious and seemed to be on easy conversational terms with the Almighty. Having on one occasion prayed for guidance and received guidance that she thought ill-judged, she said: "Oh Lord, think again." Apparently He did, and the revised guidance proved acceptable. "My husband", she once said to a surprised visitor, "accuses me of flirting with the Holy Ghost." And her reply to a rather conventional Dartmoor neighbour, who said that he could not attend Communion in the local church after breakfast but was not prepared to fast until noon, was: "Well, I am not going to let a little bit of bacon stand between me and God!" It was while walking through Brookwood cemetery after my grand-mother's funeral that, feeling somewhat oppressed by its opulent marble tombs, she broke the silence with: "If our Lord had seen the use they've made of his cross in this cemetery, he'd have wished he'd died on something else." This remark was made to one of my Brinton aunts and was not well received.

The third tier of the Rendel Connection was, of course, the grandchildren. There were nineteen of them ranging from Leila Rendel, the eldest, to Jane Rendel, the youngest, who was born at about the time when the Connection was disintegrating. She had scarcely time to realize its existence. Like the uncles and aunts, all the grandchildren knew what all the others were doing and where they were. When Ellie Rendel was saving up for a camera, or when Harry Ricardo was saving up for a second-hand lathe with which to make engines in the Bedford Square basement, it would be generally known that any gifts should take the form of cash. And it may here be mentioned that Harry did make engines. He has made, invented, and designed engines ever since; and has told his own story in his book: *Memories and Machines: The Pattern of My Life.** I have indicated Leila as one of the two most distinguished of the grandchildren. Harry was, of course, the other.

* Constable, 1968.

Leila will never write the "pattern of her life", so I shall have to do the best I can with it in the next chapter. But surveyed as a group, the grandchildren were not a bad brood. They included two gallant regular army officers, two female doctors, one very eminent film art-director, and one *Times* foreign correspondent. I can only boast that I followed in the footsteps of Great-Uncle Stuart by becoming not, alas, a millionaire, but a member of the peerage.

It should be added that the coming of the telephone, and its extension to Rickettswood, greatly facilitated the process of integration. But the advent of the motor-car did not occur in time to make the thirty-mile drive from London anything but an adventure; so the line from Victoria or London Bridge to Horley remained the link between Rickettswood and the metropolis.

But motor-cars came into the picture at a very early stage and Rendels were pioneer car owners. My grandfather was among the most adventurous. There were, for instance, the White steam car, whose boiler on one occasion fractured, enveloping its passengers in clouds of steam: the Wolseley, whose body-work resembled a wagonette, entered by a door at the back: Uncle Herbert's two-seater steered not by a wheel but by a tiller: and of course Harry Ricardo's motor bicycles, with trailer, forecar or side-car as their evolution proceeded. Many types of Rendel or Ricardo cars were seen on the roads round about Rickettswood, and their passage would be observable at a distance by the clouds of dust they threw up—necessitating the use of motor veils by females and goggles by all. During these early years their passage would often be slowed down by considerate spells of immobility at the roadside while frightened horses were led past what they naturally regarded as unfamiliar, noisy and malodorous competitors.

The last of the Rickettswood cars was the great Daimler; by which time my grandfather had developed the curious and uncharacteristic view that cars—or rather this particular car—should not be overworked. When assured by mechanically-minded members of his family that it was really good for the engine to be activated, he suggested that the Daimler might be raised from the ground or suspended from the roof of the garage, in order that the engine might be activated while the car remained stationary. This sounds unreasonable; but he was not an unreasonable man. He had, as doubtless we all have, a few eccentricities and one of them was excessive modesty.

When, during one of many internal reconstructions of Ricketts-wood, an awkwardly placed pantry was converted into a lavatory for male persons, this presented a problem. He observed that when its outer door was opened a passage leading from the washbasins to two inner W.C.s could be seen. This would not do. He therefore insisted on the construction of a wooden partition which prevented those entering the W.C.s from the washbasin area from being seen entering that passage in order to visit what lay beyond. So far so good—but not good enough. The outer door of the washbasin area opened on to the hall and opposite to it on the other side of the hall was another door, that of the smoking-room. Anyone emerging from the smoking-room might see anyone else entering the opposite door. This would not do. The hall had therefore to be bisected by a substantial partial wall which served as a visual barrier between the two doors. This did not improve the appearance of the hall and certainly impeded progress from the smoking-room to the hall, not to mention the washbasins and what lay beyond them. But decency was served.

It must by now be clear that the Rendel Connection, as indeed other comparable groups such as that described in the *Forsyte Saga*, rested on a wide substructure of domestic service. But that which sustained Rickettswood was, I suspect, wholly *a*-typical. In some cases domestic staff were engaged on the ground that they would be unemployable elsewhere. And once employed, as in the case of a very unsatisfactory chauffeur, my grandfather felt it necessary to retain his services on the ground that he could not honestly be recommended for another job. Therefore, having once left my grandmother sitting alone in the Daimler outside a public house on the road from Horley, while he refreshed himself within, his employment continued. But since he could not be trusted not to do this sort of thing again, my grandmother was not allowed to be driven alone by him in the Daimler unless accompanied by another man: if necessary the under-gardener would be mobilized as bodyguard on the seat beside the driver. But I think the outstanding deviation from the conventional pattern of Edwardian domestic service was the Daley family.

Aunt Edith, as an active Poor Law Guardian in St Pancras, was naturally in touch with its least privileged citizens. Among these who lived in the back streets north of the Euston Road were many Irish. There still are. It is notable that Jews as a rule are less static.

Starting in Whitechapel, later generations emerge in Bayswater or Hampstead.

Exactly in what year Aunt Edith was faced with the collapse of the Irish Daley family I cannot remember; but I do remember that the collapse was total. Mr Daley, a heavy drinker, had disappeared from view. Mrs Daley, after heroic attempts to keep the family together, was in the act of dying or had died. An elder sister had also died when Aunt Edith became cognizant of their plight. There remained Bridget and another daughter whose name I forget but who was happily employed in London, and a young brother called Denis. Bridget and Denis were brought to Rickettswood and integrated into the structure of Rendel domestic service. After being trained as a hairdresser Bridget became lady's-maid to my grandmother. Denis was installed as footman. He was a difficult boy with a tendency to violence; but in due course this tendency found scope in the First World War and he died fighting gallantly with the Canadian Army. But he was never a good footman and one way and another gave a certain amount of trouble. Bridget was a more enduring liability. Thanks to Aunt Edith's affection for her, she became a very well integrated member of the Connection. But my grandmother never came to terms with her habit of referring to the aunts and uncles by their christian names, nor with the undefinable vulgarity of her appearance as a companion in the Daimler. It is certain that if my grandmother could have chosen her own personal maid, she would not have chosen Bridget.

As the years rolled by, less and less was Bridget *persona grata* with other members of the Connection; but the more others criticized her, the more protective did Aunt Edith become. When Bridget became engaged to the brother-in-law of the bailiff's daughter, who kept a garage at Romsey, there was a sigh of relief. But when he pulled out of his engagement he evoked general sympathy. And yet Bridget had qualities which were at times endearing. She was on the whole good-natured, though her gossip did not always reflect this quality. She would do anyone's hair for the asking, and when encouraged she would "do the splits"; a gymnastic feat which she had doubtless learned in St Pancras. I suspect that Aunt Edith spoiled her, and that if the rest of us had loved her more, Aunt Edith might have loved her less. With Aunt Edith's death and bequest to Bridget of a modest competence, she passed out of our lives.

It must not be assumed that all members of the Rendel domestic staff were, from a professional point of view, sub-standard. Lucy, parlourmaid-in-chief during the whole Rickettswood era, was a superb administrator. She managed to survive and dominate a succession of sub-standard male assistants, including Denis, with unruffled authority. In fact she dominated her employers as well. She was tall and gaunt and resembled a camel more closely than I can remember any human being resembling any animal. She appeared to be continually chewing something, and since chewing-gum had not then become a feature of our Western civilization, some of us used to wonder whether some internal deviation required her to chew the cud, as I believe camels do. But at some time romance must have touched her life, for she had a favourite niece who was thought, but not said, to be an even nearer blood relation.

One other circumstance is connected with Lucy. She received periodically, from a firm called Price-Jones in Wales, a consignment of drapery goods which she would retail, presumably at a reasonable profit margin, to fellow-members of the domestic staff. I remember Sarah's embarrassment when these consignments arrived. She did not want the stuff, and did not regard it as cheap; but felt that out of respect to Lucy she ought to buy some of it. It is possible that other domestic colleagues felt the same.

Outside the immediate household staff, there were three outstanding personalities who remained an integral part of the Rendel Connection during the whole Rickettswood era and are inseparable from its memories. One was Jack Wicks, the gardener. He was a tireless worker, gentle, and wholly lovable. He had no wife or family, but at one time a Wicks brother called Jim functioned in the stable; at another, a junior Wicks called Bert assisted in the garden. But Jack was always there, and his rather untidy potting-shed was a haven of pleasure for members of the third generation.

The second personality was Murphy, the Irish bailiff in charge of the farm. He, too, was always there. He lived with his wife and daughters in a very comfortable house close to the farm buildings, which contained a dairy controlled by his resident daughter Kate who was liked by all. My grandfather was certainly devoted to Murphy, whom he appointed at the time of acquiring Rickettswood (see Plate 4b). The two would walk round the estate arm-in-arm apparently deep in conversation, though what they talked about I do not know. My grandfather was not particularly interested in farming and I presume that Murphy would indicate what he wanted done, and my grandfather would say: "Do it, dear boy." I think that Murphy was in some respects illiterate. He could certainly read because he read *The People* on Sundays; but there is no evidence that he could write—for that he could rely on his daughters, one of whom was a schoolmistress.

Murphy was undoubtedly a well-known personality in the neighbourhood and knew everybody for miles round Rickettswood. He was also able to exercise some patronage in the matter of pheasant shooting in which, as far as I remember, no Rendel took any interest; though Harry Ricardo asserts in his autobiography that he sometimes did, and he should know. But Murphy was certainly able to make his own arrangements with his own friends.

I doubt if the farm was well-managed; it was certainly a financial liability, and though none of us got typhoid, my memory of the cow sheds and milking arrangements suggests that these were, even by Edwardian standards, scarcely hygienic. When Rickettswood was sold after my grandfather's death, and Murphy had to be pensioned off, his valuation of the perquisites which he had enjoyed for many years as resident bailiff and for which he required compensation caused some amazement.

But expensive or not, well-managed or not, the farm is among my golden memories. Over a garden fence, across a field, and there it was, cows, carthorses, chickens, pigs, cats with kittens, and one incarcerated resident bull, all to be visited; haystacks, strawstacks, chaff-cutters, grain stores, all the agricultural processes going on under our eyes and becoming familiar to us. How I wish my grandchildren could have had that experience! As for my great-grandchild, she will never know the sounds and smells of a real farm. She will know only of silos, batteries, and a test-tube bull.

Another outlying feature of the integrated Connection was The Cottage, the special province of the third and most notable of its extra-mural personalities. This was Mrs Relf. She, too, like Jack Wicks and Murphy, was always there. From October to May she resided at the great house, and took complete charge of it. When we sojourned in it at Easter she was there to cook for us in its big kitchen. During the summer months she resided at The Cottage, about a mile away across the fields, where she cherished, washed, dressed and fed, and when necessary nursed, relays of convalescent or undernourished children brought from St Pancras by Aunt Edith. She had never received any training in the modern sense, but was infinitely competent on all fronts. I was told that at one time she had functioned as "handy-woman" for the delivery of local infants. She seemed to be familiar with all the processes of nature and could make a non-poisonous salad out of the weeds of the field. Incidentally, she was the only person who could control a donkey called Neddy who lived with us for many years. Had Mrs Relf taken the place of Balaam on his historic cursing expedition, angel or no angel, there would have been no turning back.

Her most permanent resident at The Cottage was Maurice Whelan who first arrived there as a St Pancras convalescent lacking one leg. Thereafter he walked, and later cycled with a wooden one. He was one of many Rendel adoptees, since his mother was not regarded as fit to look after him. Indeed it was thought that, in a state of alcoholic irresponsibility, she had been largely to blame for the loss of his leg. For some years she would appear on the doorstep of the Rendel London headquarters and demand him back—not, it was thought, because she wanted him, but because the threat of removing him to her own home, if indeed she had one, might have induced some philanthropic Rendel to pay her to keep away. In the end, bribed or not, she did keep away. And since there were no adoption acts and no children's officer to take him "into care", into the *de facto* care of the Rendel Connection he was taken. He remained with Mrs Relf, who loved him as a son. He was a well-behaved boy, and though not very intelligent, was intelligent enough to be trained as a carriage painter at Handcross, after which he emigrated to Canada, but continued to write from time to time, though not as often as she would have liked, to Mrs Relf, to whom he owed more affection than he was perhaps capable of feeling, or at any rate expressing.

It would have been interesting, but perhaps tactless, to inquire into the pre-Rickettswood life of Mrs Relf. The fact is, she was not Mrs Relf, nor Mrs anything. She was Miss Roffey, and had early in life produced an illegitimate son, a wild and at times violent man who now and then bullied his mother for money. He seduced a nurse (or so I was told, and it seemed a likely story) at a local hospital and begat a daughter, Kitty, with whom Mrs Relf kept in touch, and who had a daughter called Gladys. And when poor Kitty was said to be dying and deserted somewhere in Catford, two

Rendels hurried to the spot and returned with the infant Gladys to Rickettswood, and there she remained, cherished and loved by her great-grandmother. She repaid Mrs Relf's care and affection by similar care and affection when her great-grandmother lived in retirement at Dorking. She is now happily married and living in Canterbury where from time to time I visit her and exchange reminiscences of Rickettswood and talk about the people we both knew and loved.

But it was not only a great-grandmother who formed part of the background of Gladys's life. She had also a great-great-grand-mother. A colourful feature of Rickettswood life was our frequent visits to Mrs Relf's mother, known to us as Granny, who lived in an ancient cottage on the Newdigate Road. She had been married to an agricultural labourer and I was told that they had together walked to London for their honeymoon. But she long outlived him and was over 100 when I remember her. With her bonnet, her flowered print dress, her screen made from Victorian magazine prints, her stone-flagged downstairs room, the glass jars from which she sold boiled sweets, and her own wrinkled face, she might have been a creation of Walter de la Mare. She sold, in addition, "prize packets", mixed biscuits and soft drinks in bottles. We often visited her, and as a rule 2*d*. would facilitate the purchase of four different articles—except for the drinks which cost 1*d*. Towards the end of the Rickettswood era Granny became too in-firm for independent existence and was transferred to the care of relatives at Merstham, where she died, having well outlived her century.

A full recital of Rendel domestic personalities would prolong this record unduly, and would· have to include the children's nurses, who, in addition to Sarah, were a feature of Rendel family life (see Plate 2b). But the senior nurse deserves mention. This was nurse Adamson, known to us all as Scotch Nurse, who lived with the James Rendels until long after her five Rendel charges were all grown up. She had in earlier days served the family of a Presbyterian missionary in Africa and had remained a pillar of rather austere Christianity: of the Presbyterian Church when in Kensington, and at Rickettswood, of a small corrugated-iron place of worship in the precincts of the Norwood Hill Post Office less than a mile from Rickettswood. Here prayers were on occasion offered at her suggestion for the moral regeneration of the Rendel family, who were not precluded by conscience or convention from playing cards on Sunday and even, on occasions, playing Pope Joan for money. But this was the measure of her great love of them and devotion to their interests—a love combined with austere discipline amounting at times to autocracy. She was a familiar figure at Rickettswood, treated with respect amounting to awe by her fellow-nurses, and usually to be found during the summer months sitting in the orchard, which was our playground, with its sand-heap and swing, a basin on her knees and a bucketful of garden peas at her side, absorbed in the business of shelling them.

I had always thought that it would be interesting to see the Rendel Connection through the eyes of its domestic staff, and this, many years later, I was enabled to do from the angle of the most subordinate rank of its hierarchy. We had for a few years at Queen's Gate Terrace a high-spirited and adventurous nursemaid called Ethel Harvey, who went where we went and was greatly liked. She was full of fun not unmingled with audacity. When she left us we lost sight of her, though one of her many sisters later appeared as housemaid at Rickettswood. In 1954 a broadcast of mine suggested to her that Mary Stocks of the B.B.C. might be the Mary Brinton she remembered. She wrote to ask, signing herself Ethel Crewe. I replied that I was indeed Mary Brinton, and was she Ethel Harvey? Yes, she was, and there followed a correspondence from which I quote the following passages:

"I must have been 14 or 15 years of age when I was nursery maid with you. I am now 74 but that period of my life stands out as the happiest time of my girlhood. I often wonder why. I remember so many things connected with that time and all the people I knew. Poor old Sarah, she seemed old to me but I don't suppose she was; the tricks we used to play on her, but she took it all in good part. . . . The lovely time we had at Rickettswood; Sarah used to say, 'We will go to Charlwood this morning, Ethel' and you used to say to me, 'We don't want to go do we? Let's hide,' and we did, sometimes on the top of a haystack . . . and she would have to go off without us with the donkey cart, the donkey would sometimes go and sometimes not. . . . I feel I must keep saying, do you remember, there are so many things and people. Mrs Relf who did the cooking, Mr Murphy the Bailiff who lived at the farm

[37]

where we loved to visit, Lucy the parlourmaid of whom everybody was afraid . . . the three brothers Wicks in the garden
(one in the stables), even Gilbert the boy used to bring the
milk from the Farm. The orchard where we used to play . . .
the copse where we used to look for eggs where the hens laid
astray. In London, too, do you remember how we used to
roam around the Museums, especially the Natural
History. . . ? I often wonder why these memories remain
when I have forgotten lots of other things. I used to take you
and Master Ralph to Lancaster Gate every Sunday morning
when fine while Sarah went to Church but I don't remember
her going out on her own any other time. You will be tired of
reading this but there is much more I would like to write
about."

At which point she told me all about her own family and her fifty
years of happy marriage to a gardener. In a later letter, replying to
one of mine, she resumes her reminiscences:

"Dear Madam (I feel I must write 'Miss Mary'), your letter
gave me so much pleasure . . . I felt I was back at Queen's
Gate Terrace and you a little girl again. Of course I remember
going to Folkestone with you and all the excitement of it. It
was the first time I had seen the sea . . . what a thrill it was
. . . I certainly do remember going to Plymouth. I have never
been that way since but can never forget the lovely times we
had there—Miss Hobson was so good, those glorious picnics
when we went over by ferry-boat to Saltash I believe. . . .
Yes I do remember Ellen and I did play tricks on her—one
time making a dummy and putting it in her bed, and she ran
out of her room screaming saying there was a man in her
bed. . . . As you say I really was naughty and my family say
I have not improved with age. . . . I am always dreaming
about Mrs Brinton and have done for years. I am back in the
nursery. I always call it my nursery dream."

But this second letter also referred to my suggestion that she
should come and meet the family and renew acquaintance, if not
with the nursery, at any rate with some of the pictures she remembered. Alas—she suffered from a heart condition which prevented
her from moving about. And when I offered to come to West

1. The author at the age of four, 1895.

2 (a). The lawn at Rickettswood. The author's mother, Constance Brinton, leaning against tree; to the left Halsey (on garden seat) and Kate Ricardo; on right Lady Rendel (seated) and, in the hammock, Philippa Strachey and Edith Rendel.

2 (b). Nurses and children in the orchard at Rickettswood. 'Scotch Nurse' seated in the centre with Sarah standing to her right.

Wycombe where she lived, I received a letter from her daughter to say that she had died. And for years I had been driving past her house *en route* from London to Oxford without knowing that she was there!

For many young women in those days, domestic service in a large household must have produced a more abundant life than is suggested by sombre pictures of Victorian and Edwardian slavery. But perhaps life in the Rendel Connection offered features not encountered elsewhere.

When at Rickettswood, the Connection was relatively isolated, though a select number of non-Rendels were accepted and integrated. There were the Brinton Aunts, there was Beatrice Hale, the daughter of the family doctor, who became the wife of Harry Ricardo, and there was Harry's cousin Ralph Ricardo. There was Ethel Nettleship and my father's cousin Winifred Broome and Ray Costello, Newnham friend of James Rendel's daughter, Ellie, who was loved by all and especially by my grandmother. Ray, who had been brought up by her own grandmother, had a peculiar capacity for cherishing old ladies. When, later, she married Oliver Strachey, she gave the same devotion to his mother. And of course, constantly at Rickettswood was the adorable Pippa Strachey— fully integrated, though her youngest sister Marjorie was not.

Apart from such limited integration Rickettswood was a closed Rendel community. It had almost no social contacts with the surrounding countryside. No vicar called. It did not visit neighbouring houses, nor was it visited. Nor did it desire to be. It was self-sufficient.

This meant that no responsibility rested on the domestic staff to answer the front door bell. On one occasion it was indeed rung by a Brinton Uncle who happened to be staying in the neighbourhood and rightly considered it to be good manners to pay an afternoon call on Lady Rendel. Being an Eton housemaster and familiar with upper-class social usage, he naturally expected that a manservant or maidservant would respond to his ring. None did. The domestic staff was, it seems, all having tea out in the orchard. He rang again —still no answer. He wandered on to the lawn where an adult Rendel granddaughter was playing with a croquet ball. He asked where he could find Lady Rendel. She replied, "I don't know", and resumed her play. He then abandoned his quest and went home. A day later my grandmother received a letter from him explaining that he had been unable to receive any response to his bell-ringing and adding that he had been treated with scant courtesy by a young woman who, he presumed, was one of the grandchildren.

On receipt of this letter, and I happened to be at breakfast when it was read, my grandmother was very angry. Not with the domestic staff absenting themselves *en masse* when somebody should have been available to answer the bell. Not with my cousin Ellie Rendel, for being, to say the least of it, unhelpful. But with the caller who had dared to criticize a Rendel grandchild.

One could run on with reminiscences of life in the Rendel Connection, as indeed I do run on in thought to an increasing degree as I advance towards nostalgic senility. The Connection did not survive the First World War, during which Aunt Edith died, then my grandmother and lastly, in January 1918, my grandfather. Rickettswood was then sold; first to a resident who cherished it, later to a country club which desecrated it. I am told that it fell into decay and was eventually demolished. I have no doubt that property developers have been busy on its site and on the green fields which surrounded it, for that part of Surrey is well within the stockbrokers' commuter area. But I do not choose to go and see what they have done.

The death of the grandparents and the sale of Rickettswood and 23 Russell Square naturaly involved the disintegration of the Connection, and war service scattered its members. Meanwhile, the family proliferated unto the fourth and fifth generation. But contacts between Rendels, Brintons and Ricardos continued when special interests or neighbourhood proximity brought them together, and those of the second and third generations share memories which are revived by contact. They share the experience of having lived in a golden age, singularly free from personal tensions and sex problems, and wholly at variance with a modern tendency to decry the family as an obsolete or even vicious social group.

My own closest contact was with my cousin Esther, the youngest of the three Ricardos. There were Sundays at Bedford Square, reached by a red horse-drawn bus which ran from Hammersmith to Tottenham Court Road. But best of all were Easter holidays at Rickettswood under the auspices of Uncle Halsey and Aunt Kate, with Mrs Relf presiding in the kitchen, and Sarah with the

Ricardo's nurse Louisa in the nursery; because my father couldn't leave his practice and my mother wouldn't leave him.

Esther and I usually shared a bedroom; and on the first morning of the Easter holidays, which seemed illimitable though one soon found they weren't, one awoke to a country smell through the open window and the sounds of the farm in the distance. One knew that the fields would be luxuriant and the clearings in the woods full of primroses; that there would be no school; and that when the lamps were lit after high tea, Uncle Halsey would read to us while we drew and painted.

What one didn't know was that our world was moving inexorably towards a break-up of much that made life gracious and secure for the privileged classes of the Edwardian Age.

4

The Birth of
the Welfare State

IT MAY APPEAR PARADOXICAL, having presented the Rendel
Connection as something in the nature of a closed self-sufficient
community centred on Rickettswood, to present it now in the
guise of a powerhouse of far-flung political preoccupations and
social reform. But such indeed it was.

What, for instance, did Rendels talk about? It is easier to remember what they did not talk about. They did not talk about sex.
They did not talk about religion or sport, so far as I can remember.
They talked about one another, and what they were doing, and this
opened many doors, because when not at Rickettswood they were
all doing different things and enjoying different outside contacts.
They talked about pictures and architecture and the theatre and
books, and the queer goings-on of the domestic staff. During the
bicycle era, when everyone had bicycles and took pleasure in turning them upside down to clean them, and mend their punctures,
they talked a lot about bicycles, as later about motor-cars. They
talked about national politics at the time when Asquith was fighting his battle for the Parliament Act of 1911, and they talked very
continuously and vociferously about Women's Suffrage from 1905
till the dissolution of the Connection. But this last subject involved
disagreement only as to method. No member of the Connection
was an anti-Suffragist.

The most constant and ever-present subjects of conversation
were social conditions and social reform; and this was mainly
London-centred; because to members of the Connection the North
of England with its great working-class communities and its trade

union problems was foreign soil. The co-operative movement was embodied as far as they were concerned in the Army and Navy Co-operative Stores; the trade union movement in the problems of sweated factory girls or out-workers in East London. But the deficiencies of the Poor Law, its workhouses and children's homes, the poverty of St Pancras and North Kensington, the squalor of the elementary schools and of the houses where their pupils lived—all these and cognate problems were brought right into the Connection by those members of it who were active philanthropists.

Foremost among them was Aunt Edith. When she, being in London on Poor Law business, was unable to visit The Cottage, other Rendels visited it. We knew its children and we knew why they were there. In London, in addition to her Poor Law guardianship she ran the St Pancras Girls' Club for young women employed in neighbouring factories. In those days class differences were reflected in dress, and reference to old volumes of *Punch* containing cartoons by Phil May will give a good idea of what our St Pancras Club girls looked like. They were a cheerful, genial crowd, and on August Bank Holidays they were usually entertained *en masse* at Rickettswood. There, one of their chief delights was to sit in deck-chairs on the lawn; during which time my grandmother would be incarcerated in the house since she would have found their presence disturbing. In fact it was.

The headquarters of the Club was in Woburn Walk, behind St Pancras Church; and by virtue of its occupancy Aunt Edith acquired a St Pancras local government vote. In those days Woburn Walk was almost a slum. Today it has gone up in the world and is featured in John Summerson's *Georgian London** as a perfect specimen of Regency planning. Various members of the Connection were roped in to support the evening sessions of the Club. These included one of the Brinton aunts, and on occasions my mother.

One of Aunt Edith's Club patrons was my father's patient, Miss Nix. Miss Nix would not have felt at home on Club premises, nor would she have made easy contact with its members. But she devoted a great deal of time, and doubtless a lot of money, to buying and packing parcels of gifts for each individual girl, to be

* Pleiades Books, 1945.

distributed from a gigantic Christmas tree at a Boxing Night party held in the big hall of the neighbouring Lancing Street elementary school. The selection and purchase of these gifts—and each parcel contained three separate items—must have been a major occupation for Miss Nix during the weeks preceding Christmas. It was, of course, important that such parties should be sufficiently attractive to compete with the pleasure of getting drunk and perambulating arm-in-arm up and down the Euston Road, and perhaps concluding the evening with a night in a police cell or "a fate worse than death". They were indeed surprisingly successful. A good time was had by all.

Another devoted helper at the Club was Aunt Edith's eldest niece, Leila Rendel. Leila, having to earn her daily bread, trained as a teacher of gymnastics: a vocation for which, even in early days, her figure was ill-suited. On certain evenings the Lancing Street school hall would be made available for a Club physical training class conducted by Leila. And in this connection I must temporarily forsake the Rickettswood era for an excursion into the future, in order to demonstrate how, in the history of our British social services, one thing can lead on to another.

After a brief and unhappy excursion into the Civil Service as Inspector of Physical Training, Leila was able to follow the dictates of her heart. She had not only a penetrating understanding of children, but infinite patience with them and an individual interest in each child. She also had the power of inspiring a willingness to accept authority. I had experience of this at a very early age—I must have been nine or ten and she in her teens—when she decided to teach me the Catechism. She had no authority to do this, nor, I believe, had my mother suggested that she should. But into a small room at Rickettswood, known as the library, I would be incarcerated morning after morning while Leila worked on me. And it never occurred to me to say that I didn't want to learn the Catechism or that she had no authority to make me. In fact I am very glad she did, because its answer to the question: "What is thy duty towards thy neighbour?" envisages an admirable moral order though it errs a little in the direction of uncritical submission to one's betters. If I had not been taught the Catechism by Leila I should never have learned it; for the confirmation class which I attended at the age of fifteen in a neighbouring South Kensington church did not require any such effort. Indeed, its only result was to deter me from taking part in any Church service for many a long year.

It was of course natural that Aunt Edith and her niece Leila, with common interests and sharing the same domestic background at Rendel headquarters in London, should be close friends, as indeed they were; and subsequent events provided a pattern of continuity for their work. There came a time when the old Club premises behind St Pancras Church had to be vacated. Aunt Edith then acquired a larger house for the Club in what was then called Burton Crescent. This crescent consisted of elegant terrace houses curved round a communal garden. Readers of Trollope will recall it as an area of respectable if not top-class boarding houses at one of which young John Eames lodged during his courtship of Lily Dale. But by the time Aunt Edith acquired it, Burton Crescent had become far from respectable.

Clearly much had to be done and was done in the Club's new home before it became habitable. And then Aunt Edith was struck by a solemn thought: here was a spacious house in a densely populated area, used only for a few hours in the evening. And here, in St Pancras, over-driven working mothers were forced to park their babies in the most unsuitable surroundings. Clearly a crêche was needed; and in due course a crêche was established in the new Club headquarters. By day the rooms were full of cots, and by late afternoon, when the mothers came to retrieve their offspring, the cots were cleared away for the activities of the incoming Club.

Soon, however, another problem arose. The crêche babies grew older and became toddlers. But as toddlers there was no suitable provision for their needs. They were, in fact, facing an awkward and unfilled gap between infancy in a pram or cot and infancy in the lowest standard of an elementary school. What was to be done?

It is here that Leila comes back into the picture; because the answer was: a nursery school.

Languishing in the official corridors of power, Leila was spending much spare time with a fellow child enthusiast, Phyllis Potter, who ran a nursery school or nursery class under the auspices of Whitfield's Tabernacle in the Tottenham Court Road. Why not organize a nursery school for the growing toddlers of Aunt Edith's crêche? This, in fact, was done. But it could not, of course, be done properly on the Burton Crescent premises where the crêche was still operating. So the next-door house in Burton Crescent was acquired for the nursery school into which the crèche children graduated.

At some point in this series of events Leila abandoned the Civil Service and devoted her whole time, in partnership with Phyllis Potter, to running the nursery school in Burton Crescent. Phyllis Potter had an independent private income. I have always understood that the income which enabled Leila to devote herself to full-time voluntary service was guaranteed by my grandfather, who felt that money spent on enabling her to do such work at full stretch was well spent—as indeed it proved to be.

But the new house and its internal decoration required more money, and both Rendels and Potters were mobilized as subscribers to the venture. Internal decoration was served by collecting and dissecting the Caldecott picture books on which young Rendels had been brought up, and making their picture pages into a frieze round the children's playroom.

In its early stages Leila and Phyllis operated on Montessori principles which at the time represented pioneer progress. But as time went on, by a process of trial and error, they evolved methods of their own; and in the end achieved what has always seemed to me a rare synthesis of two commonly dissociated qualities: freedom and order.

The Caldecott Community did not long inhabit its first home in Burton Crescent, because it was borne in on its two directors that most of its children lived under conditions which made full and healthy development impossible. It was therefore moved into the country as a boarding school, and its children grew up in it. Today it serves all ages. Its youngest pupils are toddlers, its seniors may be working for university entrance at a local grammar school. Its history covers a series of financial crises and changes of location, all of which it survived, and for many years my youngest daughter, Helen, was a member of its staff.

The most serious blow it suffered was the defection of Phyllis Potter in 1931. Among her many gifts was love of music, and a genius for dramatic production which brought fame as well as money to the Community. The cause of her defection was a growing addiction to orthodox Anglicanism and a determination to work under Church auspices. I cannot help feeling that had she been instructed by the vicar who prepared me for confirmation, this might not have happened. But it did happen, because Leila was equally determined that the Caldecott Community should remain non-sectarian and that its chapel should pursue its own devices free of ecclesiastical control.

The full story of the Caldecott Community will, I hope, some day be told in a volume of its own. From its early days in Burton Crescent its work attracted the attention of individuals and societies, and, in due course, of education authorities and government departments. Nor did Leila's capacity for profound interest, and deep understanding of deprived or difficult, or for that matter normal children, ever wane. Her patience with them remained infinite; her perpetual emission of original new ideas for their betterment, was mentally disturbing. She was listened to with respect by educationalists and consulted by experts. That is why I put her into the top class of Rendel grandchildren alongside of her brilliant cousin, Harry Ricardo, with his impersonal engines. She died in 1969 at the age of eighty-six, having just completed a plan for her own withdrawal from active directorship in favour of a married couple selected by her for the succession.

It is time, however, that I returned in memory to the world of Aunt Edith, her workhouse, her Club, and her crèche. After her death in 1915 the Club faded out, and the administration of the crèche fell into the very competent hands of my mother—until the development of local child welfare services made it redundant. But I think the name of Edith Rendel was long remembered in St Pancras and will never be forgotten by her nephews and nieces. If I were asked who among many friends and relatives were the principal influences in my life, I should name three—in chronological order: Edith Rendel, John Stocks and Eleanor Rathbone.

Apart from being great fun as a companion, an ardent theatregoer, an Ellen Terry lover, and in ideas something of a revolutionary, I was as a child tremendously interested in Aunt Edith's work and wanted to do the same sort of thing myself. I used to accompany her on visits to the St Pancras workhouse. Unlike most Poor Law guardians, she was on friendly personal terms with very many of its inmates. I got to know them too: Granny Lamb aged 103 in the infirmary, and the Belgian seamstress who had lain there for many years and had many more years to lie; and in the old women's block, Irish Mary, so beautiful in old age and of such captivating charm, but alas, so incapable of going out without being hospitably treated and returning, or being returned, very

[47]

drunk. There were no old-age pensions in those days, so the old people's blocks contained many inmates who might nowadays live on their own—though I doubt if Irish Mary could have done so. There they sat, hundreds of them in vast bleak day-rooms, gathered round tables on hard chairs; some reading; if women, some knitting; if men, some smoking—but of course no radio, no television, only occasional visitors; so that even a teenage girl visitor was welcomed and felt flattered by the welcome. All the more welcome in the men's ward, if she brought twist tobacco, then obtainable for 3*d* an ounce and used, I believe, for chewing.

On one occasion Aunt Edith took me down to the St Pancras Poor Law school at Leavesden, Hertfordshire. Here children past the toddler stage were cherished and educated until at 13 or 14 they went out into the world as wage-earners: for the girls this would mean some form of domestic service or laundry work. I do not remember that any provision was made for the further education of specially able children. This type of Poor Law school was classified, most appropriately, as a "barrack" school.

Another active Rendel philanthropist was Aunt Edith's eldest brother James, known to us as Uncle Jim. He, too, was a devoted Poor Law guardian, but had less free time to give to it owing to full-time work in the City. His Strachey wife, Aunt Elinor, used to say that she had no idea what he did there, and for all she knew he might be a burglar! He was, I think, concerned, at the London end, with the administration of an Indian railway. He had been one of a notable vintage of Balliol undergraduates during the Jowett era, and I was told that he had originally intended to become a barrister, but marriage and early family responsibilities necessitated a more immediate and secure form of breadwinning.

In 1904 he became a Poor Law guardian in Kensington where he lived, and in due course was elected Chairman of the Board. From my earliest years, the Kensington workhouse in Marloes Road was a familiar feature of walks from Queen's Gate Terrace. And though it was a less forbidding building than its opposite number in St Pancras, as a child I regarded it with distaste because the word "workhouse" was associated with the idea of friendless and utter destitution. Later, when Uncle Jim took me to visit it, and I learned that Aunt Elinor and one of the young Rendels were personal friends with some of its inmates and ministered to their hobbies, I came to terms with it. Today, though badly scarred by German bombs, it functions as St Mary Abbots Hospital, and as a Kensington inhabitant I have benefited by its ministrations. The fact that one of its wards bears the name of Rendel indicates the debt which it owed to my uncle in its unregenerate days. Indeed the period of his chairmanship, which ended with the break up of the Poor Law in 1930, covered many humanitarian reforms for which he shares responsibility with some notable Kensington women guardians.

His principal interest was with the children; and though Conservative Kensington pursued a notably tough policy in regard to outdoor relief, its treatment of children was enlightened. Instead of a barrack school it maintained a community of cottage homes at Banstead in Surrey. For many years Uncle Jim was able to transport a group of its boys to a summer camp organized by him in a field on the Rickettswood estate. When the First World War engulfed many old boys from Banstead, he kept in touch with them by correspondence and sorrowed over the casualty lists on which so many of their names appeared.

Both Kensington and St Pancras Boards of Guardians were well in the van of such progress as there was. Children were segregated from the aged and indigent, the sick from the non-sick, the sane from the insane. Very different was the old-fashioned mixed workhouse at Bridport which I once visited with Aunt Edith when she was staying with us at West Bay. I doubt if it had undergone much change since the establishment of the Bridport Poor Law union under the 1834 Act. Its children, housed in the same building with the aged and infirm, went out to the local elementary school labelled as workhouse children by their unmistakable uniforms.

The third philanthropist of the second Rendel generation was Uncle Herbert, who lived with his parents and Aunt Edith until his marriage in 1909. But even before this he had acquired a holiday home of his own next door to our terrace house at West Bay. Here he did much entertaining. Rendels, of course, and others visited him, many of whom added greatly to the social amenities of life at West Bay, as also did his somewhat erratic pioneer Dolphin car designed by Harry Ricardo. But it was noted that some of those he entertained were selected on the principle that they were unlikely to be welcomed elsewhere.

He was happy and at ease with children and accepted responsibility for at least one—and I think more—*de facto* adoptees. I seem to remember that jointly with my mother and Aunt Edith he was responsible for the first Rendel adoption—that of a high-spirited and intelligent youth called Percy, who eventually went off to South Africa as personal servant to James Rendel's former Balliol friend, Alfred Milner,* and I believe did very well there.

It was probably through the St Pancras Girls' Club that he got in touch with a neighbouring girls' club leader in the Saffron Hill area. This was Miss Mary Canney, daughter of the Vicar of St Peter's Church, Saffron Hill, and the most public-spirited member of his large and distressful family. Mary Canney was pale, thin, habitually dressed in rather dusty black, and wholly selfless. Much of her time was occupied by the various distresses of her own family, but much remained for public service to her father's parish, and beyond it to the working girls of her area. She was responsible for an organization called, I think, the Factory Girls' Country Holiday Fund, which worked on much the same lines as the Children's Country Holiday Fund. Uncle Herbert became its Treasurer, and worked in close association with Miss Canney. Indeed, on one occasion she was a guest in his house in West Bay, and with the best will in the world the family's effort to assimilate her was not wholly successful. I do not think she was really happy there—indeed, I do not think she was really happy anywhere. Nor had she reason to be. But I am sure that Uncle Herbert was the light of her life and that she worshipped him.

She became very fond of my father too, who gave much voluntary service to her pioneer maternity welfare centre, and was even prepared to eat the stew which was perpetually on the boil in a flat in Lambs Conduit Street, where she cherished two younger brothers after the death of her parents. Edible material was from time to time thrown into that stew, and lunches for guests were spooned out of it. But whether its saucepan was ever completely evacuated and a fresh start made, we never knew.

The chronicle of second generation Rendel philanthropists would not be complete without bringing my mother into the picture—though with a smaller public part to play. Her principal role was played within the family circle. If any member of the

* Later Lord Milner.

family were ill, or otherwise in a state of crisis, she would be there. If any sick member required to be cherished otherwise than in his or her own home, Queen's Gate Terrace supplied the alternative. And the curious thing was that, though a naturally irritable person and liable to be over-anxious, the minute my mother entered a sick-room she radiated calm and could produce order from chaos. I have experienced this myself and observed its effect on others. She would have made a superb nurse, and her capacity for competent management would have been of value to the hospital service. Indeed I think this is what she wanted to do, and would have done had not Roland Brinton intervened and carried her off into domesticity.

But humanity at large had to be served; and this she did through the Charity Organization Society, known to us familiarly as the C.O.S. The C.O.S. was certainly doing admirable pioneer work in directing limited charitable funds into channels where they could be most constructively expended. This involved inquiry into the circumstances of applicants for relief, in order that such help as was available could produce some effective and permanent reconstruction, instead of merely enabling a drunkard to go on drinking, a lie-about to go on idling, or a slattern to go on muddling. Such an approach to the problems of destitution sometimes required investigations which might appear inquisitorial, and a subsequent classification into "deserving" and "undeserving" poor, which many critics regarded as sanctimonious. The association of this method with the word "charity" did some disservice to the popular connotation of the word itself; for "charity" is a beautiful and gracious word, and its full savour emerges when one is asked to "take a charitable view of someone's behaviour".

An important branch of C.O.S. work was the care of old and lonely people in the days when there were no old-age pensions or National Assistance. The C.O.S. would give pensions up to the limit of its funds to selected old people, who could thus be enabled to live alone in their own rooms instead of joining the dreary regiment in the workhouse ward. These pensions were administered by voluntary visitors of which my mother became one. A number of pensioners were allotted to her, and she would report to the C.O.S. on how they were getting on. During school holidays I would sometimes accompany her on her rounds, which covered the Ladbroke Grove and Kensal Green area.

I am sure that today many critics would say that it was degrading for these old people to receive pensions as of charity and not as of right, especially after being vetted to make sure that they were "deserving" recipients and not spending their money on drink, or providing accommodation for whores. Indeed a problem did arise when it was discovered that a very elderly couple on my mother's round possessed no marriage lines. My mother took a "charitable" view of their conduct; but some members of the committee thought otherwise, and a belated marriage service was held. But degrading or not, the impression I gained from those visits was that the personal contacts they engendered were a great joy to the pensioners. I remember one of them, who was almost blind, describing her pleasure at seeing my mother come in at the door, with her beautiful blue eyes and golden hair. My mother's eyes were in fact brown and her hair was black turning prematurely to white. But the mistake suggests that the visit represented for the old lady a sudden incursion of beauty into drab surroundings.

Behind these individual activities, stirring events were afoot in the world of social reform. The first cyclical trade depression of the twentieth century was well under way and was reflected in mass unemployment with its resulting destitution, on which charitable relief schemes made little impact. But under Asquith's exceptionally able Administration, the welfare state was being born.

Asquith inherited three things from a previous government: the 1902 Education Act which opened the way to state secondary education, the Unemployed Workmen Act which involved a tentative admission that national responsibility for the unemployed did not end with the offer of deterrent Poor Law relief; and a sitting Royal Commission on the Poor Law. The appointment of this Commission might have been conceived as evasive action in face of popular unease. In fact I think it was; and this could be said of many Royal Commissions. But as things turned out it was more in the nature of a delayed action bomb which went off with a loud bang in 1909, when a profound dichotomy of social philosophies, not to mention personalities, among its members produced two conflicting reports. A majority report recommended the continuance of the Poor Law as a general destitution authority drastically reformed and under a new name. A minority report demanded the total abolition of the Poor Law and its replacement by specialized statutory social services aimed at the causes of destitution and involving an intensified measure of communal, or as some critics put it, socialist responsibility.

Mrs Sidney Webb, as a member of the Royal Commission, was the author of the minority report. With an astuteness which William Beveridge was to show under comparable conditions in 1942, she used the machinery of an official inquiry to secure the publication of a spectacular comprehensive blueprint of her own social philosophy. On this Commission there also sat Miss Octavia Hill, a pillar of the C.O.S. but with an almost pathological distaste for the legislative solution of any social problem. It was certain that neither of these two ladies took a charitable view of the other, yet week after week they had to sit at the same table.

Meanwhile, outside the Royal Commission's acrimonious discussions, Liberal social legislation was proliferating. In 1905 came an Act which allowed education authorities to provide school meals; in 1907 an Act which required them to provide medical inspection. A year later came the Children's Act with a host of provisions for curbing exploitation or parental neglect, and in the same year came a first Old-Age Pensions Act. In 1909 came the Labour Exchanges Act and the Trade Boards Act. William Beveridge had already published his classical analysis of unemployment, which presented it as a "Problem of Industry" and not, as so many contemporaries supposed, a problem of individual inadequacy or mischance. As President of the Board of Trade, Winston Churchill had accepted Webbian advice and let loose Beveridge on constructive labour legislation. There followed in 1911 Lloyd George's National Health Insurance Act, with its tentative advance into the unexplored field of unemployment insurance, though neither of these two innovations were wholly in accord with the Webbian blueprint of a welfare state.

How was all this, and more, to be paid for? With Lloyd George at the Exchequer, the answer was differential direct taxation: for better or worse an infinitely expansive instrument of progressive social reform.

All these goings-on were the subject of Rendel table-talk. They were certainly distracting and disturbing to me as I ploughed through the final stage of my school career. This was happily curtailed, when I reached the fifth form at the end of my sixteenth year, by a failure to pass "Higher Certificate": an examination equivalent, I imagine, to O-level G.C.E., and which, given a certain number of passes, would constitute matriculation for entry to London University. But clearly I was not of university quality. Indeed no subject then taught at St Paul's Girls' School inspired me with the desire to study it further in depth. English literature as expounded by Miss Macirone certainly delighted me, but I felt confident that it would continue to do so as a spare-time hobby.

There were in those days no opportunities for training in social service, no social science diplomas, and indeed few social services to train for. But thanks to my family's affluence and the prevailing climate of opinion which did not require girls to earn their living, it was not thought necessary for me to earn a salary. It *was* however thought necessary for me to repair the disgrace of no Higher Certificate, by accepting part-time coaching to enable me to re-sit for enough of it to produce documentary evidence of having passed. This, however, left plenty of time for social work and indeed for much else. The question was: what social work?

When I left school in 1908 the Royal Commission on the Poor Law was still on the boil, but the Rendel Connection was not unaware of what was going on inside it. Leila's friend and one-time physical-training colleague, Flora Carter, was indeed employed by Mrs Sidney Webb on some of the researches which provided ammunition for her minority report. Flora Carter was a frequent visitor at 23 Russell Square and on occasions at Rickettswood. Mrs Webb and her activities were thus often under discussion in Rendel circles—though I do not know how it happened that at so immature an age I came to be invited to one of Mrs Webb's tea-time "at homes" in her Grosvenor Road drawing-room overlooking the Thames. It may have been Flora Carter's doing. If so, I am grateful to her, because a personal encounter with Beatrice Webb seemed to bring her social philosophy to life; though I suspect that "impersonal encounter" would be a better description of the experience.

Meanwhile, another sphere of activity was coming into view. Given her attitude to legislative action and her affection for the Charity Organization Society, Miss Octavia Hill was not at her best on the Poor Law Commission. She represented reactionary negation; as her deplorable memorandum to its majority report makes only too clear. Here she refers to "the poor", and expresses fear that the majority's modest scheme for medical relief "opens the door too widely to free medical relief". And to their sugges-

3. Some of the family at Rickettswood. *Left to right:* Roland and Constance Brinton (author's father and mother) with Ralph on his mother's knee; Esther Ricardo, Herbert Rendel, the author (aged about ten), Anna Ricardo.

4 (a). Edith Rendel.

4 (b). Sir Alexander Rendel discussing the farm with his bailiff, Murphy.

tion for the promotion of public works schemes to meet times of depression, she invokes the fear that such relief will undermine the resolution of our workers to find the places where they are wanted and make adequate provision for times of crisis by saving and insurance.

But in her own sphere Miss Octavia was supreme, imaginative, original, and in the best sense of the word, charitable. And her sphere was, as all the world now knows, housing.

Natural scientists are familiar with the fact that two otherwise neutral substances may, when combined, produce a very potent mixture. This may happen also in the social sciences, as it did when the Rochdale weavers discovered in 1844 a formula which effectively combined the ideal of human brotherhood with a natural desire to obtain cheap groceries. Their formula was the dividend on purchase, and the outcome of their successful synthesis was an expansive and enduring consumers' co-operative movement. Miss Octavia achieved a comparable synthesis between philanthropic concern for the welfare of slum tenants and the desire of their landlords for a reasonable financial return on their property. Her formula was: educate and establish a human relationship with the tenants and show the landlords that if they provide decent housing conditions the tenants are more likely to eschew vandalism and pay the rent regularly. Do slummy tenants make slum property or does slum property make slummy tenants?

The story of Miss Octavia's housing achievement has been well told in her biography written by Miss Moberly Bell.* We can there follow its development from its early beginning with the renovation and administration of some decaying house property in Marylebone, to its recognized "system" of housing management, involving a training course leading to a diploma conferred by the National Association of Housing Managers. Whether Miss Octavia herself would have welcomed the eventual wide adoption of her system by the appointment of salaried managers for subsidized municipal housing estates, may be a matter of doubt. What is not a matter of doubt is the imagination with which she conceived her system, the tenacity with which she drove property owners, beginning with John Ruskin, and going on to the Ecclesiastical Commissioners, to entrust their property to her management, and the personal example she set to the voluntary rent-collectors whom

* *Octavia Hill,* by E. Moberly Bell. Constable, 1943.

she trained and who in due course trained others to work on her lines.

Another debt we owe to Miss Octavia is the foundation of the National Trust and the pleasure we now get from the unspoiled beauty which it is still able, though I fear precariously, to preserve from the rapacity of predatory local authorities and speedway addicts.

Something of Miss Octavia's work on housing I was well aware of from another angle, even when I envisaged her as personified reaction confronting Mrs Sidney Webb. One of my Conservative Brinton aunts, Aunt Marion, was an active Borough Councillor in Kensington, and among her friends were two who supported Miss Octavia's housing activities. It was through her, or them, that I was invited, while still at school, to Miss Octavia's tea-time "at homes" in the Marylebone Road, and this I regarded, very naturally, as a great honour. I feel sure that Miss Octavia envisaged me as a future recruit to her rent-collecting team—and that is why she gave me a bound volume of her "Letters to Fellow Workers" which I still cherish, together with the personal letter which accompanied it, dated April 1908. It concludes: "Some day you may be able to see, to hear, or to help in similar work and you may care to know something of the history of its earlier stages." So there was I, about to emerge from the shackles of school life, conscious of those two power houses of social service adventure, and fascinated by both. So much divided them. Yet they had two things in common.

One thing that divided them was colour. Looking back through half a century I seem to see Octavia Hill's domestic environment at 190 Marylebone Road as rich dark brown; Beatrice Webb's as light blue-grey—the colour associated with bound volumes of Hansard. Octavia Hill's household consisted of elderly ladies: her sister, Miss Miranda, a devoted fellow-worker called Miss Harriot Yorke, and a more shadowy elderly lady called Miss Sim who poured out tea. Miss Miranda was beautiful in old age and very gracious. She would keep an eye on the guests and see that to each came the opportunity: "Now you must come and talk to Miss Octavia." Young as I was, I was not left out. Miss Octavia, as I remember her, was not beautiful. I think Sargent's portrait does her more than justice. She was somewhat shapeless and wore strange Victorian clothes with very wide sleeves. But she was certainly impressive.

The atmosphere at 41 Grosvenor Road was wholly different. Slim, dictatorial, unconventional, clear-cut, few people seemed to talk individually to Beatrice Webb—she talked to many, most of them young and male. More than two miles of London streets separated those two households. They were separated also by irreconcilable social philosophies.

Yet two things united them. One was the intensity of their selfless devotion to the cause of human betterment. Octavia thought in terms of distressed individuals whom she referred to collectively as "the poor". Beatrice thought in terms of terrifying impersonal statistics. But their personal dedication was the same. Their second common characteristic was the awful austerity of their catering. Seldom have such insufficient teas been offered by so few to so many.

So what with one thing and another, these were great days for social workers, young and old. New ventures were in the air, and all those engaged in social work were conscious of the clash of social philosophies. This gave to their smallest acts of neighbourly charity or their most revolutionary efforts at pioneer reform the dignity of logical integration with high policy or wide principle. And it was one particular piece of pioneer reform which in the end engulfed me as I emerged from St Paul's Girls' School on the eve of my seventeenth birthday.

A notable adherent of the Rendel Connection and a frequent visitor to 23 Russell Square was Miss Margaret Frere, known to us all as Margy Frere. She was a relation of the Stracheys and lived in Ladbroke Square. She dressed elegantly, indeed somewhat flamboyantly, was extremely lively, and very intelligent. She was also a devoted member of the London County Council Education Committee and was, I think, largely responsible for the inquiry into the health of schoolchildren which precipitated the legislation of 1905 and 1907 relating to school meals and medical inspection. She was certainly responsible for planning the system of school care-committees devised for the implementation of these services in the London County Council area.

This system involved what was then, I think, an unusually close integration of voluntary workers administering public money under the direction of a statutory authority. It is now a familiar feature of our social scene and one which facilitates experiment and expansion.

Under Miss Frere's scheme, to every London elementary school was attached a care-committee of voluntary workers responsible for keeping in touch with the teachers, finding out which of the children required free school dinners, and visiting their homes to make certain that they really did. The committee was also required to collect reports of the medical inspectors and see that any treatment required was carried out. It also had to make arrangements for the service of the dinners and send in the bill to the responsible statutory authority. For an active care-committee member this meant quite a lot of work, and incidentally involved much writing up of case papers and consideration of special cases requiring the attention of the N.S.P.C.C. or the local cleansing department. For the encouragement and guidance of all the London care-committees, the L.C.C. appointed two salaried organizers: Miss Moreton and Miss Wragge.

Inspired by Margy Frere, on leaving school I became Hon. Secretary of the Saffron Hill Elementary School Care-Committee. My mother stipulated that I should not myself do the actual home visiting, on the ground that it was unsuitable, not to say impertinent, for mature mothers of families to be visited, and possibly cross-questioned, by an inexperienced teenager. But there was much else for me to do, including the preparation and presentation to the committee of case-records compiled at random and not always legibly by individual members.

My most difficult assignment, however, was explaining to Miss Octavia that I had committed myself to this statutory service. She took a very dim view of it. Free meals, she said, were undermining the responsibility of working-class parents for the support of their own children. I argued that it was hard on the children to suffer from malnutrition and that their welfare should be our first consideration rather than the dubious moral fibre of their parents. Miss Octavia reminded me of the authority by which it had been said that "the sins of the fathers shall be visited on the children". The fact that I dared to argue with Miss Octavia—a thing I should not have dreamed of doing at any later or wiser period of my life—shows, I fear, that I was unduly "set up" with my new position as a responsible adult social worker operating under the auspices of an official body.

I think that Miss Octavia would have been on surer ground if she had said: "You are undertaking a job for which you have neither experience nor training; go, get you to a C.O.S. office and learn how to deal with philanthopic agencies and keep accurate case records." For, in fact, my sole training consisted of one evening spent with Miss Canney in her inexpressibly dreary ecclesiastical surroundings, since she had herself undertaken the work of the newly established care-committee pending a permanent appointment and knew from experience how that sort of thing should be done.

Miss Canney handed over to me an official L.C.C. minute book, and told me how to write minutes and prepare agendas. She also handed over a supply of official L.C.C. stationery and a sheet of postage stamps pricked with the letters L.C.C. to preclude improper use—and told me how and where to indent for more when required. She also told me who Miss Wragge was, and the kind of situation that might require her advice. That was that. I did not then know anything about the pattern of administrative machinery of which my care-committee was the end product. But in due course I learned of the existence of a Chief L.C.C. Education Officer who used to sign his directives: "Your obedient servant, Robert Blair." I later learned that Robert Blair was no man's obedient servant, least of all mine, and that he was among the L.C.C.'s most distinguished and dictatorial permanent officials.

Saffron Hill was, and indeed is, an interesting neighbourhood with individual features of its own, including an Italian community and an Italian church. It boasted a street market in Leather Lane, a settlement of diamond merchants in the misnamed Hatton Garden, and a line of second-hand bookstalls in the Farringdon Road. Where it got its "saffron" from, I do not know; but it bore that name in a 1794 map of London which I bought from one of the bookstalls. And Mrs George describes it in her book on London as "a den of iniquity in the time of Dickens, and notorious for its brothels in the time of James I". By 1908, when I knew it, its brothels seemed to have moved westward, and it was not, as Seven Dials still was, but no longer is, an area where one would hesitate to walk alone at night.

As a neighbourhood in which to live, it was congested, poverty-stricken, dirty, and far removed from any expanse of green grass. Its elementary school was a familiar version of the tall London School Board pattern with class-rooms opening on to a steep stone staircase, and an assembly hall in the basement. Many such school buildings survive, because they were solidly built. This particular school happily failed to survive the attentions of the Germans, and "the place that knew it, knoweth it no more". Its surrounding streets were dignified by tall grey tenement buildings with open staircases from which most of our children came. These, too, were solidly built, with no chance that a minor internal explosion or an abnormally high wind would cause them to fall down. Indeed most of them are still there, but for social reasons we now describe them as "flats" rather than "dwellings" or "tenements".

One early feature of our care-committee was the fact that several of its members did not approve of care-committees at all, or indeed of any extension of state provision for impecunious persons whose energy and economic foresight might be at risk. One of its most unsympathetic members was Miss Canney's clerical father. And when an early medical inspection diagnosed a heavy incidence of defective eyesight, our efforts to persuade parents to buy spectacles, and raise money to subsidize those who could not, were made the more difficult by his widely expressed view that such interference was all nonsense. Parents knew best.

As for me, I lived and learned. Gradually the shape of L.C.C. administration became coherent, and the work of its care-committee opened up new contacts with London local government and its problems. At which point I was told by Flora Carter, in the course of one of her visits to Russell Square, that there was a place where I could, as a full-fledged university undergraduate, study in depth all the subjects which—unlike those encountered at school— interested me profoundly. It was called the London School of Economics. She said anyone who had a chance to go to a university would be a fool not to go.

There was, fortunately for me, no competitive university entrance examination, no selective interview. All I had to do was to work up enough elementary chemistry to provide the right combination of subjects to turn my Higher Certificate into London Matriculation, and that done, present myself to Miss Mactaggart, the secretary of the school, as a candidate for the degree of B.Sc. (Econ.). This I did in the autumn of 1910.

In those days it was as easy as that, at any rate for someone who could live at home free of charge and produce ten guineas for the first year's tuition.

5

Votes for Women

MY FIRST CONSCIOUSNESS OF the disabilities suffered by women was concerned with dress. It dawned on me at a very early age that, unlike my male cousins, I was about to face an intensification of discomfort and constriction that would in due course become intolerable. In due course it did. Skirts would become longer and as a result heavier. Waists would become tighter to hold the skirts in place. Neckbands would become higher, to the point when they required whalebones to keep them upstanding. And longer whalebones would be inserted into my Jaeger "stays" which would some day, like those worn by my mother and Sarah, have to be laced up from behind. And hair, which had to be kept long and tied with ribbon, would at 17 or 18, have to be "put up" —not merely twisted into a bun at the back supported by hairpins which tended to fall out, but also fluffed up at the sides because that was the way female hair was then worn. Convention was inexorable and so, at this stage, was my mother, who naturally did not want her daughter to look noticeably unlike other people's daughters. But horror of horrors were the hats, which did not sit firmly on the head but had to be balanced on the hair, speared with hat pins, and always, but *always*, worn out of doors.

These growing constrictions were particularly deplorable during summer holidays at West Bay. I remember watching my young male cousins going off in shorts and shirts with bathing trunks, to undress and swim under the cliffs. How freely they moved, how uncomplicated was their dressing and undressing! My own, in comparison, was quite a business; and even my bathing dress had in due course to sprout an embryonic skirt. But decency had to be preserved. The result of it all was that I declared war on dress and

What M.D.B thinks M.D.B's mother would like.

What M.D.B's mother thinks M.D.B would like

What M.D.B would really like.
(She daren't say so)

have failed to come to terms with it since. It was fortunate for me that I was quite a nice-looking girl with a good figure, so that although doing as little as possible about it, I choose to believe that I did in fact manage to survive into old age without looking positively repellent. And today so many conventions have fallen away that it is possible to be comfortable and move freely without being regarded as noticeably eccentric. Meanwhile, I have managed to save quite a lot of money on cosmetics, hairdressing, nylon stockings, matching handbags for all occasions, and undergarments designed for pulling in, or propping up, the figure.

But if at this early stage I had been able to dress, as my granddaughters do today, in a tunic and tights, and wear my hair short or long as fancy directed, and bathe in a bikini—there can be little doubt that I should have come to terms with dress, thought seriously about my appearance, and advanced into middle age as a well-dressed woman; because I really was a nice-looking girl. At any rate one man thought so.

But these feminine restrictions were but the shadow of larger and more serious disabilities. At the time when I left school most professions were closed to women. They had no part in the administration of the law. Oxford and Cambridge examined them, but gave them no degrees. They were not legal guardians of their own children.

And they were voteless. One could not grow up in Rendel and Strachey circles without being acutely conscious of this particular intolerable and frustrating disability. Between 1905 and 1914 the Liberal administration was demonstrating as never before the potentialities of legislative enactment as an instrument of social reform. It did in fact during its seven years of office kindle popular faith in the possibility of change by legislation, which a previous administration had done all in its power to damp down. At the same time Asquith was exerting his very considerable influence over a pro-Suffragist majority in his Cabinet and in the House of Commons, to exclude from responsible participation in democratic politics the sex most intimately concerned with social reform. Why he adopted this attitude, which was certainly inconsistent with his professed liberalism, I do not know. The contribution of women to victory in the First World War—which was really inconsiderable compared to that of men—happily provided him with a bad reason for doing the right thing in the end, and lending his support to the final campaign for a limited women's franchise in 1918.

Among the Rendels there was a dichotomy of allegiance on the question of women's suffrage, but this did not go very deep as they all supported it. From 1903 to 1914 there existed two major organizations concerned with the achievement of votes for women.

There was, and had been for many years, the National Union of Women's Suffrage Societies, whose activities dated from the days of John Stuart Mill, and whose President was Mrs Henry Fawcett (later Dame Millicent Fawcett). It was a federal organization with branches in various parts of the country, and its policy was to promote the cause of women's suffrage by conventional lawful means, such as meetings, petitions, publications, lobbying of M.P.s, and in due course open-air demonstrations such as processions; but always within the bounds of law and order. It was a sad fact that the great majority of citizens, and indeed of unenfranchised women, knew very little about it, and the Press showed no interest whatever in its activities.

[63]

In 1903 a new organization took the field under the leadership of Mrs Pankhurst and her daughter Christabel. It was called the Women's Social and Political Union, and its policy may be defined as "getting a move on" by methods more dynamic and less conventional than those of the existing N.U.W.S.S. This it succeeded in doing with a loud bang in 1905, when the Liberal Party staged a great election meeting in the Manchester Free Trade Hall. Christabel Pankhurst and her friend Annie Kenney attended it, attempted to extract a pledge on women's suffrage from the party leaders, refused to keep quiet when their question was evaded, were roughly thrown out, and finally arrested and imprisoned for causing a disturbance in the street and obstructing the police. This incident has been frequently described, and is now commemorated, as indeed it deserves to be, by a plaque in the Manchester Free Trade Hall.

These prison sentences were the first of many served by Mrs Pankhurst's followers, and by Mrs Pankhurst herself. It was the beginning of what was described as the militant campaign which lasted until 1914, and which involved, in addition to normal propaganda activities, numerous angry confrontations with the police, police-court appearances, and in the later stages of militancy, hunger-strikes by prisoners leading to the agonizing and undignified process of forcible feeding by prison officers. But the W.S.P.U. had done what it set out to do: it had blown apathy and inattention sky-high. From 1905 onwards, women's suffrage was headline news. And the older N.U.W.S.S. was conscious of an invigorating fresh wind blowing through all its own humdrum activities. Mrs Fawcett was among the first to recognize this debt to the Women's Social and Political Union.

Since then, there has been much argument concerning the effective contribution of militancy to the ultimate triumph of women's suffrage. There were, and indeed still are, those who say that it did nothing but harm. Baroness Asquith (formerly Lady Violet Bonham Carter) expressed the view that militancy did nothing but harm to the suffrage cause, because it exasperated the public, and encouraged women to make themselves look ridiculous —as indeed they sometimes did when scuffling with the police. It is difficult enough at any time to look dignified when so engaged. It is even more difficult when one's enormous hat slips sideways over one ear, one's long hair comes down, scattering hairpins

[64]

Votes for Women

on the pavement, while one's feet get entangled in a trailing skirt.

On the other hand, and this has been particularly true of much that has been written about women's suffrage during its jubilee year 1968, many former adherents of Mrs Pankhurst, as well as journalists and historians relying unduly on contemporary Press cuttings, have created the impression that the effective women's suffrage movement began with Mrs Pankhurst's organization, and ended with its dissolution in 1914, after which "all was over but the shouting"; so that with the patriotic participation of women (including Mrs Pankhurst herself) in the war effort, an instalment of women's suffrage fell like a ripe plum into the women's lap. Such indeed was the impression created, and doubtless honestly conceived, by a *Times* article and a B.B.C. television programme in February 1968 to commemorate the first measure of women's suffrage accorded fifty years earlier. It is the impression left by Roger Fulford's book *Votes for Women** published in 1957, which contains an excellent history of the militant campaign.

Both these versions of the suffrage movement are misleading, and both contain a grain of truth.

Baroness Asquith, as daughter and constant companion of Mr Asquith, was, as it were, at the receiving end of militancy. And as exasperation grew, Mr Asquith, as "public enemy number one", was the victim of the most irritating, and indeed sometimes dangerous, attentions of Mrs Pankhurst's followers. Seeing the suffrage movement from this personal angle, and indeed from the inner ring of the corridors of power, Baroness Asquith could scarcely have realized the impact that the militant movement was making on women all over the country, even on those who deplored militant methods.

The real truth is that the advent of the W.S.P.U. in 1903 and its spectacular activities after the Free Trade Hall incident in 1905, did make a major contribution to the cause. Thereafter it could not be ignored and because what the women were demanding was fundamentally reasonable and just, the more public attention was called to it, the better.

There came a time—one might say after 1912—when militancy assumed harsher and even dangerous forms, involving senseless acts of sabotage, and it did then seem as though such activities were a liability to the cause. N.U.W.S.S. meetings would be

* Faber, 1957.

[65]

broken up, their speakers harried, missiles thrown, in revenge for militant acts for which their organization was in no way responsible.

But even so, the daring and courage of the militants and their heroism under the ordeal of forcible feeding, did provoke admiration and a demonstration of how deeply women cared. This was so when one of the less balanced of Mrs Pankhurst's followers, threw herself under the feet of the king's horse in the Derby of 1913, bringing down horse and jockey and causing herself fatal injuries. Her action could scarcely be described as a rational expression of women's political aspirations; indeed such was the general view of her exploit. And yet, when the W.S.P.U., with its habitual mastery of dramatic occasion, staged an impressive funeral procession for her through London, the crowds which turned out to watch it pass were silent, awed, and deeply moved. I, with my brother Ralph, was among them; and later in the evening I wrote a letter to John Stocks describing the event: here is my impression of it:

We took the tube to Holborn in the fond hope of seeing Miss Davison's funeral; but when we got near the church we found the densest crowd I have ever seen—right along Holborn and all down those little streets that lead off to the British Museum. We tried to get up to a window but they were all full and we only succeeded in seeing the tops of moving banners; so we again set out, to cut it off at its goal (Kings Cross Station); and after struggling through more dense crowds all along Euston Road, finally secured a position of vantage on the steps of St Pancras Railway Depot—overlooking the whole of Kings Cross and the entrance to the station. There we saw a most remarkable sight; for the whole space was dense with crowd except for the little winding passage which the police with great difficulty kept clear for the procession. They evidently hadn't expected anything like half the crowd—nor had I, when I abused the W.S.P.U. for making a public funeral. On the whole it was the most beautifully arranged thing they have done—and it really succeeded in being very impressive. I was much interested to watch the attitude of the crowd—and most of them I think were thoroughly taken by surprise. But what a strange thing the London public is! It breaks up meetings and throws clods of earth at unoffending law-abiding National Unionists, and it turns out in its thousands, with its hat in its hand and tears in its eyes, to watch the funeral of the most destructive militant who ever milled. Truly there is some excuse for the people who throw reason to the wind and address it in its own language!

I was reminded of this scene in 1969 when watching a television recording of scenes in Prague at the funeral of the young student who burnt himself to death in protest against the Russian occupation. So senseless an act—so wasteful of a young and potentially valuable recruit to Czechoslovak resistance! And yet—if a man, or woman, could care so much for a cause as to die for it, there must be something . . .

In fairness to the militants, I think it must be admitted that in a sense the respectable N.U.W.S.S. was parasitic on the unrespectable W.S.P.U.—at any rate up till 1912. The dramatic exploits and personal courage of the militants stirred the enthusiasm of keen suffragists who were not themselves prepared to break the law or condone disorderly action by those who were so prepared. For that enthusiasm, the constitutional movement provided a satisfying outlet. The fire kindled by Mrs Pankhurst's organization helped to heat the furnaces of Mrs Fawcett's.

And yet in another sense, Mrs Pankhurst's organization was parasitic on Mrs Fawcett's. The N.U.W.S.S. had a long record of political experience, and its officers were in close touch with political personalities. When Mrs Pankhurst announced that she was going to lead her deputation to the Prime Minister or the House of Commons, her announcement was intended as a challenge to the police to stop her from getting there, as in fact they always did: and the W.S.P.U. was able to chronicle one more spectacular happening which became headline news next day, and a few more Bow Street appearances and prison sentences which kept the headlines in print for a week or so longer. When Mrs Fawcett announced that she was going to lead a deputation, time and place was duly arranged. She did in fact get there and was politely received. It is true that for many years her good sense bounced off the stone wall of Mr Asquith's obstinacy. But her organization inspired goodwill and trust and was taken seriously by leading political personalities. This meant that from the first, political leaders who might otherwise have shrugged their shoulders and passed on unconcerned in face of militant action, were induced to take women's suffrage seriously; while the militants went gaily forward with the important job of attracting public attention, demonstrating heroism and stirring enthusiasm.

It was not only a difference of method, or as I have tried to show, a difference of function, which provided such interesting contrasts between the two organizations. There was a difference of structure and a difference of personality.

The N.U.W.S.S. was a democratically controlled federation of branches. The W.S.P.U. was, almost from the first, a highly centralized dictatorship: a militant army taking orders from an accepted (not elected) leader. As early as 1907 Mrs Pankhurst tore up such constitution as the W.S.P.U. had possessed, and precipitated a break-away of those members who, though pursuing militant methods, were not prepared to dispense with every vestige of democratic control. Thereafter the W.S.P.U. was a London-based organization, centred on its G.H.Q. in Clements Inn and taking orders from its leader. The year 1907 was indeed not the only occasion on which Mrs Pankhurst demonstrated a capacity for ruthless dictatorship, reminiscent of what subsequently occurred on a larger and more effective scale in Germany and Russia.

In 1912, when parliamentary events precipitated a new frenzy of exasperation with Mr Asquith and his acquiescent government,* Mrs Pankhurst advocated an intensification of militancy involving wilder and more reckless acts of sabotage, amounting, indeed, to civil rebellion. Two of her most devoted colleagues, Fred and Emmeline Pethick-Lawrence, who had for years acted as treasurers and editors of the W.S.P.U. paper, *Votes for Women*, ventured to disagree. Emmeline Pethick-Lawrence was a wizard money-raiser, Fred a very able administrator whose ability was shown later when he served as Financial Secretary to the Treasury and Secretary for India in Mr Attlee's Government. He was a rich man and had been brought face to face with bankruptcy in the service of the W.S.P.U. In 1912 they believed that militancy had no further to go without disastrous results. After all, a militant policy cannot stand still—it must either develop more extreme forms and move towards civil war, or cash in on its achievement of publicity, and

* These events are accurately chronicled in Chapter XI of Ray Strachey's life of *Millicent Garrett Fawcett*, published in 1931 by John Murray.

proceed on more conventional lines. Moreover in twentieth-century England, a minority of women cannot with the worst will in the world conduct an effective civil war. This was the view taken by the Pethick-Lawrences. They had ventured to disagree with Mrs Pankhurst and Christabel, and as an immediate result were ruthlessly thrown out of the W.S.P.U. In a letter to John Stocks dated October 17, 1912, I expressed the surprise this event created in the Suffrage world, by writing: "I feel as if the Trinity had broken up, the Holy Ghost seceded, so incredible is the event."

The Pethick-Lawrences went without any attempt to precipitate a sympathetic breakaway movement, without a word of protest or self-justification—if they had done either of these things many fellow-workers would doubtless have rallied to their side. But they knew that in 1912 any sign of internecine strife in the suffrage ranks would harm the cause and tempt the enemy to blaspheme; so they held their peace.

Looking back many years later, and a decade after the death of Mrs Pankhurst, Emmeline Pethick-Lawrence refers to this Hitlerian incident in her autobiography: *

> There was something quite ruthless about Mrs Pankhurst and Christabel where human relationship was concerned. This ruthlessness was shown not only to us but to many others. . . . Men and women of destiny are like that. . . . Looking back on these events that happened so long ago, it seems to me a miracle that for six years there could have existed a fourfold partnership like ours in which each member played a unique and important part.
>
> Thus in October, 1912, my direct participation in the militant movement came to an end. The cleavage was final and complete. From that time forward I never saw or heard from Mrs Pankhurst again, and Christabel, who had shared our family life, became a complete stranger. The Pankhursts did nothing by halves!

The selfless generosity of the Pethick-Lawrences on this occasion is easy to explain. They were the kind of people who did that kind of thing. I got to know Fred personally many years later after Emmeline's death, and grew to love him. He well deserved the great happiness which a second marriage to a former suffrage

* *My Part in a Changing World.* Gollancz, 1938. Chapter XVIII.

colleague brought him a few years before his death in 1961 at the age of 89.

But why did members of the W.S.P.U. accept such dictatorship without question and with unabated personal devotion? I can answer that question too—but at greater length.

One driving force of the militant movement was hero-worship, and Mrs Pankhurst was, in very truth, a hero. Nobody who can recall her physical presence or hear, in memory, echoes of her very beautiful voice, can fail to experience a reminiscent thrill of excitement. I often heard her speak to great crowds in the Albert Hall, a thing few people could do effectively in that pre-microphone age, and to small groups or in the hurly-burly of a street scuffle. Once I saw her in confrontation with the police; once in the last stages of exhaustion after a hunger strike in prison. And once I was taken by a friend to lunch with her at a hotel in Lincoln's Inn Fields where she lived in the intervals of prison sentences and speaking tours. For me that was a memorable occasion.

Mrs Pankhurst's statue now stands in the Embankment Gardens, under the shadow of the Houses of Parliament, and she deserves that it should. But she is here portrayed as a gentle middle-aged lady with one hand outstretched as in a gesture of pleading. I feel sure that if Epstein had made that statue it would not have created that impression; for Mrs Pankhurst was gentle neither in word nor deed. She was an extremist on whatever subject she touched.

She had, however, a gentleness of manner and an unshakeable dignity of bearing which made it impossible for people to say or think in her presence the scurrilous things that Press accounts of her doings might cause them to say or think when not in her presence. Behind this dignity her fanaticism glowed and crackled. But it never broke through and shattered the dignity. I believe that of all the many militant prison hunger-strikers who were forcibly fed, Mrs Pankhurst who nearly died of repeated hunger strikes, was never forcibly fed. One can see why.

When I describe Mrs Pankhurst as a spellbinder I know what I am talking about, because with many others, including so wise and experienced a pioneer as Dr Elizabeth Garrett-Anderson, I was myself spellbound by her. Doubtless the late Miss Unity Mitford would have said the same of Hitler. But unlike Miss Mitford, whose hero-worship led her to accept Hitler's leadership and policy, I was among those who expended enthusiasm kindled by the militant campaign in the service of the constitutional organization.

The contrast of organization and method as between the two suffrage organizations was dramatically emphasized by the contrast of personality in the two leaders. Indeed, one hesitates to apply the word "leader" to Mrs Fawcett in view of its possible translation into such words as "Führer", "Duce", or "Caudillo", with associations which might be appropriate to Mrs Pankhurst but wholly inappropriate to Mrs Fawcett. Never were two women who served the same cause so wholly unlike one another.

Mrs Fawcett was a leader in so far as she was the elected and trusted President of her organization during the most momentous phase of its history. During that time, being wholly reasonable herself, she never doubted that reasonable methods would triumph, and her service to women's suffrage was thoughtful, persistent and dogged. One dared not say that she believed "passionately" in her cause, because she resented the implication of the word "passionate". It suggested unreasonable lack of balance. That she inspired personal affection must be admitted because she was a most lovable person; but the expression of it was liable to cause her embarrassment, and anything approaching hero-worship would occasion acute distress. This it did on one occasion when, leading a delegation to an international suffrage congress in 1929, she found herself surrounded by a bevy of Greek ladies who very naturally wished to express admiration for a great Englishwoman, and did so with uninhibited intensity.

Some people seem more English than others and Mrs Fawcett always seemed to be very English indeed—perhaps because her roots were in East Anglia, which I believe is the most English part of England. She had a great respect for the English constitution and was, from an early age, steeped in its traditional liberalism. I write this word with a small "l", because spelt with a capital letter, it has associations with a political party; and indeed with the one which failed so deplorably to live up to liberalism between 1905 and 1914.

One other incident, which occurred in connection with an international suffrage congress in Paris in 1927, is typical of Mrs Fawcett. Among the British delegates was Maude Royden, that silver-tongued preacher whose own Church refused to accept her

considerable gifts because she was a woman. The American
Church in Paris did however, and invited her to preach at one of
its Sunday services. The British delegation, including Mrs Fawcett, attended in force. At the close of the service the congregation
sang the American National Anthem which is set to the same tune
as "God save the Queen". On emerging from the church with her
friend Kathleen Courtney, Mrs Fawcett was heard to whisper: "I
sang it. Yes, I sang it. But I sang my own words."

One endearing feature was Mrs Fawcett's quiet but irrepressible
sense of humour. I doubt if Mrs Pankhurst had any sense of
humour at all—though I do not hold that against her, because
many of our greatest compatriots have had none: Lord Shaftesbury, for instance, Mrs Sidney Webb, and others still with us,
whom I will not name for fear of hurting their feelings. It is
possible to have too much sense of humour, and as a result to
laugh when one should cry, or mock when one should revere. But
Mrs Fawcett had enough to lighten the burden of frustration, or
disappointment, and make her company a delight to those privileged to enjoy it, without ever showing malice or undermining
respect.

She was very kind to juniors, and when in the year of our partial
victory in 1918 my son was born, I dared to ask her to stand
godmother. She said that she would, and gave him a complete
Temple Edition of Shakespeare's plays for a christening present: a
gift that he was scarcely able to appreciate at the time but has since
greatly valued.

With this background, let us return to the Rendel Connection
and the impact on it of these various occasions and personalities.

Aunt Edith and Leila joined the W.S.P.U. and wore its purple,
white and green colours. But apart from attending meetings and
walking in processions, neither adopted militant acts or suffered
imprisonment. Harry Ricardo's fiancée, Beatrice, and her two
sisters also wore the purple, white and green, and the younger of
the two sisters worked as a secretary at the W.S.P.U. headquarters,
and from her we got inside news of its affairs.

The rest of us joined the N.U.W.S.S. whose colours were red,
white and green. But we were all more conscious of the cause
which united us than of differences of method which scarcely
divided us at all, and with varying degrees of energy most of us
took some part in suffrage activities. There was, of course, Strachey

influence at work. Pippa Strachey, whom we all loved, was full-time secretary of the London branch of the N.U.W.S.S.; she organized its processions and we walked in them. Elinor, daughter of James Rendel, was a very active adherent, and her Newnham College friend, Ray Costello, later Mrs Oliver Strachey, was more active still. She and Elinor, with a group of college friends, organized a propaganda caravan tour. And during one of Ray's many stays at Rickettswood, we conducted a series of open-air meetings in Redhill, to the embarrassment of Murphy, but with the active collaboration of Elinor's brother Dick.

This was an age when public school boys, especially when, like Dick, they became cadets of the Woolwich Royal Military Academy, might feel tempted to dissociate themselves from the public suffrage activities of their female relatives. Dick was not thus constrained. In the winter of 1907 when the first suffrage procession, known to history as "the mud march", walked three thousand strong from Hyde Park Corner to Exeter Hall in the Strand, Dick walked alongside of it. He was precluded by his embryonic military status from marching in it, but he marched near enough to engage in conversational exchanges with Aunt Edith who did. "Now then young fellow," said a policeman who observed these exchanges, "no sparking here if you please." "If a fellow can't spark with his own aunt, who can he spark with?" replied Dick in a lordly manner. I do not remember whether he then possessed the monocle whose insertion could make such remarks sound even more lordly.

I was still at school when all this began. Though spellbound by Mrs Pankhurst, I was allergic to dictatorship, and was an active adherent of the democratically organized N.U.W.S.S. I carried a banner in the 1907 "mud march" at the head of which walked Mrs Fawcett, Lady Strachey, Lady Frances Balfour, and that indomitable liberty boy, Keir Hardie. As we moved off through the arch of Hyde Park Corner we met a barrage of ridicule from hostile male onlookers. "Go home and do the washing," "Go home and mind the baby" were the most frequent taunts flung at us. As we proceeded along Piccadilly it was observed by some of the marchers that the balcony of the Ladies' Lyceum Club was crowded with members looking down from their safe vantage. Some of the marchers looked up and shouted: "Come down and join us." I do not know whether any of them did.

It was a great adventure for a sixteen-year-old; and on returning to school on the following Monday I was uncertain how my public exploit would be regarded by authority. I need not have worried. All the mistresses were suffragists, as indeed were all salary-earning professional women, with the outstanding exception of Miss Home, the Headmistress of Kensington High School, who declared herself an anti. Though unenlightened and a traitor to her sex, she deserved an accolade for courage.

This commitment of professional women proved to be an asset in later processions, as banners became more colourful and marching groups more defined, because women with university degrees marched in academic dress, and the women doctors with their red robes and multicoloured hoods made a spectacular show. Meanwhile, behind the processions staged by the N.U.W.S.S.—and the militants had some very good processions too—was the organizing genius of Pippa Strachey. She plotted the routes, negotiated with the police, gave the group marshals their marching orders, did all that had to be done for the orderly success of such occasions—without ever appearing in the limelight and seldom being seen on a platform.

Apart from marching, there was plenty of menial work for me to do under the auspices of the N.U.W.S.S. I stewarded at meetings, distributed literature, attended annual conferences and acted as crowd whipper-in at open-air meetings. On one occasion, instigated by my betters, I addressed a street corner meeting in Hackney. But when this effort came to the notice of my mother—perhaps I boasted of having done it—it was not well received; and I was told not to do it again. I fear I did—though only once—at The World's End in the King's Road. The temptation to hear my own voice raised in public for so great a cause was, I fear, compulsive; and I suspect that I did it rather well. But the nearest I ever got to breaking the law was chalking notices of a meeting on pavements in Edinburgh and running away before the police could tell me not to.

After the outbreak of war in 1914, as an adult married woman, I graduated on to the Executive Committee of the N.U.W.S.S. and played a minor part in the very carefully planned and effective campaign which was precipitated by the Government's commitment to a general overhaul of the parliamentary franchise before the end of the war. The story of our successful effort to get a women's suffrage clause inserted into the government's reform Bill, has been well told by Ray Strachey, and need not be retold here. It ended with a dramatic debate in the House of Lords, in which Lord Curzon, leader of the anti-suffrage party as well as leader of the Upper House, brought a violent diatribe on the dangers of women's suffrage to an abrupt end by reminding members that since this mischievous clause had been passed by an over-whelming majority in "another place" he must regretfully urge them not to vote against it. Thus the first important breakthrough of women's suffrage was achieved in time for women to vote in the 1918 General Election, with the blessing of a preponderantly anti-suffrage but effectively cowed hereditary upper chamber.

I achieved a seat behind the bar for the closing stage of that momentous, and until its last moment, precarious debate. It was my first experience of the House of Lords in action; and one which I shall remember vividly when all later experiences in that place have become merged in the mists of senility.

This was not, of course, the end of the fight for women's suffrage. Our demand for the vote "on the same terms as it is or may be granted to men" was not achieved without another active campaign leading to final victory in 1928. Meanwhile the N.U.W.S.S. had broadened its activities to cover other measures of special concern to women, and changed its name to the National Union of Societies for Equal Citizenship. And Eleanor Rathbone had in 1919 succeeded Mrs Fawcett as its President.

I do not think the story of these later activities has yet been adequately told, and though it is worth telling I am not going to tell it here. But there is one feature of the constitutional agitation for women's suffrage that should be recorded and is often for-gotten. Because of its structure and its methods, the N.U.W.S.S. made a notable and enduring contribution to the education of women in the technique of democratic government and political agitation. Its branches all over the country were in continuous touch with the national executive committee and officers at head-quarters. They elected delegates to its annual conference, after studying its agenda and briefing their delegates. When policy decisions were under discussion they were made aware of the views of those who stood for election to the national executive.

There were occasions when policy decisions raised acute con-troversy. It happened in 1913 when the N.U.W.S.S. adopted the policy of selecting constituencies where Labour Party candidates were fighting anti-suffrage Government candidates, and concentrating its resources on the support of such Labour candidates. The Union was and always had been and indeed remained a non-party organization. But the Labour Party had not merely declared its support of women's suffrage as a party, it had pledged itself to oppose any government reform Bill which did not include women. At a time when Labour support was a matter of concern to Mr Asquith's government, and when some measure of franchise reform was inevitable, this decision of the Labour Party was of vital importance to women. But the Union's decision to adopt such an election policy was not taken lightly and its passage through conference precipitated important resignations from the national executive committee.

This was one example of internal divisions hammered out by democratic procedure. There were, of course, others. But the fact of their occurrence should not be forgotten, because of their educative value to those who took part in them. All over the country groups of women in the branches were learning how to discuss agendas, handle resolutions and amendments, brief delegates, and think in terms of parliamentary procedure.

And for the encouragement of this education, the headquarters officers, both honorary and salaried, were admirably fitted. Successive parliamentary secretaries, Ray Strachey, and later Eva Hubback, had nothing to learn and much to teach in the matter of dealing with ministers, M.P.s and civil servants. This was to some extent a heritage of the past, dating from the days of John Stuart Mill; and from the fact that Mrs Fawcett, as wife and widow of a minister, had herself sojourned in the inner ring of parliamentary activity. Thus was set a tradition of political expertise. It was the more needed after 1918, when the objects of the N.U.W.S.S. were expanded to include, in addition to equal suffrage, the promotion of legislative reforms dealing with such complicated matters as guardianship of infants, legitimacy, nationality laws, affiliation and maintenance orders and divorce. And with all these matters the branches would be kept constantly in touch, so that when a bout of political pressure was required, a directive would go out to the branches, and M.P.s all over the country would receive urgent and well-informed instructions from their newly enfranchised female electors as to what they were expected to do.

There was one feature of N.U.W.S.S. organization which might
well be copied by other democratically run national organizations.
This was its separation of the functions of president and chairman.
It is the business of a president to influence and guide policy. It is
the business of a chairman to conduct an orderly meeting with a
show of impartiality. Mrs Fawcett and later Eleanor Rathbone
were elected as presidents because both were great women and
their views on policy commanded attention. Mrs Rackham was
elected as chairman because she possessed a masterly capacity for
guiding a large conference through a maze of resolutions and
amendments without expressing personal bias, getting in a muddle
herself, or allowing delegates to do so. Presidential and chairmanship qualities do not necessarily go together, and during the many
years of her chairmanship, observation of Mrs Rackham's technique was another phase of our education for citizenship under the
auspices of the N.U.W.S.S.

Many years later, when I had occasion to visit a number of
localities all over England—in the service of other causes such as
family allowances, birth-control, international affairs, or adult
education—it was observable that many of the women who were
playing an active and intelligent part in local affairs, as magistrates, councillors, promoters of women's citizens associations,
family planning clinics, or branches of the League of Nations
Union, were the same women who had once played an active part
in the suffrage agitation. Such, in addition to the vote, has been
its gift to posterity.

It was, of course, not only the constitutional suffragists who
marched on into wider and more constructive activities. Many of
the militants turned to public service. But they did not march as
an organization nor in company with their old leader. When war
was declared, the N.U.W.S.S. realized of course that its activities
were irrelevant. There would be little use in winning the vote
unless we succeeded in winning the war. Nevertheless, the Union's
organization might well be needed if at any time a renewal of the
suffrage agitation required action. As Mrs Fawcett said: "We will
bury the hatchet but we will mark the place so that if necessary we
can dig it up again." It did indeed prove necessary to dig it up
again when the Government was faced with the problem of a
franchise reform Bill in anticipation of peace. Meanwhile the
branches continued to function as branches, but "kept their

powder dry" and used their organization for various forms of war work. The Scottish Women's Hospitals was one such activity; the training of women oxy-acetylene welders for munitions work was another.

But faced with the greater militancy of war the Women's Social and Political Union quietly dissolved, its prisoners were set free and Mrs Pankhurst, in the last stages of exhaustion from repeated hunger-strikes and rearrests, became an ardent supporter of the war effort under her own steam. As Emmeline Pethick-Lawrence said, the Pankhursts "did nothing by halves". Mrs Pankhurst helped to promote a recruiting campaign, she waged a passionate campaign on behalf of violated Serbia; later, having started life as an open-air speaker for the Independent Labour Party, she became a right-wing Conservative. Her daughter Christabel has told the story of these later years in her book *Unshackled**, but she can scarcely be regarded as an objective historian.

My own view is that Mrs Pankhurst was a born extremist and never well-balanced, that the outbreak of war in 1914 saved her from real mental unbalance resulting from the physical and emotional stresses of the militant suffrage movement, and that thereafter, until her death in 1928—fortunately not before knew that women's suffrage was safe—she never wholly recovered that balance. I think that the outbreak of war in 1914 saved her from herself and saved the W.S.P.U. from an ignominious end. It had shot its bolt, and what an effective bolt it had been!

In March 1928 the National Union, by now the National Union of Societies for Equal Citizenship, organized a meeting in Queen's Hall at which the Prime Minister, Mr Baldwin, was to announce his Government's commitment to the Bill which at last was to give us the equal voting right for which we had campaigned so long. It was a widely representative meeting, chaired by Eleanor Rathbone. Many old suffragists were present, and many young ones—too young indeed to have played a part in the pre-1918 suffrage agitation. Mrs Pankhurst had a front seat on the platform but she was not one of the speakers. I think that many younger members of the audience did not know who she was. She looked very frail, dignified and aloof, almost as though she did not care very much about what was happening. As I looked at her, I wondered whether she recalled the acclaim and hero-worship which had so often sur-

* Hutchinson, 1959.

rounded her on that same platform in that same hall. I certainly
recalled it; and when a few months later her death was reported, a
bell tolled in my mind for the death of a hero.

In spite of exasperation with "the law's delays, the insolence of
office, and the spurns that patient merit of the unworthy takes",
that intensive pre-1918 phase of the women's suffrage campaign
was exhilarating as well as educative. Perhaps I enjoyed it inordin-
ately because I was young; but I think that all who took part in it
did, including the prisoners—though not perhaps the hunger-
strikers. It had so many side-benefits, of which the greatest were
personal friendships generated by comradeship. For me it was an
unforgettable experience to see the great women of an older
generation at work, and achieve personal contacts with them; with
Mrs Fawcett I was destined to have other contacts at the School of
Economics. And among my contemporaries it produced enduring
personal friendships with, among many others, Kathleen Courtney
and Margery Corbett Ashby—both of them now Dames—as well
as the valued memory of friendships with Ray Strachey and Eva
Hubback. My greatest side-benefit was close association with
Eleanor Rathbone; because here personal friendship was cemented
by later collaboration in another cause of great importance to
women: family allowances.

I wonder if the young people of today get as much satisfaction
from their support—both militant and law-abiding—of nuclear
disarmament or peace in Vietnam. I doubt if they can. Partly
because their demand is less easy to define and its achievement
more unpredictable—*we* always knew that we should win, it was
merely a case of this year or next. And in addition we had in those
days fewer irrelevant distractions. We were, for instance, relatively
free from the constant emotional impact of sex problems which
today enliven student life, and provoke endless discussions and
disturbing entanglements.

Our suffrage world was a preponderantly woman's world. But I
do not regret that, because the greater part of my subsequent life—
at the School of Economics, at Oxford and Manchester, on government committees and in the adult education movement—was
passed in a preponderantly man's world, and the suffrage movement showed me what a good world women can make when they
work together.

We had, of course, invaluable men supporters in the women's

suffrage agitation. Where could we have got without them? There
were Philip Snowden, Arthur Henderson, J. H. Thomas, George
Lansbury, Lord Robert Cecil, John Simon, C. P. Scott, to name
only a few outstanding friends in the political world. There was
Gilbert Murray, Professor Geldart, and John Stocks at Oxford.
At an early stage in the agitation, I became familiar with the frequent appearance on open-air suffrage platforms of an earnest pale
young man named Theo Gugenheim, who was later to become a
close friend and fellow-student at the School of Economics.

The fact that such men were working with us, ruled out any
element of sex war which such a campaign might have engendered.
But even if it had existed, it would, in my own case, have been
effectively dispelled in 1912 by the incursion into my world of
John Stocks.

6

The London School of Economics

THE LONDON SCHOOL OF ECONOMICS at the time when I clocked into it with such easy informality in 1910 at the age of 19, was a small institution in a tall Edwardian building; but it had already begun to overflow into a huddle of temporary one-storey classrooms on a neighbouring cleared site. These were described by the Director, Mr Pember Reeves, as "the shedifice". In its main building it had basement cloakrooms and lavatories; on the ground floor it had a long library with basement storage and a large hall for public occasions. On the first floor were administrative offices for the Director and Miss Mactaggart the Secretary, and above that, classrooms. At the very top were student common-rooms and the refectory, with a kitchen somewhere in the background. There must have been a senior common-room, but I forget where it was, and I never set foot in it.

The school's clientele was mixed, as regards age, nationality, social background, and sex—though it was preponderantly male. I imagine that first-degree students, like myself, were in a minority. There was an army class consisting of officers seconded from their staff college for a course in public administration. As they were the product of an agreement between Haldane, as Minister for War, and H. J. Mackinder, a former Director of the school, the group was known as "Haldane's Mackindergarten". They were the only group which kept itself to itself. Perhaps they found the rest of us a bit odd. Perhaps they were unaccustomed to working on free-and-easy terms with females; and, having served in India, one of them was, it seems, rendered uncomfortable by the sight of white female students mixing happily with black males.

Another more mature group which did, however, mix freely, was concerned with the special study of railway economics. And in 1912 a diploma in social studies was created which produced a mainly female group working under Professor Urwick, to which we gave the name "Urwick's harem". Some of us who were working for the B.Sc.(Econ.) adopted an attitude towards these potential social workers which can only be described as tainted with intellectual snobbery; but "Urwick's harem" proved to be the embryo of an important department; and at an early stage Clement Attlee, who had started his pilgrimage to Labour premiership as a social worker at Toynbee Hall, became one of its lecturers.

In addition to these groups there were a number of postgraduates at work on research projects, one or two delightful Irish students financed by Dublin Castle, and a number of casual visitors attending particular lectures or seminars. Flora Carter, who first introduced me to the school, must have been such a one.

A notable feature of the school was the duplication of its lectures and classes for the benefit of evening students. Most of these were fully employed during the day, and their academic life began at about 6 p.m. This duplication must have imposed a heavy workload on the academic staff whose teaching day would thus often extend until 9 p.m. But the evening students were mature and enthusiastic learners, and must have been a delight to teach. Many years later, when I became an adult education tutor in Lancashire, I was able to appreciate the opportunity of working with students who had been ready to sacrifice leisure and pleasure to the hard pursuit of learning.

In those early days professors, and heads of departments who were not yet professors, undertook first-year teaching of degree students—so that in my first year I was able to sit at the feet of leading members of the staff and get to know their ways. Before I left the school in 1913, heads of departments had produced a number of first-class honours students who could be used as assistant lecturers and thus relieve the professors of much elementary teaching.

The first-year degree course consisted of lectures on a wide range of allied subjects economic theory, public administration, banking and foreign trade, economic geography, economic history

—and a choice between logic starting from zero and mathematics starting from logarithms. The gap between this mathematical starting-point and the last chapter of my matriculation manual drove me to logic and thus prevented me from becoming a statistician. On these various subjects we wrote essays which were handed back to us in the porter's lodge with appended comments. Of tutorial class-work there was, at this stage, none for first-year students, so far as I can remember. But with the help of text-books and lectures, plus the stimulus of fellow-students, I found my first year exciting and not unduly discouraging. It ended with an exam known as "Inter" which required passes in all these subjects.

This might sound a tough assignment for a complete beginner, but in fact in one respect it was far less tough than it would be today owing to the increasing complexity of the subject-matter since 1910, and the vastly expanded range of economic textbooks. Banking, currency and foreign exchange presented in 1910 a simple self-adjusting mechanism based on the operation of the Gold Standard and manipulation of the discount rate. One could get to the bottom of it with the help of two popular volumes by Hartley Withers. Apart from Cunningham and Ashley and Samuel Smiles's biographies of the engineers, economic history had yet to be written. The Hammonds had not yet appeared on the horizon. With hard work and lecture notes, and the mastery of a few standard textbooks, one could survive "inter"; and in fact I did.

Only first-year economic theory as expounded by Professor Edwin Cannan gave me, and indeed others, serious trouble. His intermediate course appeared to me almost wholly unintelligible. His own superb small textbook "Wealth" was not published until 1914, and we worked on Alfred Marshall's large single volume— which I did my best to supplement with John Stuart Mill. But I soon learned that Mill was all wrong; and Cannan's first-year lectures on Marshall suggested that he was all wrong too. "There's not much in that," was a Cannanical phrase which seemed to echo through those lectures like a liturgical response. In fact we used it later as a chorus in a student variety entertainment entitled "Economic Extravaganza". I handed in two essays to Professor Cannan during that first year and both were returned marked "O". I do not know how I managed to survive the economic theory paper in "Inter"; but I am very glad I did, because the two years which followed brought a realization of what a great man Cannan was: original in exposition, destructive in criticism, and wholly allergic to verbiage or cant. His approach to his subject was clean, clear, and cutting. He lived in Oxford and commuted from there to London—on occasions doing the fifty-mile journey on a bicycle. Later I got to know and love him and his wife as Oxford neighbours.

Very much more encouraging during that first year were the economic history lectures of Dr Lilian Knowles, head of her department though not yet a professor. She was a brilliantly stimulating lecturer, and a magnificently flamboyant personality. In politics she was an unashamed imperialist, and her interpretation of the industrial revolution of the eighteenth and early nineteenth centuries was coloured rather by admiration for its technical and commercial achievements than by consciousness of its distressing social consequences, which from 1911 onwards were so effectively highlighted by Barbara and J. L. Hammond. One curious paradox about Lilian Knowles was that though her lectures and tutorials were unforgettable, the minute she committed her learning to paper, it became as dust and ashes.

Though academic contacts with the staff were impersonal during that first year, social and cultural contacts were quite otherwise. The centre of the school's social life was the refectory. There, staff and students mixed informally. There were only two fixed stars in the whole galaxy. At the head of a centre table sat Mr Pember Reeves, the somewhat withdrawn Director, with Miss Mactaggart the Secretary on his right hand. It has been said that the Director reigned and Miss Mactaggart ruled.

And here one peculiarity of Miss Mactaggart is worthy of note. She did not approve of women smoking, and in 1910 very many women did, though it was still regarded as unconventional. She was unable to impose a rule on this matter because this would have violated the principle of sex-equality which was dear to the school. So she asserted that though no rule existed, there was a "convention" that women did not smoke in the refectory—a convention which was certainly not observed by either Mrs Sidney Webb or Mrs Pember Reeves who frequently lunched at the Director's table. But the rest of us observed the "convention" by refraining from smoking until Miss Mactaggart had left the room. Her attitude was absurdly antediluvian, and she had no right whatever to impose her prejudice on others. But common politeness and respect for the foible of a senior and well-liked member of the staff demanded restraint. I would like to think that L.S.E. students of today would show similar consideration; but I fear not. I fear rather that if a senior staff-member was known to attempt any such veto, the students would assert their right to smoke by smoking all the more under his or her nose. However, by the end of my sojourn at the school, Miss Mactaggart had come to terms with current usage; though whether she herself was ever seen to smoke, I cannot remember.

There was, I think, a tendency for seniors to gravitate to the central table with its two fixed stars, nevertheless there was no clear separation of students and staff. Anybody sat anywhere, and a raw first-year student might find himself sitting next to Edwin Cannan or Lilian Knowles, or Graham Wallas or L. T. Hobhouse, participating in conversation which was an education in itself, and far more satisfying than are the conversations of the great heard on radio or seen on television today. To me, these great ones did indeed seem great, and I felt for them what can only be described as "reverence". This is a sensation which, according to my daughter and doubtless to many of her contemporaries, no human being or institution should be allowed to inspire in other human beings. Doubtless one could evade the issue by saying: "It all depends on what you mean by reverence."

One cannot, however, exclude from any reminiscence of the L.S.E. refectory one of its leading and unchanging personalities: Mrs Sergison. I do not know how far she was responsible for its finance and catering. But whenever the refectory was open, Mrs Sergison was at the cash-desk by the door. She knew everyone, and everyone was her friend. She can best be realized by readers of Dorothy Sayers's detective novels, who are familiar with Lord Peter Wimsey's colleague, Miss Climpson. Miss Climpson was an outwardly austere, thin, high-Anglican spinster, a shrewd but humorous assessor of character and a wearer of little religious medallions. Except that she was not a spinster—indeed I think she had a grown-up daughter—when I met Miss Climpson in fiction I saw Mrs Sergison in memory.

Some years later, during the First World War, I encountered a thin lady in military uniform, including riding breeches, busily engaged on the platform of a railway station, supervising the transport of Army forage. It was Mrs Sergison—so different, yet the same.

Moving from the attic to the ground floor, another unforgettable but unchanging personality will be forever part of early L.S.E. life. This was Dodson, the head porter, who came to the school from the Royal Navy and presided over the lodge. Had he survived with full vigour into the nineteen-sixties I feel sure that there would have been no nonsense with disorderly students; and had anyone died of a heart attack precipitated by such disorder it would not have been Dodson, but rather somebody whom he had restrained.

He used to hand back our essays to us, and I suspect that he observed and remembered the marks obtained by us, from which he was able to make a fairly accurate forecast of final class results. Those students who were prepared to bet on their own destinies were likely to be the losers; because either from modesty or fear, one always tended to under-rate one's chances. Thus it may have been a profitable game for Dodson. On balance he probably knew more about the individual students, their ability, their assiduity, and indeed their social habits than did their own professors or their fellow-students. But his integrity and discretion were absolute.

The School of Economics opening into Clare Market was—and still is—situated in an interesting part of London, though thanks to redevelopment its surroundings do not look the same. To the West of it was the Strand, then as now a gay theatre land. To the East of it was the City, Fleet Street and Lincoln's Inn Fields. One approached the School either through Portugal Street, off Kingsway, Houghton Street, off Aldwych, or through a passage which ran between the Law Courts and the tall flats of Clement's Inn. That was my own usual approach from the Temple underground station. It had special interests of its own. In a Clement's Inn basement was the office which operated Mr and Mrs Sidney Webb's campaign to break up the Poor Law. There I worked for some years as a volunteer on Saturday mornings, directing envelopes and sticking on stamps, until the Webbs abandoned their effort in face of the Poor Law's obstinate survival, and went off to China, leaving the Poor Law to be effectively broken up, very much on the lines they had planned, by a Conservative Government in 1929.

Another special interest offered by Clement's Inn was the fact that it also housed the headquarters of the militant suffrage campaign, and was the home of Mr and Mrs Pethick-Lawrence and Christabel Pankhurst. During the last cloak and dagger, hunger striking and forcible feeding phase of militancy, Christabel was on the run; and entering or leaving Clement's Inn one would be aware of policemen on the look out for a homecoming and possibly disguised fugitive from justice. She was, in fact, conducting her campaign from a safe hideout in Paris. And I have little doubt that her lodging there was comfortable as well as safe; because I learned, having once accompanied Christabel on a twenty-four-hour journey from Switzerland to London, that, unlike her heroic mother, she appreciated the amenities of gracious living.

The L.S.E. was in those days very politically-minded, as indeed it appears to be today, and as the nature of its studies requires it to be. The Students' Union brought us distinguished speakers, and the fact that we were a London institution gave us easier access to them. So that during my three years we had, among others, Bernard Shaw, Norman Angell, Mrs Fawcett, Father Benson, and Hilaire Belloc. This last arrived slightly drunk, and in the course of the evening during discussion referred with extreme insolence to our President, who was an Indian, and also to a third-year student with a Jewish name whom he repeatedly referred to as "Uckstein", though this was not his name. We resented his behaviour and determined never to invite him again; but we did not show our resentment by hustling him or shouting at him. He was, after all, our invited guest, and we were civilized adult students.

One excellent school of politics was the Union's Clare Market Parliament, which met on alternate weeks. Its deliberations reflected current politics. In my second year I served as President of the Local Government Board in a government led by Theo Gugenheim as socialist Prime Minister, with Vera Powell as President of the Board of Trade and William Piercy as Chancellor of the Exchequer. I remember that Piercy finally brought down his government by a proposed tax on mineral water, but not before we had carried adult suffrage, Irish Home Rule, and a considerable measure of unilateral disarmament. And I succeeded in carrying an Unemployment Bill based on the recommendations of the Poor Law Commission's minority report. It was strongly opposed by Hugh Dalton, a postgraduate student from Cambridge, who led the Liberal Party. He denounced my Bill as "academic", and I like to remember that in 1934 its main provisions were carried into law under the nose of the Rt Hon. Hugh Dalton, M.P., who was by that time a leading member of the Labour Party.

But these were mainly, as far as I was concerned, second and third-year happenings. It was at the beginning of the second year that work for the B.Sc. (Econ.) became intensely absorbing. One chose an honours subject in which to specialize and thus became the special charge of the head of department whose subject had been chosen. I chose economic history and thus became the charge of Dr Lilian Knowles. As such I found myself one of four history honours students.

Two, Theo Gugenheim and William Piercy, were evening students who had achieved L.C.C. scholarships which enabled them to abandon the hard life of wage-earning plus evening studies, and become full day-time students for their second and third years. The third was Vera Powell, now Vera Anstey, who, though two years older than I was, started her first year at the same time; so we had already become friends. Together the four of us attended Dr Knowles's weekly tutorials. Together we habitually occupied the same small table in the refectory. Together we played politics in the Union and the Clare Market Parliament, and for a year William Piercy and I were joint secretaries of the Union. Together, after Union meetings, we would adjourn to drink beer at a restaurant in the Strand called Appenrodt—now, alas, no more. Together we dined with Dr Knowles, and together we entertained her to dinner.

This fourfold association was a heaven-sent benefaction for me because the other three were all brilliant students, as their subsequent careers show. Vera Powell married a fellow-student, becoming Mrs Anstey at the end of her third year. Thereafter she accompanied him to India on his appointment as head of an Indian college. After his death in 1920 she returned to the school where later she became Reader in Indian History, and Dean of the Faculty of Economics. She has recently retired as an eminent and well-loved member of the school senior staff and a notable authority on Indian history.

William Piercy rose to eminence in big business and finance, and died in 1967 as Lord Piercy. My own promotion to the House of Lords came just in time for him to act as one of my sponsors at

the ceremony of my induction as a fellow-member of that enchanting social club.

Theo Gugenheim, as member of a German Jewish family, was
inspired with a very natural desire in 1914 to fight and if possible
kill Germans. He had already shown himself, as an open-air
speaker surrounded by angry anti-suffrage mobs, to be a man of
remarkable physical courage. Having failed owing to his German
origin to achieve a commission in the army, which normally a man
of his academic standing would receive, he changed his name to
Gregory and enlisted as a private in Kitchener's Army. Alas—
thanks to a letter forwarded by a fellow-student who had foolishly
scratched out his old name and added his new one on the same
envelope—the authorities learned of his Germanic origin and cast
him out of the army. This caused him great disappointment; but to
his friends it was a matter for rejoicing, because for that particular
vintage of Kitchener's Army, an infantryman on the Western
front had a poor choice of survival. In the end his disappointment
enabled him to pursue a distinguished career, undisturbed by war
service, first on the staff of the L.S.E., later as Professor of
Economics, and through a number of important financial assignments, to his post at the time of writing, as Sir Theodore Gregory,
Financial Adviser to the British Economic Mission to Greece.

Thus, being closely associated for two crucial years with three
brilliant fellow-students, I had to exert myself to keep in step with
them. In the end we all four got firsts; in fact out of five firsts
achieved by the L.S.E. in 1913, four of them fell to the credit of
Dr Knowles. This pleased her greatly, though in my case she
indicated a cause of success other than my own natural wit—with
which I will shortly deal. Describing her reaction to the results in
a letter to John Stocks dated November 29, 1913, I wrote:

> There is one other first beside us four—an Indian Banker
> named Subedar. . . . None of Lees Smith's people have got
> firsts and none of Hobhouse's. Fortunately I found Dr
> Knowles in her room—dressed in ermine and silk and with
> the smile of a mother whose children are superior to anyone
> else's children.

Looking, today, at the considerable collection of economic
history textbooks in my bookcase, I am reminded of what we had
not got when we started on our second and third year of honours

work with Dr Knowles. Hammond's *Village Labourer* lightened our darkness in 1911. But there was no Clapham, none of those important studies of special areas, special industries or individual firms, which have since brought economic history so vividly to life; no Bland, Brown and Tawney's *Select Documents*; no three-volume collection of *Tudor Economic Documents* edited by R. H. Tawney and Eileen Power. Among my collection stand three well-worn massive volumes of Cunningham's *Growth of English Industry and Commerce*, kept I fear for its sentimental value, but long since superseded as part of my later stock-in-trade for the teaching of economic history. We had, of course, access in the school library to early nineteenth-century blue books which told us what later generations learned at second-hand from the Hammonds and others about conditions in mines and factories, about the reconstruction of the Poor Laws and the campaign for sanitary reform. The publication in 1912 of R. H. Tawney's *Agrarian Problem in the Sixteenth Century* came as a burst of light on rural England, and enabled me to write an essay which was marked 100 per cent.

This dearth of processed material put an extra burden on Dr Knowles. At an early stage of our second-year studies she took us to the British Museum and introduced us to the Charters of early joint-stock companies. It seems that she paid many such visits with students by ones and twos, to evade the rule which precluded the use of the British Museum for teaching purposes. This, she said, aroused the suspicion that she was using the Museum as a convenient location for meeting men not necessarily interested in the contents of the surrounding book-stacks, and thus caused her to be watched. This was not as surprising as one might suppose, because Dr Knowles did not look in the least like popular conceptions of a female don.

As with the self-contained Rendel Connection, so with the above-mentioned self-contained academic quartet, attention must be called to a paradox. Though constantly in one another's company which I think each one of us found congenial, we all had equally absorbing outside concerns and unshared interests.

In the summer of 1912 William Piercy and I were elected as joint secretaries of the Students' Union which meant quite a lot of work, though not nearly as much as would fall to a pair of secretaries today. We had our internal Union disagreements, of course, and a major conflict was sparked off by the impact of the women's suffrage movement, then in a critical phase. The Union had of course an elected working President, at the time an Indian student called Muzumdar. It had also an outside President, a person of eminence who was normally expected to do no more than shed the light of his name, perhaps give one address, and attend the Union's annual dinner. The final selection of this ornamental President lay with the committee, and the choice lay between Mrs Fawcett and Lord Avebury—the latter a known anti-suffragist, nominated precisely for this reason as a counterblast to feminist pretensions. It was a hard, and at times acrimonious, fight, but the "quartet" were all members of the committee and finally an invitation went out to Mrs Fawcett.

As things turned out it was a fortunate choice and, I think, generally admitted to be so. Mrs Fawcett, who lived in Gower Street, within easy reach of the school, accepted the invitation with pleasure. She was interested in the young and in economics, and doubtless pleased to have been selected as patron of a preponderantly male assembly. She gave us a hilarious inaugural address on the subject of "gossip", and thereafter from time to time attended and presided over Union public meetings. She became a familiar figure at the school, and to me fell the incidental pleasure of calling at Gower Street on several occasions to discuss arrangements for Union functions. There are references to such occasions in my letters to John Stocks. In February, 1913, I wrote:

> Yesterday I had tea . . . with Mrs Fawcett, and went through some details relating to the annual dinner next Wednesday, at which she is going to preside. I never can quite get over the feeling that Mrs Fawcett is a kind of anachronism and belongs more to the 70s and 80s than to the present day—not because she isn't as up-to-date as anyone, and a good deal more so than most—but because it does seem rather queer that a person who worked with Mill and Fawcett and all those people whom I seem to regard as "history" should be leading the suffrage movement today and shouldn't seem at all old.

The organization of the annual dinner was perhaps the most burdensome task which fell to the joint secretaries. It involved a tour of London restaurants involving cold rebuffs when their managers were told the maximum charge we could impose per head. Our contact with Princes in Piccadilly was peculiarly humiliating. Finally, the Criterion accepted us, and did us very well at prices our members and their guests could afford to pay. But seating arrangements gave much trouble and caused me to write:

> Piercy and I had literally to lock ourselves up in private yesterday afternoon in order to arrange the seating and be free from the multitude of conflicting suggestions that everyone was so ready to offer, as to who they should sit near. If we had adopted them all, Gugenheim would have had a large table all to himself and Vera Powell would have been the centre of a dense crowd.

Gugenheim was both liked and respected but he was at this time excessively earnest, and one can see why he would not have seemed the ideal companion for a festive occasion.

It always has been, and doubtless still is, the habit of students to form small close societies—which come into existence and go out of existence with the changing student generations. William Piercy, Gugenheim and I belonged to such an ephemeral group. Vera Powell was at the time preoccupied with the business of getting engaged to Percy Anstey, a fellow student whom she married before sitting for finals. It was called the Query Club, presumably because it could not think of a suitable descriptive name. It was a mixed group of about a dozen third-year and post-graduate students, and its leading members were Hugh Dalton and Eileen Power. It was, I thought, a great honour to be asked to join it. Its usual, though not its only, meeting place was Hugh Dalton's room in the Temple. There, papers of a serious nature would be read and discussed. I seem to remember that light refreshments would be provided, but whether alcoholic or not I cannot say. Our subjects of discussion might be political, philosophic, or aesthetic. My own contribution, produced with much pain and infinite misgiving, was a paper on the post-impressionists who were at that time represented by an exhibition promoted by Roger Fry at the Grafton Gallery.

Among all the post-graduates of that vintage—and there were some very good ones—Eileen Power shone like a star. She was intellectually brilliant, beautiful, witty, and of surpassing charm. She came to the School from Girton with a scholarship given by Mrs Bernard Shaw for research into the history of women, and was engaged on researches into medieval nuns. She inhabited a lodging at the unfashionable Pimlico end of Ebury Street, and the emoluments of the Shaw benefaction required austere living. But her tastes were not austere, particularly in the matter of clothes, and her economic fortunes would alternate between elegant living and temporary periods of extreme penury to liquidate resulting insolvency. She and I became great friends, and she was a frequent weekend guest at Queen's Gate Terrace, also on one occasion during a summer holiday at West Bay. My mother adored her, as did everybody who knew her.

Her subsequent career, as medieval historian, teacher, both at the L.S.E. and in Cambridge, and traveller in the Far East, will be familiar to all sojourners in academic and literary circles.

What is perhaps less familiar is the disturbed childhood and adolescence which she shared with her two sisters—both of whom achieved distinction in other spheres. Their story bears some resemblance to that of the two sons of Oscar Wilde, in that while still children their family fortunes were suddenly disrupted by the disappearance of their father into prison—not in his case for an unmentionable crime, but for straightforward financial embezzlement, a career which he pursued until late in life with astonishing persistence. This left his wife, who did not long survive the catastrophe, and three small daughters who did, to be cared for by his wife's family, completely cut off from that of their delinquent father and very short of money. They changed their name from Power to Raymond, and as Raymonds they grew up in the care of devoted maternal aunts—resuming the name of Power by their own choice when they reached years of discretion.

Psychologists are wont to indicate insecure and unhappy childhood experiences as a cause of subsequent mental unbalance or anti-social behaviour. It is therefore pleasant to recall notable deviations from this widely accepted pattern. Elizabeth I's childhood experiences contained all the ingredients for subsequent mental and moral disintegration. She was, however, the wisest, most intellectually distinguished and public-spirited monarch that this kingdom has ever had. The three small Power sisters, Eileen, Rhoda and Beryl, their childhood overshadowed by paternal disgrace, orphanhood, and family dissension, emerged with undisturbed mental balance, remarkable self-reliance, intellectual brilliance, and more than normal capacity for generous public spirit.

By the end of my second year, though still a well-integrated member of the Rendel Connection and a hard-working student of the L.S.E., I had at least ceased to be London-centred. A new horizon had opened out with the advent of John Stocks.

A chance encounter with Sidney Ball, of St John's College, Oxford, and his wife, beginning with a conversation on the pier during a summer holiday at West Bay, revealed to him that I was a student at the London School of Economics. He himself was a Fabian, a great friend of Sidney Webb and of its other leading personalities, such as Hobhouse and Graham Wallas. The acquaintance ripened rapidly. The prevailing atmosphere of St John's, conservative and clerical, was not wholly congenial to Sidney Ball. Indeed he had in the preceding year been rejected for its Presidency after an internal conflict which in some respects recalls C. P. Snow's book, *The Masters*.* But one of his colleagues, a young tutor and fellow of the college called John Stocks was wholly congenial. Stocks was a socialist, a Poor Law guardian and a keen member of the Oxford Women's Suffrage Society. He had all the right ideas. So, it seemed, had I. And Stocks, at the age of 28, was still unmarried. Mrs Ball was struck with an idea; and never was a matchmaking enterprise more deliberately planned and effectively sustained. I received an invitation to spend a weekend at Oxford during the summer of 1912. John Stocks was invited to lunch and deputed to show me round the colleges. There it all began; with an abruptness which took my breath away and left me speechless. But John Stocks was not deterred. He appeared in lodgings at West Bay during the ensuing summer vacation, during which I had been given time to draw breath, and by the end of that summer vacation on the eve of my third year as a student, Mrs Ball was proved right. She was not always right, in some respects she was notably eccentric. But in thinking that John Stocks and I were ideally suited for one another, and taking deliberate steps to prove it, she could not have been more right, and I owe her a deep debt of gratitude.

During the year which followed, I pursued my studies at the School of Economics and John Stocks pursued his teaching in

* Macmillan, 1951.

Oxford. But the Ball house was always open to me for weekends, and 8 Queen's Gate Terrace was open to him. Nowadays I suppose we should have got married immediately and I should have commuted from Oxford to the School of Economics fortified by the "pill". Such a possibility did not arise in 1912. Nor was the suggestion that I should throw up my studies and retire into matrimony even under discussion. John Stocks was a sufficiently committed academic to regard such desertion in the middle of an honours degree course as unthinkable. He had all the right ideas about women's education—so much so, that as one of the older members of a large clerical family he had used his comparative affluence as a newly established fellow of St John's to finance the education of his younger sister Helen at Lady Margaret Hall.

So we settled down to something more than a year's engagement, since finals occurred in the Autumn term following the completion of three years, with weekends together in Oxford or London and daily correspondence between Monday and Friday. Since he kept my letters and I kept his, together they provide a running commentary on life in pre-1913 Oxford University and life in the pre-1913 London School of Economics.

Re-reading these letters after more than half a century I am struck by a contrast. My letters are those of an immature undergraduate, rather sloppily written but perhaps attractive to him in their spontaneity. His were the letters of a mature philosopher, but a philosopher in touch with the world of politics, social problems and the eccentricities of human beings. And they are things of beauty in themselves, being written in a script which at a distance recalls a Greek manuscript, since Greek philosophy was his main subject, but are nevertheless as clear and precise as were his own processes of thought. I sometimes wonder, as indeed I sometimes wondered at the time, how his devotion managed to survive. But he was interested in undergraduates and knew their ways—and doubtless knew also that with education and encouragement they would in due course grow up.

Much of my further education during this year came from integration with John Stocks' friends and contemporaries: particularly his two greatest friends Harry Tawney and William Temple. In Oxford, Gilbert Murray came into my view—and indeed others to whom I was presented not as a third-year undergraduate, but as a newcomer to Oxford academic society at what might be described as senior common-room level. Industrial Lancashire also swam into my ken, since a Stocks sister had married a colliery owner and lived among pit-heads and cotton mills. So did the trade union movement as a live concern outside the pages of Webb's *History of Trade Unionism* and *Industrial Democracy*—for my sister-in-law Helen Stocks was a colleague of Mary MacArthur and had been engaged in organizing the chainmakers of Cradley Heath in their historic strike for a minimum wage. Most significant of all, as it subsequently proved, was my introduction to the Workers' Educational Association, which had scarcely impinged at all on our London-centred existence. How could it be otherwise with William Temple and Harry Tawney so near at hand?

All this might have been distracting and disturbing to studies. On the contrary it was extremely stimulating. I had now to keep up, not only with Vera Powell, William Piercy and Theo Gugenheim, but also with John Stocks who was no less academically brilliant but also eight years wiser. Moreover I had need to justify the long wait that my preoccupation with economics had imposed on him. My recognition of these necessities acted as a spur and caused Dr Knowles to ascribe my unexpected achievement of a first to the advent of John Stocks. Since she had watched the progress of my studies for three years, she should know. At any rate she made it perfectly clear in a letter to him in reply to one of his, congratulating her on her achievement in dragging me up to first-class level:

> Ever so many thanks for your letter. I was of course delighted at the result. It was not really unexpected but I dared not hint at it beforehand for fear of disappointment. I think a good deal of the credit is due to you . . . she always was clever but had such a youthful mind. I used to say that Miss Brinton would get a second and evolute into a first; the evolution, owing to her engagement, came early, earlier than I had hoped. She lost that immaturity of outlook this last year, and began to really handle things. I think that is due to you.

Alas, I see no trace of advance from this "immaturity of outlook" in my letters to John Stocks. But obviously he did, or he couldn't have gone on with it!

Since those early days the School of Economics has "suffered a sea change into something rich and strange". Money has flowed into it from many sources, and neighbouring sites have been occupied by it. During its middle years its two ageing parents, Sidney and Beatrice Webb, watched it with pride: delighting in its growth and deriving satisfaction from its spreading influence. That influence has been world-wide.

In 1952 I happened to attend a cocktail party in Ankara. I found myself surrounded by a group of eager young political architects of Turkey's twentieth-century new look. They all talked fluent English and wanted to exchange reminiscences of the School of Economics since they had all studied there. No doubt a visitor to political circles in other capital cities, notably in India or Pakistan, would experience similar contacts. And no doubt Oxford, fortified by Rhodes scholarships, could do as well in respect of world-wide influence.

Where does the school stand today? As I write this, its public "image" seems to be sadly tarnished by disorder and political fanaticism. *Of course* its student body is politically conscious and so it should be. *We* were politically conscious. We wanted to break up the Poor Law and secure adult suffrage and promote disarmament in response to Norman Angell's inspiring analysis of the futility of war. Many of us were active socialists. Later generations of students demonstrated in support of the General Strike of 1926, while others helped to man services paralysed by the withdrawal of labour. But work continued in the school and order reigned in its class-rooms and corridors. No police were required to abandon their proper function of restraining criminals by having to assemble round Aldwych in order to restrain heavily subsidised L.S.E. students.

If I were asked my impression of the School of Economics to-day, I should be tempted to say that it is now too big; and that having become so, it is constrained to press down what Ricardo called the "margin of cultivation" both as regards students, particularly perpetual post-graduate students, as well as junior staff. I might be tempted to add that there is too much sociology, which we used to regard as a second-rate intellectual discipline for undergraduate studies, involving a variety of subjects studied at intermediate level rather than in depth.

But one must allow for the nostalgia of an aged ex-student, who

[97]

is tempted to retreat in memory into a small Edwardian building, where staff and students mixed on easy terms, where the great were treated with respect and the non-great talked to as rational, if immature, human beings. A world in which no eccentric antic could achieve easy notoriety, since there were no television cameras to focus public attention on him.

7

Oxford before World War One

FROM 1912 ONWARDS I lived as it were a double life: in London which had always been my centre, but with thoughts always turned to what was going on in Oxford. And the more I learned of life in Oxford the more mixed became my feelings with regard to the prospect of living in it. I was a born and bred Cockney. London was my native heath and for years my weekends had been spent exploring it on foot and on a bicycle. I became familiar with the sights and sounds and smells of dockland and the Isle of Dogs, as well as with my old working area of Saffron Hill and Clerkenwell. Its contours, of which one became conscious as a cyclist, taught me the pattern of its underground rivers. The contrasting personality of particular areas indicated when one was in the centre of what was once, and in a sense still was, a village. It was fascinating to watch the social rise and fall of whole areas. Islington and Canonbury, for instance, once so respectable, then so dishevelled; now, indeed, in this present age once again rising in the social and economic scale to house migrants from Bloomsbury driven from their Georgian squares and terraces by the predatory sprawl of London University. London, so vast, so dramatic in its contrasts, so unendingly productive of newly discovered backwaters, unimagined squalors and architectural gems; how could I bear to leave London?

And London, or rather the School of Economics, and indeed London University, was an egalitarian world. Women played an equal part in it, equal in status if not in numbers, and were in no sense conscious of being second-class citizens. From no academic

[99]

activity were they excluded by virtue of their sex. No avenue of academic promotion was closed to them. And, so far as I was aware, no learned society excluded them either from its deliberations or from its social festivities.

But Oxford was quite otherwise. Its women's colleges were there on sufferance. Their students could attend male lectures, though some lecturers still resented their presence. They could sit for male examinations but could not receive the degrees to which their results entitled them. They had no part in the counsels of the University—were not indeed members of it. The centre of University social life was in the male college common-rooms. No woman could share that life, and few of the learned societies were open to them. Unless she happened to be a member of a women's college staff, a woman's academic contacts in Oxford were meagre. John Stocks was all too conscious of this situation, and, as will shortly be related, took heroic steps to end it.

But there was Oxford—so beautiful, and in those far-off days strangely withdrawn. One could watch the whole cycle of the seasons round as an Oxford resident; not only in the college gardens but in open country, by crossing the bridge in the Parks, or strolling for less than a mile along the towpath of the canal into fields where cowslips grew. One walked through fields to Boars Hill or Bagley Wood with its spring carpet of bluebells. An easy bicycle ride took one to Otmoor, a stretch of country so remote, so unwelcoming, so redolent of unhappy agrarian history that on returning from it, one felt as though one had sojourned in an earlier century or a distant foreign land. As for architectural beauty, in London one sought it out from a mishmash of commercial development. But in Oxford, there it was all within reach, all down the High Street to Magdalen Bridge, all up the Broad, and round the corner in St Giles where was St John's College, the most beautiful college of all.

Thirty years later, during the Second World War, the centre of Oxford was once seen at night under the rare confluence of three conditions: total war-time blackout, a thick pall of undisturbed snow, and a bright full moon in a cloudless sky. I hope that this threefold confluence may never occur again; but since it once did, I am very glad to have seen it. So breathtaking was its beauty that one forgot the reason why no competing artificial lamps were lit.

No doubt in London there were greater numbers of interesting and significant personalities. But in London it was seldom that one met and talked to them. In Oxford it was seldom that one did not. During the pre-war year of my sojourn there, I encountered in person Madame Montessori, James Bryce, Jim Larkin at the height of his fame as a revolutionary Dublin strike leader, Sir Horace Plunket—and immediately after the war Annie Besant, T. E. Lawrence and Nansen. In London one would read of such people. In Oxford one met them socially face to face; such was the compactness of its social circle.

But far more satisfying than these chance encounters was the immediate social circle in which John Stocks moved. Gilbert Murray and his wife Lady Mary Murray were at the centre of it. At the time of our engagement they lived in North Oxford; later, and for the rest of their lives, they moved up to Boars Hill where they cultivated a lovely garden and looked over open country. Superficially they seemed a curiously incongruous pair: Lady Mary had little sense of humour—indeed, I suspect, none at all. Gilbert had so much. When one realized that Gilbert was Shaw's model for Adolphus in *Major Barbara* and that it was possible to equate Lady Mary with Major Barbara herself, the partnership became explicable. Lady Mary was at the time a devout agnostic; so devout as to warn a young woman who applied for the post of governess that God must not be mentioned to the children. Later she became an equally devout member of the Society of Friends. She was unendingly kind to people and generously hospitable; but socially she could be intimidating. I remember making a joke in her presence; doubtless a bad one. But to be greeted with "I don't think that's funny" was not encouraging.

Both Gilbert and Lady Mary were vegetarians and teetotallers; and in a letter dated November 14, 1912, John Stocks refers thus to a Murray dinner party:

> I sometimes think that the total and ostentatious absence of all forms of alcohol has rather a depressing effect upon a party. We all drank lemonade, and I dare say most of us would not have taken much else if an alternative had been offered; but there was no alternative—so that our abstemiousness had no moral value. Lady Mary Murray offered me a lot of advice about houses, but she seemed to think I did not

mind how near Banbury I lived. She also very kindly asked if you would feel inclined to stay with her; but she became rather distracted in the middle of my reply, so that the question was never answered. I doubt if I should "star" the Murrays' house as a Hotel if I were doing a Baedeker of Oxford for your benefit.

In fact we didn't want to live in North Oxford at all. We wanted to live in the middle of Oxford, and at one time, to Lady Mary's surprise, we hankered after a flat over a shop. In the end we leased the ideal house in St Michael's Street, a turning off the Corn-market. Next door to it was a livery stable, opposite to it was a book-binding workshop. Lady Mary thought our choice of it "very original". She had, of course, been born and reared in Castle Howard. My mother, who should have known better, referred to it as "the little slum house".

It was, in fact, a perfect little house for our purpose, and what need was there for a proprietary garden, with Worcester College round the corner and St John's College garden across the road? And with the accommodation of a resident housekeeper, since in those days dons' wives, like doctors' wives, normally employed domestic servants, we calculated that it would still be habitable, given the addition of one baby; but that in due course two would precipitate a move. Alas, we did not inhabit it long enough to test its capacity. The first war put an abrupt end to our enjoyment of it, and by the time the first war was finished that second baby required extra accommodation.

But to return to the Murrays and their circle. I suspect that the dinner-party described by John Stocks was less attractive than it might have been because, as was then the custom on such social occasions, a male guest did not sit next his host; and one presumes that there was no subsequent port-drinking sex segregation at which he might have done so. As a prospective, and later, actual bride, I of course could sit next to my host, and such occasions were memorable. Gilbert Murray's conversation was enchanting; so indeed was his face and his voice. I suppose he had in a marked degree what was known as "the Oxford accent", which was, of course, pure southern English spoken with perfect clarity. But I sometimes thought I could detect in it a very faint trace of his native Australian. One lunch party during this early period I very well remember, because he told me the strange story of Mary Baker Eddy's life up to the time when, in late middle age, she emerged as the leader of an influential religion and the manager of a very profitable publishing business. It was indeed a strange story and he had learned the facts of it from a somewhat ill-natured biography which her own devotees were not encouraged to read. Many years later I read a larger biography by E. F. Dakin,* written with greater objectivity, which carried conviction. But the facts of her early life, with its strange manifestations of hysteria, were as Gilbert Murray had related them; and my interest in an extraordinary human phenomenon, in due course reinforced by admiration for her fundamental business astuteness, was kindled at the Murrays' dining table.

Thus began a friendship which lasted until his death in 1957 at the age of 91. He then lacked the companionship of Lady Mary, whose body unhappily outlived her mind. But to the end he remained active in writing, and in serving the United Nations Association in London. This last activity from time to time brought him to London for the night; when he stayed in my flat and I was able to drive him to his various engagements. On one such occasion he said: "When I was eighty I had a kind of rejuvenation; but it's very tiring being ninety." He did indeed show signs of tiredness after a day of committees, but a short sleep between tea and supper refreshed him, and he enjoyed meeting old friends at supper. This required me on occasions to address informal invitations by telephone to persons whom I should certainly not have dared to invite to my flat, had not Gilbert Murray been my excuse. One such was Rose Macaulay, and I and my youngest daughter owe to Gilbert Murray's sojourn the delight of listening to a conversation between those two.

At one point in it, Rose Macaulay referred to an unhappy case of homosexual behaviour which had been headline news in the popular Press, but not, it seemed, in the newspapers that Gilbert Murray read. He was extremely surprised. He knew, nobody better, what went on in ancient Greece. But that such goings-on could occur in twentieth-century England and among educated persons was very strange indeed. His surprise was equalled by Rose Macaulay's surprise at his innocence. "But", she said, "fifty per cent of my men friends are homosexuals." Gilbert Murray was

* *Mrs. Eddy*, by Edwin Franden Dakin. Charles Scribner's Sons, 1929.

more surprised than ever. "But my dear Rose, how do you *know*?" "One does," said Rose Macaulay.

Turning over old Oxford papers I find a letter from Murray to John Stocks dated March 1910. It seems that John Stocks had invited Jane Harrison from Cambridge to speak on the same day as another important university meeting. It runs as follows:

THE BURDEN OF LEOFRIC*

Tear thy garments, O maker of meetings; make a great noise, O secretary of the Philological Society.

Howl aloud unto Clark for help; play upon the harp until Richards shall pity thee.

Shalt thou find mercy in Grundy, or shall Wells deliver thee from the roaring of lions?

For, behold, ye have asked a Virgin to play before you, a virgin from Cambridge to tear wild bulls and the like:

And on the same day and the same hour you yourselves shall be dancing to others; yea, dancing like unicorns before Lord Cromer.

How shall ye skip and mock before the lord of Egypt, how shall your hearts not sink within you?

When you know that Miss Harrison is in your empty room, reading alone to a magic lantern and a blackboard.

Shall ye not either invite her for the 18th instead of the 6th; yea, for the last day of April if need be:

Or else make the Classical Association invite her for the afternoon; to sweeten their tea with fair songs about Palaeocastro?

Is this not a kettle, saith the prophet; yea, a pretty kettle, a kettle of fish?

Among Gilbert Murray's latest works are his reconstructions from fragments of Menander's Greek comedies. I am told by classical scholars that there is more Murray than Menander in the result. Indeed he signed the copies he gave me as from "Menander & Co"; and I am sure that the adventure of an errant nymph who had been turned into a forest bear in Act I of *The Arbitration* is pure Murray; as also is the rollicking drinking song at the end of

* Leofric was in fact John Stocks's second name, though he never used it, and its existence was unknown to many of his friends.

that Act. To have recaptured in his eighties and after much sad-
ness and family disappointment, both the ecstasy of the nymph and
the drunken abandon of the reveller, shows that however tired he
might have been, Gilbert Murray's capacity for understanding and
sharing human experience was never impaired. Rose Macaulay's
revelation doubtless opened yet another avenue of understanding.

To return to pre-1914 Oxford where it all began: John Stocks
shared an interest with Murray other than Greek philosophy and
literature. That was the stage. A group of Oxford stage enthusiasts,
including Murray, Robert Bridges and John Stocks, had organized
a committee whose purpose was to invite good repertory companies to play for a season at the Oxford New Theatre since the
present Oxford Playhouse was as yet unborn. Among those invited
were the Horniman company from Manchester and the Irish
Players from Dublin; and these guests would be entertained
socially by members of the Oxford committee. On one such occasion John Stocks commiserated with Miss Horniman's producer,
Lewis Casson, on having lost to London managers two excellent
leading ladies. Casson admitted the loss, but added that he didn't
really mind, because he had now acquired a young woman worth
all the rest put together. Her name, he said, was Sybil Thorndike.
This all happened before my incursion into John Stocks's life; but
it enabled me to boast in later years to Sybil Thorndike that I had
seen Lewis Casson before she had. I had, in fact, seen him as the
Sidi el Assif in *Captain Brassbound's Conversion* in 1906 before
he ever joined Miss Horniman's company.

It must have been left to Robert Bridges to negotiate these
Horniman Oxford seasons, because on being asked what it was like
to have business dealings with Miss Horniman, all he could say
was: "Lions and tigers, my dear Stocks. Lions and tigers!"

Such was the lighter side of John Stocks's existence, in due
course to be shared by me. It is clear from his letters that he carried a considerable burden of college teaching in addition to meetings of learned societies and Boards of Guardians. In the summer
of 1913 he was appointed Junior Proctor. This involved him in
much university administration at high level and much university
ceremonial in addition to the disciplinary duty of taking turns with
the Senior Proctor in patrolling the streets of Oxford after dark,
accompanied by the Proctor's Marshal and his attendant "bull-
dogs", otherwise two of the university police. This would mean

[105]

the further duty next morning of dealing with any delinquent undergraduate whose "name and college" had been taken the night before, for such peccadilloes as drunkenness, frequenting "out of bounds" cafés or failing to wear academic dress. The usual penalty would be a fine. There were, of course, from time to time more serious matters such as "an awkward disciplinary case" recorded in a letter dated April 24th, 1913, "of an undergraduate who frequents the society of a lady of inferior class to his own." What form his attentions took is not precisely specified; but the "poor fellow was pitifully afraid and seemed very contrite."

Proctorial status with its multifarious duties meant a curtailment of the honeymoon in Italy after our wedding in December 1913. It involved, however, one very significant privilege. A Proctor has ex-officio the right to move resolutions in the Hebdomadal Council. John Stocks decided to use this privilege to raise the question of women's degrees. In a letter dated November 16, 1913, he explained the matter to me:

Today has been most thrilling. I lunched with the Geldarts to discuss the prospects of Women's Degrees; and since then I have had a long talk with Miss Rogers.* G. was benevolent and rather chilling—suggested other people to consult, etc. Miss Rogers was in a state of wild excitement, already girding her loins for battle. (Is that womanly? I fear she is not.) She agrees that I must consult these people, but seems already to have concluded that I shall make the motion. The V.C. said if I wanted to move I had better do so. I have not yet heard any valid reason why the matter should be deferred any longer. The people I have got to consult are Heberden, Gerrans, G. Murray, and Miss Penrose. The matter was last raised by resolution in Congregation in 1896. The lovely thing is that if I move, the Council cannot refuse a committee on which they will have to put me; and after I go out of office they will have to continue me on the Committee, and I shall be able to give nearly all my spare time—since I have very few business engagements apart from Proctorship—to the business. So I hope that my movement won't be nipped in

* Miss Annie Rogers was Secretary to the Delegacy for Women Students, a body which provided the official contact between the women's colleges and the university.

the bud. It would take a full year, I expect, to draft a workable and acceptable scheme.

Among those he was advised to consult was Heberden, Principal of Brasenose College, who had just retired from the Vice-Chancellorship; and Heberden gave him an important piece of advice. "When you have to talk to Annie Rogers," he said, "always go to *her* house, do not invite her to yours. It will thus be possible for you to end the conversation when you wish." After the war, when John Stocks took the field again, and the women's degree campaign involved detailed negotiation, he adhered to this advice and was assured of its wisdom. One can understand Miss Rogers's point of view. After long service to the Oxford women's colleges she could see the prospect of full membership of the university as "the glory of the coming of the Lord." And if the man most responsible for that vision had also other fish to fry, she was not conscious of their importance.

I choose to believe that St Anne's, the newest of the Oxford women's colleges, was called after Miss Rogers. I am assured that it was not, but I still choose to believe that it *was*—or that if it wasn't, it ought to have been.

Two days after his first declaration of intent in a letter to me, John Stocks wrote:

I have advanced yet further today in the Women's Degree Campaign. I interviewed the great Gerrans and was not repulsed—so that now, I take it as settled that the matter will go forward. It only remains to decide the form and date of the motion. I expect that will mean a deal of conference and correspondence.

It did indeed. What other university privileges should undergraduate status carry with it? What about the discipline of women undergraduates? Would it be safe to press for complete equality of university status or be content with something less to begin with? John Stocks's letters reported progress up to our wedding on December 14th, after which, letters were no longer necessary for this purpose.

But alas the campaign was in fact "nipped in the bud". In the autumn of 1914 John Stocks was occupied with O.T.C. training. By Christmas, he was due to leave Oxford for full-time training in camp as a lieutenant in Kitchener's Army. At the end of July he departed for the Western front as a captain in the King's Royal Rifle Corps; and five days after his disappearance to an unknown destination our eldest daughter was born.

When he left Oxford, so did I. I returned to Queen's Gate Terrace and to the School of Economics; where, owing to a wholesale stampede of male staff into active service, I was in due course employed as assistant lecturer in economic history. Thus, since contentious university questions could not be discussed in war time, the women's degree campaign was, if not effectively "nipped in the bud", at any rate put into cold storage. So, too, were the contents of 17 St Michael's Street.

Thus ended my acquaintance with an Oxford whose social and academic climate failed to survive four years of war and political upheaval. Its atmosphere was largely monastic; its society serene and class-conditioned. Since there was no retiring age, heads of colleges might continue to inhabit their dignified residences and enjoy their substantial emoluments without any necessity of rendering service. Some, like the Provost of Queen's, had long been incapable of active participation. Some were "personalities" whose eccentricities added charm and variety to Oxford life, and provided a store of good-natured anecdotes. Some were gifted administrators and worked hard.

St John's was presided over during these years, and indeed during very many subsequent years, by the Rev. Dr James, a bearded headmaster, who had been brought from Rugby to keep the left-wing Sidney Ball out of the Presidency. He brought with him an elderly widowed cousin called Mrs Williams who kept house for him and entertained his guests. Her presence raised the question of whether she should be accorded the status of a Mrs James, had there been one, when he was invited out to dinner. And here opinion seemed to be divided. There was one unhappy occasion when a group of inebriated undergraduates assembled in front of his house and chanted: "Who lives in sin, who lives in sin." Lady Mary would doubtless have said: "I don't think that's funny." But considering the impeccably respectable personalities of the two persons concerned, I think perhaps it was.

Dr James was certainly not idle. He performed his college duties with dignity. And he cannot be said to have become senile, because having come to us with a mental age of about fifteen he maintained the undimmed interests and mental clarity of that age as long as I can remember. His hobby was stamp-collecting, and on one occasion, when a young cousin who was then at Rugby came to stay with us, Dr James was exceedingly kind to him.

Apart from a minute minority of deviationists, St John's College was at this time notably clerical. But so indeed was Oxford. I doubt if compulsory chapel was helpful to religion, though it was certainly an encouragement to early rising. But New College Chapel and the services in Christ Church Cathedral *were* helpful; so, too, were bells ringing through the quiet Oxford streets on Sunday mornings. As Dorothy Sayers said, writing twenty years later in her novel *Gaudy Night*: *

> Here was the great Anglican compromise at its most soothing and ceremonial. . . . Here were the Universities and the Church of England kissing one another in righteousness and peace, like the angels in a Botticelli Nativity: very exquisitely robed, very cheerful in a serious kind of way, a little mannered, a little conscious of their fine mutual courtesy. Here, without heat, they could discuss their common problems, agreeing pleasantly or pleasantly agreeing to differ.

By that time my memories of a disastrous confirmation class had begun to fade; and I had married into a clerical family. John Stocks was one of eleven children of the Archdeacon of Leicester, later Canon of Peterborough. Two of his six brothers were clergymen and his four sisters were all devout churchwomen; but one sister, Helen, whom I first got to know in connection with her trade union activities, had a capacity for laughing aloud in church which I have never seen equalled. It is an incontestable fact that anything mildly comic has, if it occurs in church, a peculiar touch of whimsicality. Usually on such occasions one cultivates a muted merriment. Helen's laugh was clear and uninhibited, and dangerously infectious.

John Stocks, writing on January 23, 1913, repudiated an accusation by Lady Mary Murray that he was a High Churchman:

> I certainly try to be as free in my thinking as possible. I believe that is the duty of philosophers. But I fear my

* Gollancz, 1935.

> thoughts on religion are so vague that I could hardly claim to be a free thinker in the technical sense. And am I not a prominent member of the C.S.U.* which is restricted, I think, to communicant members of the Church of England? I am afraid I am not at all a regular communicant; but I don't regard that as sufficient reason to justify resignation. On the whole I should describe myself as a pretty ordinary specimen of the common or garden sham Christian who is the backbone of the British Empire and the despair of missionaries.

If his thoughts on religion were vague, mine were even vaguer. Apart from my confirmation class vicar, and Aunt Polly's curates, I had never encountered the clergy, and my introduction to the Stocks family might have been intimidating had it not been that they were all so kind to me as to make me forget that I had entered a strange new world. I was at the time, and have remained, incurably religious, and if the flame of my faith is damped down, as unhappily it often is, by hearing a sermon or reading an ecclesiastic utterance, I can always rekindle it by turning to the humanist literature of Margaret Knight or Professor Ayer. Meanwhile, Mrs Sidney Webb seemed to me to put religion in its place in a lecture which she gave in the autumn of 1913. It was the last of a series of Fabian Lectures and was entitled "The Bankruptcy of Science". I retailed it with crude enthusiasm in one of the last letters I wrote to Oxford before letter-writing became an unnecessary means of communication. In it she expounded a simple view of the relationship of science and religion—in this case of course social science, to which, as a disciple of Herbert Spencer, she regarded the scientific method as applicable. Science, she explained, deals with the process of life—it answers the question: how? When it comes to the purpose of life—an answer to the question: why?—science is bankrupt. Here is the proper field for religion—and indeed the necessity for it. This simple thesis has since been expounded by her in her autobiography, and indeed in other works, including her diaries. I found it comfortably satisfying in 1913 and have been content with it ever since.

The Christian religion has absorbed, if not digested, a number of strange ancient and even pagan myths, such as the virgin birth,

* If these letters stand for Christian Social Union I think John Stocks was wrong in assuming any such restriction.

the scapegoat, and the blood sacrifice, dating from "a time whereof no memory is". If traces of them appear in the creeds and the articles of the Church of England, it no longer causes me distress provided we recognize them for what they are. As a twelfth century Arab philosopher said of religion: "Men must grasp it at whatever level their intelligence permits." It is the business of the Church today to present religion at a level that intelligent men may grasp, while not denying comfort or colour to those who are less intelligent or perhaps not intelligent at all.

I have said that in this pre-1914 Oxford the academic status of women left almost everything to be desired; though *qua* wives, their social contacts could be satisfying. In my case, this needs qualification. Women students could attend tutorials with men tutors and men students on rare occasions with women tutors. My School of Economics' record enabled me to undertake tutoring of students of both sexes in economics, because in that subject tutors were then few and far between in Oxford. My first pupil was a student from St Hilda's called Doris Odlum; she was a year older than myself. Her subsequent career was in a high degree distinguished, and I should like to be able to boast that my tutoring in economics had laid the foundation of greatness in that subject; but alas its effect was quite otherwise. She deviated almost immediately into medicine and rose to world-wide fame as an authority on psychiatry and psychological medicine.

Far more significant as regards my own academic activity, was contact with the Workers' Educational Association. I had realized at the outset that in marrying John Stocks I had married the W.E.A. Even before the first marriage was celebrated the banns were up for the second. While still a spinster resident in London I had been dispatched on a visit to W.E.A. London headquarters in Red Lion Square, and there been given my first assignment, due to begin immediately on my appearance as a married woman in Oxford. This was to an afternoon class for women in a completely rural Cotswold area: Ascot-under-Wychwood. Its members were farmers' and labourers' wives, and its subject was economic history. One reason why the W.E.A. had taken the field in so remote a spot was the fact that Sanderson Furniss and his wife had a country house there. He was the Principal of Ruskin College, and both husband and wife were socialists and naturally, because of Ruskin, concerned with adult education. In addition Mrs Furniss was in touch with rural life, and had in fact established a district nurse in the village.

Looking back on my dozen sessions in the village hall at Ascot-under-Wychwood, I know that I did in an extreme form what any inexperienced adult education tutor should at the outset be told not to do. I exuded concentrated information. I led them through the Industrial Revolution, the enclosure movement, the origins and reform of the Poor Law; I even attempted to explain the suspension of cash payments and the reorganization of the Bank of England. All this my class endured with undiminished attendance. It was held in a warm room and made a nice change for its members. At the end, the district nurse served tea and a good time was had by all.

But there *was* another reason for its endurance: Joseph Arch had visited that village in the eighties, in the course of his historic campaign for agricultural trade unionism. It had been a troubled area—there had been a lock-out of intrepid and dangerous trade unionists. There was still in the village an aged lady who had been sent to prison in Oxford for "intimidating" non-unionists. Economic history clearly *had* something to do with real life in Ascot-under-Wychwood. I was thus confirmed in my belief that it was an entrancing subject—if only I knew how to teach it!

I hope that my wanderings round university politics, religion, and adult education have not resulted in a somewhat over-austere presentation of my philosopher husband. He was far from austere. Incidentally, he was exceedingly handsome, and anyone who wants to know what he looked like at this period has no need of photographs. Giorgione's "Young Man", familiar to Medici print collectors, is an excellent portrait of him.

He had one interest which I could not share: this was games. All the Stocks brothers and sisters were ardent players of games, especially hockey. Here, since there were eleven of them, they could have produced a powerful mixed eleven. Three of the brothers and two of the sisters had played for England. When John Stocks couldn't play hockey or cricket, since both involved numbers, he could content himself with golf or tennis. Alas, I couldn't play anything. Even St Paul's School had failed to stimulate co-operation. For what is the use of including in a hockey team a member who is only too anxious, if somebody else wants the ball, to let them have it, instead of selfishly trying to hook it away from them.

He could, however, not only play ball with a material round object, he could play ball metaphorically—by responding to any play of conversation or imagination. And he was an ardent reader of poetry. I needed no introduction to Browning, having, like him, been a Browning addict since an early age, and during our brief residence in St Michael's Street we read much Browning aloud to one another. But he introduced me to his friend and contemporary, Gerald Gould, whose poetry is now, so far as I know, scarcely remembered. But poets have a way of being brought to life and appreciated, many years after their death. Let us hope that Gerald Gould will some day be thus resurrected.

Our lifelong devotion to another contemporary poet dates from July 10, 1913, where it is thus recorded in a letter from Oxford: "I got today a very charming book of verse (by one Walter de la Mare) which I will bring with me." He did bring it to Ricketts-wood for the week-end. It was *Peacock Pie*: the first volume of our de la Mare collection. Some of its verses he later set to music, and I illustrated all of them in water-colour. Since he had never learned to play an instrument, and drawing was one of the subjects which had floored me in Higher Certificate, I think our joint effort was creditable: a poor tribute, but the best we could do, to Walter de la Mare.

One feature of pre-1914 Oxford which would cause most astonishment to my granddaughter's generation was its elaborate machinery for frustrating social contacts between male and female undergraduates. The visiting of one another's rooms in college was severely restricted. The gates of women's colleges were closed of an evening and late night ingress required special leave. Early marriage, involving still earlier engagement, was not yet the fashion, and very many of the men and certainly most of the women were more interested in their own separate activities than in one another.

One regular annual feature of St John's College academic life was an exclusively male "reading party" led by Sidney Ball to some pleasant resort where work and country walks could be happily combined. For many years, unknown to me until 1912, John Stocks had thus sojourned at West Bay during Easter vacations. Such reading parties were a familiar feature of Oxford life.

Meanwhile the women's colleges were largely inhabited by young women with a special bent for academic studies, or inspired by a determination to pursue a career other than marriage.

Thus the policy of *apartheid* was probably not as irksome as it was destined to become. It did, however, present complications. It involved, for instance, arrangements for chaperonage. Any married woman, however junior, was qualified to act as chaperon. Accordingly, when Gilbert Murray's daughter Agnes, then at Somerville, wanted to attend tea-time meetings of the Oxford University Fabian Society, a chaperon was required. Fortunately I was qualified. Accordingly, the President, G. D. H. Cole (then a Prize Fellow at Magdalen), and I went hand in hand to Miss Penrose, then Principal of Somerville, to assure her that the correct procedure would be observed. It was explained that I would always be present at such orgies, even should they take place in G. D. H. Cole's rooms. One feature of them was the enormous consumption of buttered scones, buns and cakes which accompanied discussions. But discussions were none the less serious; and one could trace in them the revolt of the Oxford Fabians, led by Cole, against the orthodox Webbian presentation of socialism conceived in terms of consumer control. Such socialism, said Cole, would merely perpetuate the wage system. His challenge to the Webbs on this fundamental matter eventually erupted into Fabian Society politics at top level. But looking back on those Oxford meetings I think it would be fair to say that the germ of the subsequent Guild Socialist movement was fostered there, even if deeply embedded in buttered scones, buns and cakes.

Fresh from the School of Economics, and the uninhibited yet wholly un-sexconscious and decorous companionship of William Piercy and Theo Gugenheim, this sex *apartheid* seemed very odd to me. So far as I could understand it, it appeared to be based on the fear that young males and females could not be trusted to mix freely without emotional entanglements which might disturb their work—not to mention worse complications too unthinkable to think about. At the time I found this fear wholly baseless. I find it less so today.

8

World War One

THE WAR YEARS WHICH followed our retreat from St Michael's Street in 1914 have been so well documented by so many writers from so many angles that any further record of their progress would be superfluous. John Stocks endured eighteen months of trench warfare in France, including front-line fighting on the Somme. It ended, as far as he was concerned, with a wound incurred during the subsequent autumn, which brought him a long spell in hospital followed by a cadet training job in Pirbright Camp near Brookwood in Surrey. It also brought him an award for gallantry, which enabled me, fifty years later, to be described in my patent of nobility as "Widow of our trusty and well-beloved John Leofric Stocks Esquire, Companion of our Distinguished Service Order".

The telegram which brought me news of his wound contained the best tidings I have ever received by post, 'phone, or wire; for it ended a period of acute and unrelieved personal anxiety. What we did not then know was that his wound left him with an unsuspected internal scar for which his heart, overworked during twenty years of subsequent strenuous life, paid the penalty.

As far as I was concerned, the war years began with a return to Queen's Gate Terrace, later followed by periods of residence at furnished houses in the neighbourhood of Pirbright camp; but thanks to the blessed institution of middle-class domestic service, I was able to carry on various committees in London, part-time work as assistant lecturer at the London School of Economics, and during the final year of the war, full-time work as economics lecturer at the Domestic Science wing of King's College (which has since become Queen Elizabeth College) on Campden Hill.

[115]

And thanks to a very competent children's nurse, the appearance of daughter Ann in 1915, and of son John early in 1918, produced only brief temporary interruptions to these activities.

My own immediate family was indeed fortunate at a time when so many of our fellow citizens were not. John had survived the carnage of the trenches. My brother Ralph survived the war at sea, including the Battle of Jutland. And my father, on joining the R.A.M.C., achieved the nearest he ever got to a naval career, by serving in the Mediterranean on a hospital ship. This craft, though brightly lit and clearly marked with a red cross, was finally torpedoed by a German submarine in the English Channel but happily only after it had landed its casualties at Avonmouth. However, the Germans who torpedoed it presumably didn't know that. The adventure of being torpedoed and brought ashore as a survivor afforded my father intense pleasure; indeed I think he enjoyed the first war as much as my naval officer son enjoyed the second. But I doubt if his Kensington medical practice ever recovered from this exhilarating interlude. Some old patients had died and potential new ones had attached themselves elsewhere.

The two world wars through which I have lived seem to have little in common except that large numbers of people got killed and there seemed no obvious way of ending the conflict once it had begun. But two outstanding differences leap to mind, and both were conditioned by the fact that when the first war broke upon us it found us new to the whole conception of total war and taken unawares by the problems it presented. The first notable difference was the disastrous waste of man-power precipitated by a helter-skelter rush of men into the fighting forces, without any official pre-determination of how their specialized talent and experience could best be used for the furtherance of the war effort. One of many examples of this was the recall of John's Oxford colleague, Guy Dickens, from the Western front, when it was realized that his unrivalled knowledge of Middle-Eastern geography and demography could be of vital importance when that area became a theatre of war. Alas, his recall coincided with his death as an infantry officer on the Somme.

The second differentiating feature was the inept development of food rationing and the slow evolution of machinery for its application. But both these features have been adequately stressed in a multitude of publications.

There is, however, one aspect of this First World War which is in danger of neglect or even distortion. The indiscriminate rush of men into the army was, in the vast majority of cases, inspired by a genuine belief that they were fighting evil forces. A similar belief was so readily understandable during the events which precipitated the Second World War that one tends to forget the part it played in the first.

When peace, or rather British non-involvement, hung in the balance before our declaration of war on August 4th, 1914, John Stocks and I were in Lancashire staying with members of the coal-owning Fletcher family into which his youngest sister, Kitty, had married. They were *Manchester Guardian* addicts and unlikely to be responsive to a crude "King and Country needs you" appeal. In fact they, and many others, were actively preparing to engage in a great peace campaign supported by the *Manchester Guardian*'s influential editor, C. P. Scott. The Cabinet was itself at sixes and sevens as regards British participation and the precise nature of our obligations to France. Meanwhile Russian mobilization had seemed to obscure responsibility for bellicose intentions, and we had not then learned—what subsequent publications made clear— that Germany could be regarded as peace-breaker number one, still less regarded as a nation capable of ruthless brutality. Then came news of the German invasion of Belgium, and with it, farewell to peace activities.

Looking back on very vivid memories of those weeks, I have no doubt that the revulsion of feeling on learning of the Belgian invasion, which brought our Lancashire circle into wholehearted support of the war effort, reflected public opinion throughout Great Britain as well as in the "corridors of power". It was seen as a monstrous, wicked, unprovoked act of aggression against a small neutral country which we were in honour bound to assist. The issue was as simple as that. Whether subsequent analyses of the remoter causes of the war uncovered more complex motives is another matter. Except for a small number of dedicated and obstinately consistent pacifists, in August and September 1914 the issue was as simple as that.

But though accepted as inevitable, the outbreak of the First World War was not accepted with the pleasurable enthusiasm depicted in the opening shots of that impressive film "Oh what a lovely War". On the day after the declaration, when mobilization was in full swing, John went off to Oxford and I did a slow cross-country railway journey *via* Birmingham and Westbury to Bridport. At every station there were crowds; but they were unhappy, bewildered, apprehensive crowds. I saw no flags wagged.

Later I asked my mother what the response had been in London. My father's South African friend W. P. Schreiner, the product of a Cambridge undergraduate contact which had survived disapproval of his pro-Boer affiliation, was dining at Queen's Gate Terrace on that fateful day. He had come post-haste with his sister Olive from Berlin, which was already on a war footing. He described scenes of joyful enthusiasm in Unter den Linden where crowds had marched up and down cheering for the Kaiser. He suggested that he and my parents should go after dinner into central London, and see how crowds there were taking it. This they did, and Schreiner was struck by the contrast. The Whitehall crowds were not marching and cheering. They too were unhappy, bewildered, apprehensive.

Pity can, alas, be "chok'd by custom of fell deeds". Today we have become accustomed to witnessing unprovoked assaults by one nation on the integrity of another. We take such events more calmly. But in the civilized twentieth-century Europe of 1914 such behaviour hit us hard and left us gasping.

Nor did events which occurred during the first year of the war obscure this initial moral judgement. The atrocities committed by Germany before and during the Second World War have been on such a scale as to obscure the realization by later generations of atrocities committed in Belgium during the first. To begin with, during the autumn of 1914, many of us accepted with a grain of salt highly coloured Press reports of German cruelty in occupied Belgium. But it was not possible to discount facts subsequently presented in the report on Belgian atrocities by a select committee of jurists and historians appointed by the Government to inquire into the truth of these allegations. Its chairman was Lord Bryce.

The committee sat for three months. It received, checked and compared numerous depositions, and alas it was found that the allegations published in the Press were only too true. Lord Bryce, an old friend of Germany who owed much to its scholarship, wrote* that it was "an unspeakable grief to find that such things had been done by members of a nation among which he numbered so many

* See *Life of James Bryce*, by H. A. L. Fisher. Macmillan, 1927, 2 vols.

warm personal friends". And the worst of it was that such acts were not committed by isolated and undisciplined individuals, but by a disciplined army "on a system and in pursuance of a set policy". It was, in fact, a policy of calculated ruthless terrorism such as was, twenty-five years later, applied to Rotterdam. Thus the belief that we were in truth fighting something evil was further strengthened.

I have dwelt on this particular aspect of the 1914–18 War because we live in an age which seems to take a peculiar delight in debunking virtue and hurling accusations of hypocrisy against earlier generations. The men who so gallantly and indiscriminately poured into the army in 1914 genuinely believed that they were fighting something evil, and indeed I think that they were not deceived. Like the Israelites who answered the call of Deborah at the battle of Megiddo, "gain of money took they none; they fought from heaven". Unfortunately one cannot add, as she did, that "the stars in their courses" fought for them. The stars were regrettably unpropitious. After four years of savage mutual killing, moral issues became blurred and the cry of: "Hang the Kaiser and make the Germans pay," on which Lloyd George rode to victory in the General Election of 1918, left us in some doubt as to whose face was the dirtiest: the pot's or the kettle's.

As far as I was concerned, during these anxious and restless years, which also covered the disintegration of the Rendel Connection and the sale of Rickettswood, two constructive developments lightened my darkness. These were the triumph of one good cause, votes for women; and the initiation of another, family allowances. Eleanor Rathbone played a leading part in the first, and was initiator and, to begin with, a lone pioneer in the second. Active co-operation in both brought me working contact and later warm personal friendship, with a very great woman—whose biography I was destined to write at the invitation of her family after her death in 1946.

As an active social worker in her home town of Liverpool, Eleanor Rathbone was of course well acquainted with working-class conditions. Indeed she had, before the war, published an analysis of casual labour in the Liverpool docks which William Beveridge acknowledged as an important contribution to the problem of unemployment—and he should know. It was during the chaotic opening phases of the war in 1914 that she found herself responsible for improvising in Liverpool machinery for the administration of separation allowances to service men's wives, through the existing Soldiers' and Sailors' Families Association. In due course the position was stabilized and the organization worked.* But the experience gave a new direction to her thoughts. She had learned even more than she already knew about the stresses and strains of family life lived on the razor-edge of destitution.

What caught her imagination was the fact that in spite of its distresses and anxieties, war had, for working-class wives of service men, produced a new element of security. Small as the dependants' allowances were, and they were small even by 1914 standards, they did produce a family income which bore some logical relation to the size of the family; and incidentally put spending-power into the hands of the mother: hers by right because of her service to the nation in bearing and rearing children, and not merely something on which her husband might, or might not, choose to spend his wages as an alternative to beer and tobacco. Thus a feminist slant might be observed in the contemplation of dependants' allowances, in addition to the observable fact that a relatively small amount spent on them declared a really surprising dividend in terms of health and a sense of security.

This partial war-time experiment in family allowances was Eleanor Rathbone's starting point for the penetrating analysis of the economics of motherhood which she published under the title of *The Disinherited Family*† in 1924, by which time her campaign was well under way.

My own involvement in it began with an invitation to join a small committee of sympathizers which she assembled in 1917 for the purpose of working out a practicable scheme of family allowances applicable to all mothers. She did not lose sight of its feminist implications, one of which was its relevance to the problem of equal pay, at that time in the news following a claim by women bus conductors. All men must be paid more than all women, it was argued, because men have families to keep and women haven't. But it could be shown that at any given time most men haven't families to keep either because they were as yet unborn, or because they had grown up. And thinking in terms of an adequate universal minimum wage, a sum adequate for the families

* See *Eleanor Rathbone,* by Mary Stocks. Gollancz, 1949.

† Edward Arnold, 1924.

that are not there as well as for the families that are, would amount to a wage bill that our existing level of productivity could not carry. But the statistical exponency of this aspect of family allowances came later, though the rumblings of the equal pay controversy were making themselves felt in 1917 when the committee was formed.

Two of its members were former suffrage colleagues, Kathleen Courtney and Maude Royden. One was H. N. Brailsford, who was both a socialist and a tried feminist—as were two others, Mr and Mrs Emile Burns who undertook to act as secretaries. I was a sixth member, and felt it a great honour to be included in such company. We met at the newly formed 1917 Club, so called in honour of the fall of Russian Tsardom in that year. It occupied a small house in Gerrard Street, Soho, a few doors away from Mrs Meyrick's night club, with which the police were on occasions concerned.

It was there that we met, during the autumn of 1917, since Soho was a convenient location for all concerned, and it was there that we hammered out a pilot scheme which was published in 1918 as a shilling pamphlet entitled *Equal Pay and the Family*.

This pamphlet has long been out of print and the statistics on which its proposals were based are now of no significance. The committee which produced it also ceased to exist after its publication; and some years later the 1917 Club ceased to exist too. But the campaign for family allowances was well and truly launched, and Eleanor Rathbone's long and arduous agitation began.

A year later she converted her own organization, the National Union of Societies for Equal Citizenship, to the view that since motherhood was the largest of women's occupations, the recognition of its economic and social status was an essential feminist demand; but in so doing—to her great distress—she precipitated the resignation of her old friend and former leader, Dame Millicent Fawcett, whose individualist economic liberalism precluded the acceptance of so large a measure of socialist redistribution of income.

What, if family allowances were conceded, was going to happen to the economic incentive of the worker? That was what many orthodox liberal economists were asking, and that was the basis of widespread opposition. The answer to that question came in 1937 when the Statutory Committee on Unemployment Insurance

diagnosed a dangerous overlap between the lower levels of earnings which took no account of dependent families, and unemployment insurance benefits (or for that matter public assistance) which
did. In fact it might pay a man to remain unemployed. After 1937
it was Eleanor's turn to talk about incentive; and she did.

A more obstinate nut to crack was the habitual conservatism of
the trade unions which saw family allowances as an attack on the
conception of a standard family wage and a potential spanner in
the works of the familiar machinery by which they sought to
achieve it by collective bargaining.

By the end of the thirties the case for family allowances was
moving forward by its own momentum. Meanwhile, Eleanor had
much else to think about and indeed act about: child malnutrition,
India, African women, the Spanish civil war, Palestine, and always,
from one area or another, more and more refugees. Her concerns
were as infinite as were the sufferings and tyrannies of the world
around her; and the starting-point of all her tireless activity was
immediate compassion seen in terms of individual distress of body
or mind.

In this she provides an interesting contrast with another great
contemporary woman, Beatrice Webb. I think that Mrs Webb saw
human distress primarily in terms of statistics and defective administrative machinery. "To me", she wrote, "a million sick have
always seemed actually more worthy of self-sacrificing devotion
than the 'child sick in a fever' preferred by Mrs Browning's
Aurora Leigh." Having seen the "million sick" in terms of numbers, and having decided what could be done about them, the self-
sacrificing devotion was forthcoming for its redress. But she was
able to concentrate thought and energy on that particular problem
to the exclusion of what she regarded as diversionary or distracting
interests. That was the way she worked and the way she could
work effectively. The demand for family allowances was to her a
diversionary interest. It would arouse controversial issues likely to
complicate the Webbian blueprint for social reform. For her, international affairs, race problems, India and much else represented
"remote issues" on which she was not prepared to waste serious
thought or emotional energy.

To such "remote issues", as they beat upon her consciousness,
Eleanor's mind was always open. Here was human distress and she
must do something about it. She could not rest until she did—

which incidentally made her an unquiet companion on a holiday. But though her starting point was, I suppose, emotional, the action stimulated by emotion demanded hard thought and a meticulous marshalling and sifting of facts. Indeed, a record of her activities at any given time would suggest the image of a skilful juggler keeping a number of balls in the air simultaneously. But the result was not, as would doubtless be the case with lesser mortals, a mishmash of distrait futility, but rather a persistent and often effective drive which, especially after she entered Parliament, proved to be a terror and a challenge to ministers and government departments.

She lived long enough, though only just long enough, to see the achievement of family allowances in 1945. But the glowing tributes paid to her from all sides of the House as the measure passed smoothly into law, caused her nothing but embarrassment. That job was done for the present—meanwhile there were other things to do; so much to be done: starvation in defeated Germany, an appalling refugee problem, and things going very wrong with the British mandate in Palestine.

This excursion into the work of Eleanor Rathbone has carried my record far ahead of World War One. But even before the end of the war it landed me in a lot of work and was destined to land me in more as the years rolled by. It was a subject in demand at meetings, and indeed a subject fascinating to expound to audiences at various intellectual levels, from the British Association to a village hall gathering of very simple women.

Meanwhile another disturbing concern had loomed up. In 1915 the Women's Co-operative Guild published, under the title *Maternity*, a series of letters from working women describing the conditions under which their babies had been born; often without adequately trained midwifery and always without anaesthetics.

In spite of present day expositions of the "pleasures" of natural childbirth, I continue to regard the process as painful, messy, undignified, and potentially dangerous, and the less I know about it while it is actually going on, the better. The result, of course, makes it worth while. Having in 1915 mitigated these distresses in the spacious nursery quarters of Queen's Gate Terrace with the help of a doctor armed with anaesthetics and the ministrations of a full-time resident maternity nurse, the impact of these published letters was shattering. Of course I knew that childbirth was a very different matter for those who could not command the skill and comfort available to me. But the letters were so vivid, so personal, so immediate and so horrifying.

Family allowances might bring a modicum of economic security to mothers: but what next? It was not until 1919 that we had a Ministry of Health with a chief maternity officer, Dr Janet Campbell, who took maternal mortality and midwife training seriously. And three years after the publication of *Maternity* came another publication, *Married Love*, with which Marie Stopes, the Mrs Pankhurst of the birth-control movement, broke the silence barrier which shrouded that subject with a reverberating supersonic bang. Here, at any rate, was something that could be done, but the doing of it relates to a later chapter of this record.

Anyway there seemed to be nothing that I could do during these final war years. They were restless anxious years, though the worst of their anxieties had been removed by the return from France of John Stocks. Sometimes I was in residence at Queen's Gate Terrace; sometimes in furnished houses in the neighbourhood of Pirbright camp from which I could commute with a season ticket to London for various committees, for the teaching of economics, and, in the spring of 1918, for the birth at Queen's Gate Terrace of John Stocks junior.

November 11, 1918, found us in a furnished house at Brookwood where daughter Ann, aged three, lay "sick in a fever". It turned out to be typhoid; the result of a polluted water-supply in a local dairy farm. But it had been diagnosed as gastric influenza, not of course by my father. At that particular time all indispositions were being diagnosed as influenza; as indeed most of them were, because England was then in the grip of a particularly vicious influenza epidemic. But the treatment prescribed for gastric influenza was quite other than that which should have been prescribed for typhoid and Ann very nearly died. It was surprising that we didn't all very nearly die, not only of the milk, but of the cesspool at the bottom of our garden which every other day I pumped into Brookwood Cemetery. Its territory lay on the other side of our garden hedge, and its inhabitants were, of course, already dead.

So in our small family circle, the guns that signalized peace on November 11, 1918, did not find us in a hilarious mood, nor were we able to pep ourselves up by joining cheering crowds in Whitehall and Trafalgar Square. But thank God the killing had stopped and John Stocks was home for good. The war was over. Such a war could not happen again—we hoped. No, we actually believed.

It is astonishing what one can believe if one tries hard enough: like the White Queen who, after shutting her eyes and taking a long breath, was able, she said, to "believe as many as six impossible things before breakfast". But, as she explained to Alice, she "lived backwards" which "always makes one a little giddy at first". We lived backwards in November 1918 and it made us a little giddy at first.

9

Oxford after World War One

DEMOBILIZATION, FOR SOME REASON, doubtless a good one but I cannot remember what it was, seemed to take a long time after November 11th, 1918. But as far as John was concerned it did not take as long as we had expected. The authorities decided that for those not immediately demobilized the Army should fill in time, at any rate at Pirbright Camp, with educational programmes. So John and I set to work to devise a syllabus which we were prepared to operate. Hardly had we done so, when it was decided immediately to demobilize all teachers. What happened to our syllabus I do not know, but I do know that it was sorely needed, at any rate by one of our regular officers. His projected post-war programme involved making Germany pay the full costs of the war while at the same time achieving a world-wide boycott of German goods. When asked how then were these war payments to be made, he seemed surprised at the obviousness of the question. "Why, by cheque of course," he said.

So John returned to St John's College, Oxford, and I returned, with the convalescent Ann in an ambulance, to Queen's Gate Terrace. In the end we did not get resettled in Oxford till the autumn of 1919 because St John's House, which was destined for us, had to be reclaimed from a war-time tenancy and redecorated; and I still had an academic year to complete at King's College. However we did get settled in time for daughter Helen to be born at St John's House in the summer of 1920.

It was a pleasant house, the property of the college and within the college precincts. I had often stayed in it during its occupancy by Sidney Ball who died during the war. It overlooked the President's garden where the Rev. Dr James and Mrs Williams still walked. In one corner of its small front garden was an escape route by which errant undergraduates climbed in and out of college at unauthorized hours. Our house was never short of cushions which could often be found on the ground on our side of the wall because they were used by climbers to surmount the broken glass defences on the wall, and were not always retrieved by the climbers when accidentally kicked down. I have no doubt that as a result of these irregularities Mrs Williams also reaped a harvest of cushions on her side of the wall.

There, in St John's House, we resided for five years, long enough to experience life in an Oxford which had suffered a remarkable series of extraordinary changes, after awaking from four years of somnolent stagnation. In this first war there had been no air raid alarms in Oxford, no evacuated government departments; no incursions of refugees from London bombing, only a number of improvised temporary hospitals.

In a letter to John Stocks during the last phase of the war, our elderly St John's College Librarian, Stevenson, wrote of his solitude and nostalgic longing for "those pleasant days when the college was full of the light of ebullient (sometimes too ebullient) youth instead of being dreary, dark, and silent (apart from the hoarse words of command of the sergeants drilling in both quads the nth detachment of cadets)."

Four officers resident in college had provided an element of variety; but the younger dons had departed, and of twenty-five undergraduates, half were disabled officers. One colourful incident lightened Stevenson's gloom: a visit to his Library by Mrs Asquith "dressed in a sort of fur hearthrug—at least that is what its want of shape suggested to me—and white leather buskins on her feet, with loose uppers coming halfway up the leg". His description is interesting because it suggests that the Margot Asquith of 1918 might have felt quite at home in the King's Road of 1969.

Stevenson's account of St John's College was doubtless true of others. In fact Oxford slumbered until it was awakened by the kiss of peace to the acceptance of a new generation in a new world. But alas, for nearly a whole generation of young men there was to be no awakening, no new world: their names were recorded in long college rolls of honour.

[127]

For women in particular, the awakened Oxford certainly did present a brave new world. With minimal exposure to danger and death, the war had offered new, interesting, and really responsible opportunities for service—including service in the Forces, all of which had helped to undermine Edwardian convention. Dress was more manageable; behaviour less inhibited. The achievement of partial women's suffrage in 1918 had been followed by the Sex Disqualifications (Removal) Act of 1919, which opened a wide range of professional and public activity to women. On such a political tide the women's degree campaign was resumed and carried to a successful conclusion. On October 7th, 1920, the statute which made women full members of Oxford University came into force. Why Cambridge women failed to float to victory on the same tide I do not know—but not until 1948 did they become full members of their university.

In fact the whole of academic life was enriched after 1918 by the advent of a mature vintage of students: men who had survived dangerous war service as well as women who had gained new self-confidence from it. To Somerville came Vera Brittain, Winifred Holtby and Dorothy Sayers. To St John's came Tyrone Guthrie; and the O.U.D.S. sparkled with his early promise. It was during these years that the Oxford Playhouse was born—in a disused museum—with a youthful company which included John Gielgud.

In university administration, too, the wind of change was blowing in gusts. These old universities, it seemed, were in many ways out of date and ripe for reform. Aged senile men dozed in positions of responsibility. College kitchens reflected eighteenth-century waste. A Royal Commission on Oxford and Cambridge Universities was appointed in 1919 under the chairmanship of Mr Asquith, and its report, published in 1922, dealt among other matters with both these anachronisms. Professors and lecturers were to retire at 65; heads of colleges at 70. Those actually in office might remain *in situ* for the term of their natural lives—but thereafter there were to be no more sinecures for the senile.

In the field of catering the Commission had much to say on such matters as bulk buying and expert stewardship. A new race of domestic bursars came into being: men (and in due course women) with training in management. In St John's College an *ad hoc* committee was set up to expedite the Commission's recommendations, on which John Stocks played a leading and, in the view of some, a disturbing part. There followed a detailed inquest into kitchen arrangements, in the course of which a precise monetary valuation had to be made of the perquisites pertaining to the office of head cook. They proved to be considerable; and included such side benefits as receipts from the sale of dripping and the enjoyment of largesse given in return for the patronage of tradesmen. Time-honoured custom as well as mercy had, in justice, to be recognized in assessing compensation for the redundancies precipitated by reform; but steps were taken to ensure that such things did not occur hereafter.

In the purely academic sphere also, important changes were taking place. A new school emerged. It covered philosophy, politics and economics, and was known from the first as Modern Greats. Its emergence was, I suppose, the reflection of a new and more immediate interest of the young in current affairs; but it was not presented, nor has it since come to be regarded, as an easy option and should not be confused with sociology. My husband was, of course, concerned with its philosophy and politics. I took a small part in its teaching of economics. I do not know whether it now presents students with a selection of set books—but it did during its early experimental years. Those involved very intensive study of currency problems, banking and public finance, and—oddly enough—the first nine chapters of Karl Marx's *Das Kapital*. Why, I used to wonder, the first nine? Why, when Marx begins to draw his political moral and lead readers on a cascade of emotional rhetoric to his thunderous crescendo of capitalist exploitation, did the compulsory reading requirement break off?

I have suggested that the emergence of Modern Greats may be seen as a reflection of current political preoccupation; and during our five years of post-war Oxford life three major political pre-occupations cast a shadow over university activities; though Oxford, being what it was, could still offer sound-proof ivory towers for such as desired to dwell in them. The first was the problem of post-war Germany following the Treaty of Versailles. The second was the Russian revolution. And the third was the Irish question and the surge of public opinion against the repressive policy of Lloyd George's government. But even before these preoccupations became obsessive we had a small refugee problem peculiar to academic circles.

I suppose that Great Britain has for centuries been at the re-

ceiving end of refugee problems precipitated by tyranny or misrule elsewhere. Three centuries have passed since we ourselves
exported refugees in search of freedom. Since then we have
harboured French refugees, Italian refugees, Polish refugees,
Russian refugees, Jewish refugees—one might add Irish refugees
from famine. The opening year of the war had brought a flood of
Belgian refugees, and British hospitality flowed freely. But this was
a transitory problem. Belgians are hard-working people. They regarded refugee status with distaste, and were soon absorbed into
British war-time industry.

In Oxford the end of the war brought a small but highly select
wave of Austrian refugees whose lives had been disrupted by the
break-up of the Austrian Empire. Vienna, suddenly deprived of its
function as administrative and cultural centre of a far-flung empire,
became, until the Viennese spirit had time to reassert itself, a distressed area; and much Oxford, and doubtless Cambridge, hospitality was accorded to professors and lecturers whose background had thus fallen away. The Murrays harboured a very
eminent Austrian professor whose library, including all his research
records, had been burned—by whom I do not remember. We, at
St John's House, cherished a young lecturer called Steinermayer.
Having thought of himself as Austrian, when the map of eastern
Europe was finally re-drawn he found himself a Czech and in due
course was happily settled as English Lecturer in the University of
Brünn.

I think that Steinermayer benefited greatly from his residence
with us because it gave him good opportunities for the study of
English literature. He was particularly interested in the work of
Masefield and, for some reason, T. E. Brown. This was certainly
not due to Stocks influence because neither of us could endure
Brown's conception of a garden as "a lovesome thing, God wot".
Over Masefield we were, however, encouraging. He repaid us with
a really excellent translation into German of Browning's *Pied
Piper*. Less encouraging, however, was his encounter with Robert
Bridges, our Poet Laureate. Steinermayer had a great desire to
meet Robert Bridges and hear him speak with authority on English literature. That, we said, was easily done. We would take him
up to tea with Robert Bridges on Boars Hill. We did—and Steinermayer was prepared with his first question to the great man:
"Who, in your opinion, Dr Bridges, is the greatest writer of Eng-

lish prose?" The reply was brief and unhesitating. "Jane Austen," said Bridges. For the rest of the visit Steinermayer was silent. We did our best, on the way home, to assure him that Robert Bridges was not mocking him, but I doubt if we succeeded. I think he *had* heard of Jane Austen—but really! a novelist, and withal a woman! In his view Bridges could not have been serious.

However, this particular phase was transitory. It was not so much beaten Austria as beaten Germany that occupied our minds. Both John Stocks and I had long enjoyed friendly contacts with Germany. He had studied German there and forged links with German philosophers. I had formed ties with a Jewish family called Heimann, encountered on a winter holiday in Switzerland. Hugo Heimann was then a rich man and a publisher. At the same time he was a prominent member of the Social Democratic Party and a friend of its "Grand Old Man" August Bebel. I had stayed with them before the war in their large house in Berlin, where music and politics were the dominant interests; and they had been very kind to me—even to the point of taking me to visit August Bebel, himself an impressive figure in old age and retirement, romantically associated in my youthful eyes with the era of Marx and Engels.

By the end of the war the Heimanns had ceased to be rich. Inflation had hit them hard and the great house had given way to a flat in the Bendlerstrasse on the edge of the Tiergarten. Food was difficult, and at an early stage we began sending them parcels of coffee and tea. But socially and politically all was well with them. Their son, Peter, my contemporary, was a Professor at Hamburg, their two younger children were self-supporting, and Hugo Heimann had come into his own as an elder statesman of the Social Democratic Party. He played a leading part in the creation of a Greater Berlin local government region, was a director of the Charlottenburg Opera House, and Chairman of Committees (which presumably corresponded to our Speaker) in the Reichstag. Meanwhile, his wife, who was an accomplished pianist, was able to pursue her musical interests and sustain her friendship with Frau Siegfried Ochs, whose Jewish husband conducted the Berlin Philharmonic Orchestra. The shadow of German anti-Semitism had not yet fallen upon them.

As a result of these connections we visited Germany on several occasions during our five years in Oxford—first in the Black Forest, where a notable professor of Greek, exiled from Strasbourg

University by the French reconquest, lived, so he thought, like a peasant. As a prisoner in England John had made contact with him, and this was renewed by several visits to the Black Forest where the two classicists worked together while I wandered in the forest. My impression of Professor Krönert was that he was slightly mad and this belief was subsequently confirmed by some of his colleagues. But having previously associated only with German Jews it may be that some part of what I regarded as madness was merely German etiquette, so aptly portrayed by the author of *Elizabeth and her German Garden*. But in addition to peasant life in the Black Forest we added visits to the Heimanns in Berlin and to Herr Krüll, a friend of John's in Hamburg, who had survived the war and returned to direct one of Hamburg's important shipyards.

It was during these visits that we saw Germany in the throes of inflation connected, we believed, with the economic consequences of the Peace of Versailles. All visitors to Germany brought back strange tales of its consequences. A good example was what happened in Berlin when Frau Heimann's very distinguished music teacher, Fraulein Constanza, was found to be living in penury because the weekly pension contributed by her pupils was about sufficient in depreciated marks to buy a pound of margarine. What was to be done about it? To give her more money would have been as helpful as collecting ice cream to feed hungry children in the tropics. In the end they gave her a number of small silver objects which she could sell one by one, spending the cash quickly before its purchasing power melted.

This situation, and the post-war humiliation of Germany, was intensified by the French occupation of the Rhineland. Indeed on one occasion John and I got entangled in it, by attempting without the necessary military visas, to travel from Strasburg to Freiburg. In the end all was well. We managed to bribe a German with a car to take us by unfrequented side roads under cover of darkness across the frontier which separated the French occupied Rhineland from unoccupied Germany. Had we encountered French armed forces we were well primed with the lies we were instructed to tell as to what we were doing and where we were going.

However, as students of economic history well know, the reestablishment of the German economy was rapid and spectacular. When I revisited Berlin as delegate to an International Women's

Suffrage Conference in the summer of 1929 all was sweetness and light. Germany was prosperous and Berlin was opulently hospitable. It was also ostentatiously democratic. Women played a prominent part in the Reichstag. Taxi-drivers no longer required tips. One could walk about in the streets and visit museums without a hat—we had not got that far in England—and at the Charlottenburg Opera House the appearance of Einstein in the centre of the dress circle was the focus of reverent attention.

In Oxford these goings-on raised solemn thoughts. Maynard Keynes's *Economic Consequences of the Peace* was widely read and discussed, as were the financial events which led up to the Dawes Plan for the settlement of the German reparations debt. Moreover, the problem of bringing Germany back into the comity of nations was taken seriously. Our thoughts took shape in the form of a plan to bring over groups of representative German students for a month's stay in Oxford. First came a dozen, then another dozen; Oxford families offered hospitality. St John's House became their headquarters and we had two in residence, one after the other. Though a very few Oxford inhabitants were disposed to regard Germans with distaste, I think we were successful in making our visiting students feel that all was forgiven and forgotten and that talk of war guilt had become irrelevant. In this enterprise the Quakers played a leading part—and, of course, the Murrays.

This then was the first of our three external political pressures. The second was the Russian revolution. Its occurrence, and what was going on in Russia as a result of it, were matters of burning interest both inside and outside university circles, and publications began to pour out from those few adventurous seekers after truth who had actually visited it. In Ruskin College Marxian communism was fiercely discussed and by many found inspiring. I came in for some of it, having been invited by a delightful left-wing Jesuit named Father O'Hea to act as tutor to a group of Catholic students working at Ruskin, but cherished by him in a separate residence. They were pleasant and responsive students until, in the course of our studies, we came to Malthus; at which point their minds shut up with a click. They associated him (wrongly, of course) with Dr Marie Stopes, and were not prepared to discuss so much as the part he played in the Poor Law developments of the eighteen-thirties—still less, in an important phase of the evolution of economic thought, in connection with his population theory.

At one point Russian communism came to Oxford in the form of a visit by Krassin, I think at the invitation of the University Labour Club of which John was senior treasurer. Krassin was at that time acting as trade representative of the U.S.S.R. in London, and occupied a house in Eaton Avenue with his wife and three handsome daughters, at which we subsequently visited him. After the Oxford meeting we went round to one of the colleges where he was entertained to refreshments; but Mme Krassin and I were turned back from the porter's lodge on the ground that females were not allowed in a male college at that hour. This caused Mme Krassin to think that her husband was being lured to some doom. I took her back to St John's House, where she consented to eat some apricot jam in a saucer. But she was clearly in a state of great agitation, the more so as, knowing no Russian and she very little English, I was unable to explain a strange Oxford custom. But all was well when our two husbands arrived intact and the Krassins returned to London by car.

I fear that neither Krassin's marriage nor his period of fruitful co-operation with Stalin lasted very long. One subsequent chance encounter many years later with his widow and daughters during a summer holiday at West Bay, belongs to a later chapter—or would so belong, were I prepared to turn this serious autobiography into more of a gossip column than it already is.

The Krassin visit, and indeed many others, took place, during these years, against a political ferment which was highlighted by the Vice-Chancellorship of Lewis Farnell, Rector of Exeter College. His attitude to such events can best be illustrated by the correspondence following a request by Miss R. J. Hardy, undergraduate Secretary of the Oxford University Labour Club, for permission to organize a public meeting at which Bertrand Russell was to speak. The Vice-Chancellor's reply, dated October 14, 1921, was as follows:

Dear Miss Hardy,

My reply to your request must be an unconditional refusal. I object to your Club, which you call the "Oxford University Labour Club", holding any public meeting at all. Apart from the question whether Mr Bertrand Russell is a desirable

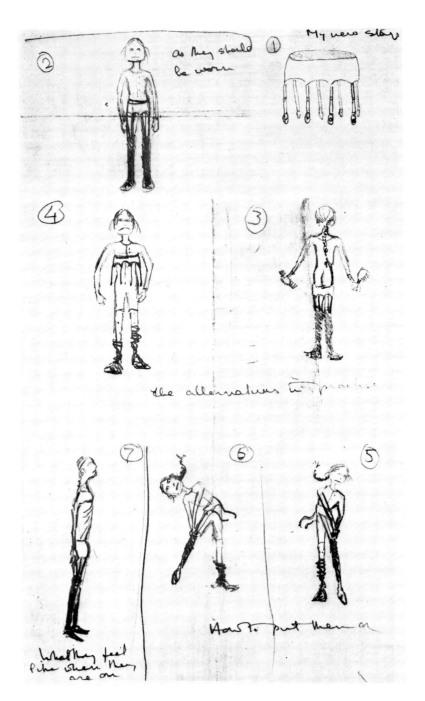

5. An incident in the dress war as recorded by the author.

6. J. L. Stocks and the author, at the time of their engagement, 1912.

person to address Oxford undergraduates on problems that involve social morality, it is against the law of the University for undergraduate members to take part in public political meetings of an agitating tendency. It is still more objectionable that they should organize them. We also object to their assuming the name of Oxford University for a party union of of class-dividing tendency. If your Club wishes to exist, it must keep itself entirely private, both in respect of meetings and publications; otherwise, we shall have to take steps. Your organizers ought to have asked my opinion before venturing to take such a name.

I will now speak a few words to you more *in loco parentis*, as you are an undergraduate member of the University and newly admitted. I earnestly advise you to concentrate on the purpose for which you have come here, which is the increase of knowledge through honest study. It is premature for you to be taking violent sides in violent political controversies. What you want to do is to think and to know more. These public meetings do not make for the increase of knowledge or for greater clearness of thought obtained by fair and careful argument on both sides. You will be more fit to deal with social problems later, if you concentrate your mind and time on the more abstract studies that you have chosen to pursue. This advice applies equally to our women as to our men students.

Yours faithfully,
(signed) Lewis R. Farnell
Vice-Chancellor

The Chairman of the Club replied as follows:

22 St Giles, Oxford
18 Oct. 1921

The Vice-Chancellor, Exeter College
Sir,

I have the honour to inform you that the letter which you sent on October 14th to the Secretary of the Labour Club here in reply to a request for permission to hold a public meeting has been considered by the Executive Committee of the Club. In view of the serious tone of your letter, and considering the implications of the statements made therein, it was considered vitally necessary that these points in particular should be cleared up:

(i) Whether you intend that the Labour Club shall hold no *public* meetings at all and shall virtually cease to exist as a public society here;

(ii) Whether in consequence of this, discrimination is to be made in favour of other political clubs; and

(iii) Whether you really consider that a club which is composed of all classes and has at heart the welfare of all the people in this country is a "party union of a class-dividing tendency".

In order to obtain a clear statement of your attitude on these points in particular the Committee appointed a deputation to wait upon you, for the purpose of having the favour of an interview with you at your convenience on any morning during the present week. This deputation is composed of:

Kenneth M. Lindsay, President, the Oxford Union, and Ex-Chairman of the Oxford University Labour Club;

J. S. Collis, Junior Treasurer, the Oxford Union, and Ex-Chairman of the Oxford University Labour Union;

S. Tetley, Chairman, Oxford University Labour Club.

We agree that the latter part of your letter affords no ground for ambiguity in meaning and we are anxious to promote its chief aim.

I have, Sir, the honour to be
Your obedient servant,
S. Tetley,
Chairman, O.U. Labour Club

At this point the matter was taken up by the senior members of the university acting on behalf of the club. Correspondence was conducted by John Stocks who acted as its Hon. Senior Treasurer. It turned on the Vice-Chancellor's right to sanction, or refuse to sanction, public meetings, as well as on his objection to the Labour Club's "class-dividing" name. It became distinctly acrimonious.

Whether in the end Bertrand Russell was allowed to speak, I do not remember. But I do remember that other meetings raised similar problems. For instance, a meeting at which Miss Maude Royden was to speak on Women in the Church was vetoed, though on what grounds I do not know. Meeting the Rev. Dr Selbie, Principal of Mansfield College, in the street one day, I raised the problem. He said he could only suppose that the Vice-Chancellor had confused Maude Royden with Maud Allan, a dancer who was at the time in some trouble over a nude show in London.

It was about this time that another distressing incident overtook the Vice-Chancellor. The popular Press had been giving much publicity to the case of a husband who had disposed of his wife by giving her poisoned chocolates. The Vice-Chancellor was therefore naturally suspicious when he received an anonymous box of chocolates on which it seemed some white powder had been scattered. Professor Soddy, a very eminent chemist, happened to be present when this gift arrived. He removed some of the powder which on analysis he indicted as an Indian poison containing ground glass. The chocolates were then handed over to the police, at which point the perpetrator of the deed confessed. It was, he said, a practical joke; the powder was stuff he had obtained from the College kitchen and its trade name was "Old Dutch Cleanser". Since it was designed for scouring saucepans it could well have contained ground glass, which might not have been lethal, but would certainly have been unhealthy if eaten in quantity. In Oxford, and, I fear, in the local Press, the powder was described as toothpowder; with the result that the incident became known as "the gumpowder plot", and must have caused the Vice-Chancellor some distress.

Farnell's Vice-Chancellorship cannot have been a happy one. He was conscious of his dignity and of that of his office, but both were constantly at risk during his reign. In some ways he resembled Malvolio for whom one cannot withhold deep sympathy and even affection when in *Twelfth Night* he was the subject of a cruel jest. It was unfortunate that the perpetrator of the "gumpowder plot" happened to be an undergraduate of St John's College; but I am sure that Farnell acquitted my husband of complicity. Indeed, some time after the incident he wrote John a friendly letter to ask whether he would like to be recommended for the post of Vice-Chancellor of the University of Hong-Kong.

The third of our post-war Oxford preoccupations, and one which involved most work, was the Irish question. Ireland was in a ferment, and the Sinn Fein movement for independence appeared to be beyond the control of the British regular army

[137]

stationed in Ireland. In face of intensified violence, including the burning of British property and the ambushing of British soldiers, Lloyd George recruited and dispatched to Ireland a special force known as the Black and Tans. Violence generates violence and outrage generates reprisals. The Black and Tan reprisals were far more savage than those of the much provoked regular army, and the villain of the piece was Lloyd George.

C. P. Scott of the *Manchester Guardian* was an old friend and admirer of Lloyd George, and his estrangement from Lloyd George on this question, as recorded in his biography* by J. L. Hammond, gives a fair picture of what all, except a minority of "give 'em hell" right-wing Conservatives, felt about British policy in Ireland. A nation-wide protest took shape in 1921, in which Asquith and Sir John Simon played a part, and protest meetings were held up and down the country. Sir John Simon was indefatigably energetic and unforgettably eloquent, spurred on by devotion to his Irish patriot wife.

Oxford was deeply concerned with all this. A group of dons, including Walter Moberly of Lincoln College and A. D. Lindsay of Balliol, went over to Ireland under the auspices of Sir Horace Plunket to see for themselves what was happening. Their report confirmed all our worst fears. We organized a great protest meeting in the Corn Exchange at which Sir John Simon, Lord Monteagle, Lord Henry Bentinck and Sir Horace Plunket were the speakers— a powerful platform, and with Sir John Simon at the top of his form as a great orator who on this occasion really felt deeply about what he was saying. I spent the preceding two days replacing notices of the meeting, which were repeatedly torn down by objectors outside St John's House. In the end the meeting was orderly enough, but not so orderly as to make it dull. At any rate, judged by modern university standards, it was Sunday-school orderly.

But the outrages and reprisals went on, and so long as they did, the agitation had to go on at full blast. We resolved that every night in Oxford there should be an open-air protest meeting, and so there was. It would have become tediously repetitive were we not fed with up-to-date facts and figures from Ireland recorded in a stencilled journal which appeared at intervals. By whom it was issued, and whether it was distributed throughout the country or

* *C. P. Scott,* by J. L. Hammond. Bell, 1934.

was peculiar to Oxford, I cannot now remember. But its contents were distressing.

In the end Lloyd George "yielded to circumstances", as C. P. Scott put it, and in the summer of 1921 opened negotiations with the rebellious Irish leaders, which ended on December 5, 1921, with a treaty involving the creation of the Irish Free State minus the six counties of Ulster. It did not end faction and disturbance in Ireland but it did end our sense of immediate responsibility for its continuance. All of which shows that in democratic Great Britain, public opinion, with freedom to write, speak, and organize, can affect national policy if a minority of activists really care.

Meanwhile our residence in Oxford was drawing to a close. My own activities as adult education tutor had multiplied and included courses of University Extension Lectures. One such course took me to Northwich in Cheshire. This involved a number of railway journeys into Manchester. Looking out over the sea of grimy roofs and factory chimneys as the train crept into the centre of the city, the scene inspired not repulsion but a sort of anticipatory affection. So I had little regret when in 1924 John answered a call to succeed Professor Samuel Alexander as Professor of Philosophy in Manchester University. He had more regrets than I had, because he owed more to Oxford and had for so many years been an integral part of it. But long tutorial hours left little time for writing, and Manchester opened out opportunities for non-academic activities in which he was interested. And in his case, personal and family contacts in Lancashire represented a pull to the magnetic north.

The person who most regretted our departure was Stevenson, the St John's College librarian, who adored our four-year-old youngest daughter, Helen, and generally accompanied us on our Sunday afternoon walks. I fear that he pined for her, and soon after her departure died as quietly as he had lived.

I wonder if his type exists in the modern world? It certainly did in the days when great nobles maintained resident learned men in their stately homes as librarians, chaplains, or archivists. Stevenson was the son of a Nottingham builder and had achieved learning by the hard way of scholarships and private benefactions, which finally brought him to roost in St John's College. His duties cannot have been onerous, and his bachelor existence in St John's was certainly peaceful and comfortable. His knowledge, beginning with working-class conditions and building techniques, seemed boundless. We wanted to know how to cut glass—he told us. We wanted to know the etymology of a word or the origin of a place name—he told us. There was nothing he did not know.

I doubt if our remaining stately homes—the few that exist—maintain men like Stevenson; but I hope that some colleges still do. The University Grants Committee today spends public money on less gracious non-essentials.

10

The Hammonds
and the Astors

AS OUR LIFE IN resurrected Oxford drew to a close, two outside
contacts developed which were carried over into our new existence.

One was friendship with Barbara and Lawrence Hammond, the
joint historians of the Industrial Revolution, whom we visited from
Oxford in their country home at Piccotts End. Theirs was an unusual
ménage. Later, the house was improved by the introduction of a
hot-water system, an upstairs bathroom, and electric light. But
when we first knew it these amenities were lacking. Though
scarcely more than a mile from Hemel Hempstead, on the Leighton
Buzzard Road, it was approached through a narrow rutted lane up
a fairly steep hill, at the top of which one was conscious of being
in deep silent country. Later, when the new town arose on the
other side of Hemel Hempstead, it was able to preserve this illusion
of remoteness; and for all I know, may do so still, though the
Hammonds are no longer alive to enjoy it.

The excuse for this rural isolation was an early diagnosis of
threatened T.B. for Barbara; but as it turned out, this was a stroke
of good luck because she remained perfectly healthy, while both
were set free from conflicting preoccupations for the writing of
history. Incidentally, it required them to sleep in the open air.
This they did, whatever the weather, in a revolving summer-
house, open to the winds, apart from a roof over their heads, but
able to be rotated so as to keep them to leeward of whatever gales
were blowing during the night.

If it were possible to think of the Hammonds as two separate
persons—which it is not easy to do—I would surmise that Barbara

contributed the scholarship and Lawrence the fine writing. As an
undergraduate at Oxford she had made history by a brilliant first
in Greats. Her achievement was commemorated, not of course in
those days by a degree, by the publication of a picture postcard
obtainable at the time, and indeed for many years later, in Oxford
shops. It depicted a dishevelled and distraught male, coping with
an examination paper, while in the corner was pictured, accurately,
a red-headed young woman, writing with easy nonchalance, above
the following rhyme:

> I spend all my days with a crammer
> And get nothing better than gamma
> While the girl over there
> With the flaming red hair
> Gets alpha plus easily d... her!

Lawrence, while writing history, continued at the same time to
pursue his original vocation of journalism, especially in connection
with the *Manchester Guardian*, and I have always supposed that
some of the finest prose passages in their joint books were drafted
by him.

There was another reason why Barbara's threat of T.B. had
compensations. It provided an excuse for the kind of life they both
liked. They could not live without animal as well as human companionship. Their close friends included dogs, cats, birds with
whom they had assignations at meal times, and two horses named
Magic and Mystery who lived in their paddock and on whose backs
they rode about the countryside. Both these animals had, I believe,
suffered traumatic experiences during war service and were treated
with special consideration. So, during one spring, did a lark whose
nest in the paddock was threatened by an owl. I was present with
Eleanor Rathbone in London when she received a telephone call
from Barbara cancelling an engagement to lunch because the situation in the paddock required constant surveillance. Eleanor was
herself prepared to be kind to animals, though she did not seek
their company, but, she thought, there really were limits to the
extent to which they should be allowed to dictate day to day
behaviour. It was not until 1943 that she herself submitted to the
domination of a small black cat.

Many years later, when only Magic (or was it Mystery?) survived as an old-age pensioner out at grass in the paddock, my

daughter Ann suggested to Lawrence that the expensive diet of oats provided for her might be suitable for a Leicestershire hunter in full work, but was unnecessary for an old-age pensioner with an adequate diet of good grass—and might even not be very good for her. Lawrence was apologetic but unrepentant. "You see, she's had so little in her life," he said. Personally I doubt if this was true. She had enjoyed for many years the love and companionship of two adorable people, which seems to me quite a lot in anybody's life.

I hope the world still contains people like the Hammonds: so sensitive, so compassionate, at the same time so gifted, so alive to what was going on all over the world, and withal so perceptive of human foibles and so well endowed with a sense of humour. To later generations who did not share the advantages of Magic and Mystery and know them personally one can say: "By their books ye shall know them." They did not tell the whole story of the Industrial Revolution of the late eighteenth and early nineteenth century, but they told it from the human angle of those who had lived through it; and the compassion which infuses their telling does not obscure the meticulous and painstaking scholarship which has set them among our great pioneer economic historians.

The other outside contact which developed during these Oxford years was with the Astors, and this took us into a strangely contrasted environment. It began, as far as I was concerned, with the interested observation of a public event, but led in due course to a personal contact in which John also shared.

The public event was the election in 1919 of Lady Astor as the first woman to take her seat in the House of Commons. I shared the mixed feelings with which my fellow-working feminists regarded this apparent triumph of our cause. Not for this had we laboured so long and so hard. We had envisaged our first woman M.P. as at best a tried suffragist—at least as a woman distinguished in local government or social service. But here was an American millionairess, known only to us by reputation, since we did not move in those circles, as a society hostess, stepping into a safe seat vacated by her husband on his elevation to the peerage not by reason of her own qualification but merely *qua* wife. We feared the worst. Only Mrs H. A. L. Fisher who, it seemed, did move in those circles, offered a word of comfort. "Wait and see," she said. "She's all right: you'll be surprised." We did: and were. Nor did we have to wait long.

The advent of Nancy Astor, M.P., certainly contributed a colourful and almost bizarre chapter to the sombre story of women's emancipation. She had, of course, initial advantages for the part she was to play: beauty, charm, physical vigour (which she owed to Christian Science) and enough money to secure expert help, both domestic and political. This last brought her the highly skilled services of Ray Strachey as political adviser and Hilda Matheson, who later became director of talks in the B.B.C., as personal political secretary. Both had her well in hand, though this was not always easy.

I have seen Hilda Matheson at work with her on a morning's correspondence requiring serious attention, patiently attempting and at last succeeding in fixing Nancy Astor's darting mind on some matter in hand. It was not only external intrusions such as dinner arrangements or telephone calls which threatened to produce chaos, but irrelevant and often highly amusing trains of thought inimical to any sustained mental concentration. Excellent speeches might be prepared for her—she was apt to ignore her notes or use the wrong ones. This occurred on one occasion at an international conference where she inadvertently used notes prepared for a meeting of the English-Speaking Union. Delegates from all over the world were not prepared to applaud a dissertation on the special relationship and civilizing influence of Great Britain and the U.S.A.

But her supreme initial advantage was that she was married to a saint-like and selfless husband who was prepared to subordinate his own political career to hers, sustaining her always, and restraining her where possible.

It was not always possible. She was alarmingly indiscreet and as courageous as a corsair. Her physical courage was to be seen many years later when Plymouth suffered an appalling ordeal by German bombing. Her moral courage was shown almost at once when she dared to provoke Horatio Bottomley, whom she regarded as a crook—which indeed he was soon proved to be. Her fellow M.P., Josiah Wedgwood, warned her to keep clear of Bottomley who was, he said, the kind of animal that spits mud. The warning was unheeded. As a result there appeared all over London, and for all I know everywhere else, posters advertising Bottomley's paper, *John Bull*, with the words: "Lady Astor's Divorce." I was told, and I like to believe this to be true, that a leading political opponent of the Astors in Plymouth lost a lucrative advertising contract by refusing to display this poster in her constituency. The divorce in fact related to an unhappy first marriage of Nancy Astor's youth in America of which she had no reason to be ashamed, and which Bottomley was able to dig up and exploit for her discomfort.

One feature of Nancy Astor's indiscretion was a rare gift of mimicry which she shared with other members of her family, and which her niece Joyce Grenfell has since shared on the stage with the public. Nancy Astor's brilliant impersonations of politicians or great ladies were not always taken in good part. She combined a bubbling irreverence with her own brand of evangelical puritanism: two qualities which are rarely combined, but when they are, produce surprising results.

Her first two lonely years in the House of Commons, before she was joined by the discreet and motherly Mrs Wintringham, must have been a gruelling experience; indeed she confessed that it was. There was no television in those days, but her life must have produced the sensation of living on a permanent TV set, with cameras trained on her from every angle. The Press were never far from her. How would she dress? What would she say? How would male M.P.s take her? What would she do next? The support of her husband and the tact of her two experienced political advisers enabled her to survive; and I suspect that some credit must be accorded to Mary Baker Eddy, whose book *Science and Health* she read with greater concentration than was accorded to any other written work.

But something else enabled her to survive: the affection and support of other women. In spite of feminist fears it was soon obvious that Nancy Astor was the fiercest feminist of us all. In a very short time women's organizations up and down the country were at her feet. The more so, perhaps, because she was so wholly unlike the eminent women who normally addressed them. She cared for the things they cared for. She wanted to meet them. Indeed she did meet them in a big way at the periodic evening receptions given in the Astor London home at 4 St James's Square, where she aimed at introducing politicians to women voters from all over the country. These gatherings became a feature of political life in the twenties; and it could be a great adventure for the officers of some small women's organization in a remote provincial

town, up in London for a delegate conference, to see the inside of
4 St James's Square and meet men and women whose names were
familiar hearsay. But, of course, it required Astor millions to entertain on such a scale, and Astor friendliness to render it congenial.

My first personal encounter with Nancy Astor was as member
of a delegation to canvass her support for a further measure of votes
for women. The encounter led to lunch at St James's Square and
later to an invitation for John and me to a week-end at Cliveden.
She told me that I had an adorable husband—which I already
knew—but she took a dim view of his politics.

This was the first of many contacts with Nancy Astor and her
family, and that week-end party was the first of many visits to
Cliveden, spanning three decades of this century and the period
when sections of the Press were attempting to discredit what they
called "The Cliveden Set". Was there a "Cliveden Set" in the
sense that a century and a half ago there was a "Holland House
Set"? It certainly did contain persons who seemed insensitive to
the danger of German aggression, including that most despicable
of responsible journalists, Geoffrey Dawson, who used his position
as editor of *The Times* to suppress news from Germany which he
thought might inflame public opinion against the Hitler régime.
But it also contained persons able to argue with them, and I doubt
if a set so mixed and so varied could properly be regarded as a
"set" at all.

At any rate much has been written about it, and doubtless more
will be. And the same may be said about Nancy Astor herself,
whom later I got to know rather well, and saw something of her
family life and its tensions. By the time this reaches readers (if it
ever does) I hope that the full and careful biography now in preparation will have told her story to the public. Indeed much has
already been written about her, including her son Michael's excellent account of his early life at Cliveden,* and I can add little to it.
I have risked repetition by retailing my own reminiscence because
there is some fear that what women owe to her for those very early
years may be forgotten.

Many of those whom one meets in contemporary life today
know only of her later years as an M.P. When she was persuaded
not to seek re-election in 1945 she was doing no good to her own
reputation as a serious politician or to the causes she had at heart.

* *Tribal Feeling*, by Michael Astor. Murray, 1963.

I think she never forgave those who persuaded her. Nor did she
forgive Harold Macmillan for not making her a Life Peer when it
became possible after 1958.

Of course the persuaders were right and so was Harold Macmillan. As she advanced into old age she could be exasperating,
often unreasonable, and foolishly prejudiced. Negroes, French-
men and Jews were among her collective antipathies. It was thus
that younger generations knew her, though her generosity, kindness, and unfailing sense of humour made up for much. But those
of my own generation, who are a rapidly dwindling minority, saw
at first-hand her impact on the feminist movement of the twenties.
Seen from that angle, she remains in the memory as a most gay
and gallant knight "with a heart of furious fancies", riding all
alone two years ahead of a later company of wise and distinguished
women M.P.s. She deserved our love and admiration and she will
command it while our memories last.

In 1956 I had occasion as a member of the *Observer* Trust,
created by Viscount Astor, to stand in for a year as its Chairman
pending the selection of a suitable successor to Dingle Foot who
had been appointed by Lord Astor. The editor of the paper was
David Astor, whose pro-African and anti-racist views were not
shared by his mother. I have heard her refer to *The Observer* as
"the *Coon's Gazette*". Her view was that niggers, with many of
whom she had been familiar as a child in Virginia, should be kept
in their place. However, personal friendliness prompted her to ring
me up and say, "I'm glad to hear that you are to be Chairman of
the *Observer* Trust". I replied that I was only a temporary chairman. She said: "Black your face and they'll want to keep you as
Chairman."

11

Manchester

MANCHESTER IN 1924 WAS dirtier than it is now and its centre was nearer to open country. Wilbraham Road, Fallowfield, where our hideous but spacious mid-Victorian house was located, led into fields, but these were in process of being developed as a Corporation housing estate. The inhabitants of central Manchester could no longer enjoy half an hour's walk into rural country at Green Heys as they could in the days of Mrs Gaskell's *Mary Barton*, but the inhabitants of Fallowfield could, and did, enjoy country walks from Wilbraham Road into fields and across the Mersey to the village of Northenden.

Closely packed round the business centres of the interlocked cities of Manchester and Salford was a ring of slums, mean streets, jerry-built as economically viable dwellings for the working-classes of the Industrial Revolution, with here and there a surviving row of gracious Georgian terraces designed for the employing classes in the days when they lived near their factories. Later, these had been abandoned to baser uses which no longer required their occupants to spend money on external spit and polish. There they remained, looking like distressed gentlewomen degraded by the proximity of the lower orders.

As one proceeded from the centre, streets became wider and their houses more comely if no less monotonous, until one erupted from the aspidistra and lace curtain zone into an area of Victorian semi-detached houses, or houses like our own, wholly detached and standing in their own gardens.

And what a good garden ours was, when once one had come to terms—as John Stocks had by a process of trial and error—with what could be made to grow well in our bleak climate. In Oxford

[148]

he had inherited ready-made, after centuries of expert management, the stewardship of St John's College garden with its superb
rockery. The garden of 22 Wilbraham Road, rockery and all, was
the work of his hands.

Whatever might be the physical climate of Manchester, its
social, political and academic climate was far from bleak. It was
warm, welcoming and exciting.

One element in its warmth was the fact that we moved straight
into a family connection. The Fletcher connection was very
different from the Rendel connection, but it was well integrated,
and it became part of our day-to-day, or rather our week-to-week,
Manchester life. It was centred on the coal and cotton areas of
Atherton and Leigh and our point of close contact with it was the
household of John's youngest sister, Kitty, who had married a
Fletcher. I think John was indirectly responsible for the marriage
because it was a Rugby friendship with several Fletchers that had
brought Stockses and Fletchers together.

We had, as I have already reported, often visited them before
we went to live among them. Kitty's husband, Leonard, was the
one Fletcher war casualty. Other young Fletchers had gone off to
the war and returned from it intact. Leonard had been obliged to
stay at home to manage the family collieries, and had died of
pneumonia—complicated, doubtless, by overwork—leaving Kitty
with three children, a large house, and a deep sense of responsibility to the workers who produced their family income. There she
remained until 1962, to serve them as a very active member of the
Lancashire County Council, a J.P., a sustainer of the local Labour
Party, the W.E.A., the Church, and indeed much else.

I never really succeeded in describing her environment to my
mother. Did Kitty live in the country? Yes, in a way, but no
country that my mother could envisage or indeed that any Rendel
had ever known. Did she live in a town? Well—in an urban district, but not such a one as any Rendel had ever lived or shopped
in. It had a garden and a tennis court, but one could not retrieve
tennis balls from the surrounding vegetation without emerging
rather black. It had fields in front and at the back, indeed the house
was called "Woodfields", but its skyline was diversified by cotton
mills and colliery winding-gear; and the sound of factory sirens
and the clatter of clogs on cobbles was part of its unforgettable personality. It was approached by a track whose undulating contours,

like those of its neighbouring small streets, indicated subsidences occasioned by underground coal workings.

Thus were my children provided with a ready-made family of contemporary first cousins, and every Sunday afternoon it became our habit to drive over to Leigh. Those Sunday drives, and indeed the whole Fletcher contact, helped us to become truly integrated Lancastrians. The drives themselves were fascinating; through Worsley, where one could still see part of the original brick structure of Brindley's Bridgewater Canal, *via* Tyldesley and Atherton to Leigh. Sometimes we would approach Worsley through Trafford Park and over the Ship Canal by Barton Bridge; sometimes through Salford and Pendleton. Nowadays the journey would pass in a flash along a banausic high-level motorway; but I am glad it didn't then.

The Fletcher connection, and indeed the whole Lancashire environment as we got to know it, provoked interesting reflections on class consciousness. We were richer than our neighbours, so was Kitty Fletcher. We had larger houses, better educational opportunities, greater mobility. We had cars, and most people hadn't. But these inequalities did not seem to be reflected in differences of social class. Lancashire as we came to know it was worlds away in this respect from London or Oxford though it is difficult to put into words exactly why.

It must, of course, be admitted that the Fletchers were atypical employers. For at least two generations relations between them and their working colliers had been closely personal. Leonard, as a manager, had worked underground and emerged black, to his bath in the basement at Woodfields. When the miners were being slowly starved during the stoppage which followed the ill-fated General Strike of 1926, the men in the Fletcher pits looked to the Fletchers for help and sympathy—and got it.

In Manchester itself our two spiritual centres were the *Manchester Guardian* and the University, and very soon there emerged a third: the Manchester University Settlement in Ancoats.

The *Manchester Guardian* was personified by C. P. Scott. Into his staff came able young men: Kingsley Martin, Malcolm Muggeridge—they came, and they went. C. P. Scott liked his own way and his way was the way that ran the paper. And what a good paper it was! *The Times* was a stuffed shirt in comparison. With decades of political experience and easy access to the "corridors of

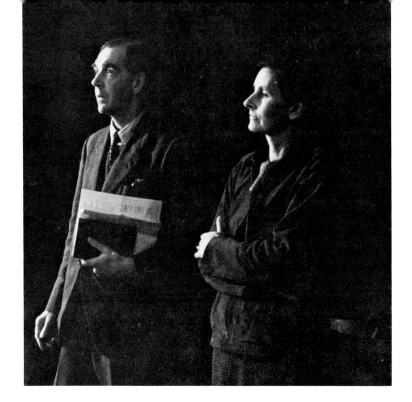

7 (a). Professor Stocks and the author at a play rehearsal at the Manchester University Settlement.

7 (b). The Stocks children on holiday at West Bay: *Left to right:* Ann, John and Helen.

8. Mary Stocks, 1953.

power", its editor had, in addition, a wholly consistent flame of political philosophy and journalistic integrity. Yet mingled with his thrusting liberalism was a grain of conservatism which conditioned his response to new or popular features, which his colleague W. P. Crozier describes so vividly in a chapter contributed to J. L. Hammond's life of Scott.

Scott's retirement from his editorial chair in 1929 was widely reported and the subject of many tributes, including one from the King. It was said that some time after this event, a member of the office staff was heard to remark that it was interesting to learn from the Press that C. P. Scott had retired.

One vivid memory of my own links C. P. Scott, the grand old man of the Press, with Professor Samuel Alexander, the grand old man of the university. It was very generally regarded as fitting that Alexander's distinguished academic reign as Professor of Philosophy should be commemorated for posterity by a portrait. It was, I think, John Stocks's idea that this should take the form of a bust by Jacob Epstein. The idea found favour, money was collected, and Epstein came to Manchester to survey his model. He was fascinated by what he saw. Alexander, who was in fact an Australian Jew, resembled Blake's conception of God. His head was massive and magnificent, his beard was long; but—one would wish so to conceive of the Almighty—his expression radiated kindness and humour and he smiled most sweetly with his eyes.

But Alexander's was not the only magnificent head in Manchester. Scott, too, had a magnificent head, and we conceived the idea, since Epstein sojourned in our house, that if Epstein could be confronted with Scott he would fall for Scott as he had fallen for Alexander. So we invited Scott to meet Epstein at high tea, since that was the meal which fitted *Manchester Guardian* hours, and hoped for the best. Tea passed, and it did seem as though Epstein's eyes were boring into Scott like gimlets; but nothing significant happened. We then adjourned to the sitting-room, and it did. Epstein suddenly said: "Are you ever in London, Mr Scott?" Yes, Scott sometimes was in London. "Would you let me make a study of you?" Yes, Scott would. And he did: and his eightieth birthday was celebrated in 1926 by the presentation of Epstein's bust of Scott to the City of Manchester.

Memories of Alexander are mainly centred on Wednesday evening gatherings in the house where he lived in bachelor retirement with a wholly undistinguished brother, one of whose occupations seemed to be the nurture of a plant which Gracie Fields would have recognized as "The Biggest Aspidistra in the World". Its furnishings were Victorian, but uninteresting Victorian, and I think it is true that Alexander, whose appreciation of the beauty of words was acute, had very little visual aesthetic sense.

Years later, soon after my husband's death, I asked Alexander to edit an unfinished work of his. His readily agreed, and I asked John's old friend William Temple, then Archbishop of York, to write a preface. This he did, and in the course of it remarked that the fact that "our greatest living English philosopher" was proud to act as editor, was indeed a tribute to John Stocks. I naturally showed Temple's MSS to Alexander since he was responsible for the book. He insisted that the phrase I have quoted should be omitted. "It's absolute rubbish," he said. "Our greatest living English philosopher indeed!" I suggested that whether true or not, an Archbishop should be allowed to express an opinion. He replied: "Well, *I* don't think an Archbishop should be allowed to tell a lie." And that was that.

Whether or no Alexander was our greatest living English philosopher, I do not know, and as a non-philosopher have no right to an opinion. But this I do know: Samuel Alexander was a very great *man*, and never was the O.M. better bestowed.

I have spoken of the university and the *Manchester Guardian* as two centres of Manchester cultural life. In fact they were closely interlocked, and cement was added to their interlocking both by business and civic interests. Ernest and Shena Simon* of Didsbury could be said to represent all four. Ernest Simon was the head of the two great firms which later became the Simon Engineering Group. He was, during the greater part of our time in Manchester, an active member of its City Council and a leading expert on housing, while his wife Shena was an equally active member of the Manchester Education Committee. At the same time, both were closely concerned with university administration, and intimately associated by personal friendships and social philosophy with the Scott family circle.

This integration of business, civic and academic interest could, of course, be seen in other large cities, in many of which university development had been conditioned by the support of public-

* Ernest Simon later became Lord Simon of Wythenshawe.

spirited business families. What gave it peculiar significance in Manchester was, I really believe, the centripetal force of the *Manchester Guardian* reflecting a consistent social and political philosophy all through the twenties and thirties. Today it has discarded its local allegiance and transferred its editorial direction to London. Whether it can survive there under the shadow of Lord Thomson is anybody's guess.

But to return to the twenties. Outside the university John Stocks had two main activities and in both I was able to share. The one which he found most time-consuming was the University Settlement. He had always been interested in Manchester, and now here it was with its shape, its streets, its buildings, its history, indeed its whole potent personality, all to be explored. This he set to work to do. Wherever in the course of these explorations he found a building which bore a date, a note of it was made in a small notebook. Among those explored was a particularly interesting group of buildings in Ancoats. Ancoats itself was an area of small, mean streets built largely for workers in the Industrial Revolution textile mills, which still dominated it. Indeed the whole area is vividly described in Engels's *Condition of the Working Class in England* written in 1844. And even in Engels's time Ancoats contained interesting features.

One was Ancoats Hall, the ancestral home of the Mosley family, former Lords of the Manor. It had become very black by 1924, and was surrounded by railway yards; but it was a good building and the Manchester Corporation maintained it as an art gallery. The other, not far from it, was a small, two-storeyed house, No. 20 Every Street, in front of which was a tombstone recording the burial there of the Scholefield family, at dates ranging from 1834 to 1855. To the back of this house there adhered a large circular building which when we first saw it had apparently been rented to a builder as a store for various kinds of junk. It was in a dreary state of disrepair. Over its outer door it bore the inscription *Christchurch 1821*. Over an inner door leading to the rear of No. 20 Every Street, were inscribed the words "Serve the Lord with gladness". This indicated that its original purpose was that of a chapel, but it was clear that for many a long year it had not been possible to serve the Lord or anybody else with gladness. Surrounding the circular building was a yard, unevenly paved with tombstones. It contained a large, dishevelled wooden structure

[153]

furnished as a recreation room. All this was at first sight discouraging. But there was that in the whole set-up, the roundness of the circular building, the architectural proportions of the little square brick house to which it adhered, the indefinable air of historical significance underlying its squalor, which arrested and fixed the affections of John Stocks and held them firmly in place for the rest of his life in Manchester.

This, together with one dreary wing of Ancoats Hall, was the habitation of the Manchester University Settlement upon whose Council John Stocks, as a man known to be interested in such social ventures, was on his arrival in Manchester invited to serve. He responded readily, and almost the first duty required of him was to move in 1925 a resolution recommending the winding up of the Settlement, then in a state of apparently hopeless insolvency.

When the Manchester University Settlement celebrated its fiftieth birthday in 1943 I was invited to write its history,* a long story which covers a significant period in the evolution of social reform and voluntary service. It also covered a notable early golden age of achievement before the dislocations of World War I threatened its continued existence. But since it has been told in detail I will not retail even that part of it which concerns John Stocks, except to record that it was not wound up in 1925. On the contrary it enjoyed a glorious resurrection and entered on a new golden age under the leadership of Hilda Cashmore, its Warden from 1926 to 1933, with John Stocks playing a significant part as its Chairman until he left Manchester.

In various ways the Settlement became part of our family life in Wilbraham Road, with Hilda Cashmore as a frequent week-end visitor. One aspect of it which gave John particular pleasure was the development of its drama (see Plate 7a), thanks to an unexpected bequest, which enabled us to reconstruct the circular ruin as a well-equipped Round House theatre in which it was indeed possible to "Serve the Lord with gladness". Among many notable dramatic achievements was a production of Shaw's *Saint Joan* in which Kingsley Martin played the part of de Stogumber while John played that of the Inquisitor, with a cold and deadly objectivity which gave it a terrifying significance.

Another way in which the Settlement impinged on life at Wil-

* *Fifty Years in Every Street*, by Mary Stocks. Manchester University Press, 1945.

braham Road was in connection with the corporation housing estate which had grown up under our eyes. Post-war housing developments had raised the problem of how to transform mushroom areas of decent houses inhabited by uprooted individual tenants into neighbourhoods where corporate activities could be pursued and human contacts developed. The National Council of Social Service in London was grappling with this problem in the south, and the Manchester University Settlement was early in the field with a project for the organization of a Community Centre on the Wilbraham Estate.

The Wilbraham Association, to which the University Settlement played the part of midwife with due concern for pre- and post-natal care, grew up and in due course went on its own way rejoicing. It began with a garden club, which brought to members the advantages of bulk buying and joint ownership of expensive implements such as rollers and mowing machines. Later it acquired a community hall in which an active amateur drama society flourished. With these activities well and truly launched, the Wilbraham Association became almost as much part of our lives in Wilbraham Road as did the Settlement in Ancoats. John Stocks was its Chairman, his study was its committee room.

John's second activity outside his day-time professorial duties was adult education. Two personal friendships had fostered his addiction to it. One was that of R. H. Tawney, a significant figure in the history of extra-mural education and tutor to the first two W.E.A. three-year tutorial classes which took the field in 1908. One was at Rochdale, the other at Longton. To these centres R. H. Tawney would travel each week. He was, of course, in addition to his professorship at the London School of Economics, the author of many notable books, whose readers will recognize him as a writer of grand English prose. Phrases from them remain in the memory.

He was the untidiest man I have ever known and the most oblivious of his personal comfort. He married the sister of William Beveridge, and from their early visits to our newly set-up house in St Michael's Street, Oxford, I got the impression that she would herself have liked a well-ordered home such as ours. But her standards broke against his odd habits, and I think that she adopted the only alternative to a life of nagging, which was to approximate her standards to his and damn the consequences. Thus she conquered her distaste for squalor, and as the years rolled by, their successive homes became increasingly dishevelled and even unclean, while accumulated debris, which nobody thought fit to throw away, piled up round them.

Their standard of life was a perpetual wonder to working-class students who were accustomed to associate such conditions with shiftless poverty. But the dignity, and indeed nobility, of Tawney's personality obscured the fact that he dressed like a tramp and might even, as on one occasion, have forgotten to put on his socks. It was fortunate for the W.E.A. that its early years were profoundly influenced by the leadership of Professor Tawney.

The same might be said of the other personal friendship which helped to forge John's contacts with adult education. This was William Temple, who had been, since boyhood, an intimate of the Stocks's family circle. It was to John, as a young man, that Temple had written the letters which throw so much light on his own spiritual and philosophical development and are described in Iremonger's biography* of Temple "as among the most revealing he ever wrote". We were fortunate in finding him installed as Bishop of Manchester on our arrival in that City. Apart from him, our contacts with the Church were slight.

Temple's passionate interest in working-class education and the devoted service he gave to the W.E.A. as its first President, and indeed up to his death as Archbishop of Canterbury in 1944, has always seemed to me something of an enigma. If ever a young man had been cherished as a sheltered darling of the gods, William Temple had. Brought up in Lambeth Palace with an archiepiscopal father and an aristocratic mother, all opportunities for advancement open to him, no amenities of cultured existence denied to him, he was, unlike many of those thus privileged, determined that what he had, others should have too. It was not only in the adult education movement that his influence was felt. His personality had somehow acquired such significance in the eyes of "the man in the street" that if Churchill had not appointed him to the Archbishopric of Canterbury in 1942, all England, with the exception of the City of London which felt that the clergy should stick to religion, would have wanted to know the reason why. So that when he died, less than three years later, a curtain seemed to fall on the fleeting vision of a national Church speaking wisdom to the people. It has not risen since.

* *William Temple*, by F. A. Iremonger. Oxford University Press, 1948.

Such were two among the many personal friends with whom our life in Manchester was bound up. Tawney stood godfather to our youngest daughter. Temple, many years later, officiated at our daughter's wedding and christened our first grandchild. And today, with the worst will in the world, I cannot regard as wholly class-divisive the system of education at Rugby which produced William Temple, Harry Tawney and John Stocks.

Adult Education made heavy demands during these years on the academic staff of Manchester University. John was not the only member of it to undertake evening tutorial classes involving difficult excursions in all weathers by car, train or bus to outlying areas. For me, since I was not engaged in a full-time job, it was less of a strain but there was more of it.

I think my most difficult assignment was Burnley, reached by road over the watershed of the Pennines. Ice was slow to melt on the road from Crawshaybooth to Burnley, and during those last few miles there were no tram-lines to steer by in foggy weather. But classes had to be served and class registers kept up to standard; if the students could get to the classes on nights when it would be pleasanter to stay at home, so too must the tutor. But how repaying it all was; to the tutor anyhow, and I choose to hope, though with less certainty, to the students too. Of the weekly run to Burnley I remember not only the precarious climb up and drop down at the end of the journey, but on clear nights, the lights in the Rossendale Valley below, the romantic thought that if one flew crow-like north-east across miles of ferocious moor one would walk in at the back door of Haworth Parsonage. And the feeling of being part of real Lancashire that one got from a night drive through Bury, Edenfield, Rawtenstall, Crawshaybooth, and over the top to Burnley, could not have been achieved in a chauffeur-driven Rolls-Royce.

It is paradoxical that though these were grand years for an adult education tutor, they were distressing years for Lancashire, and indeed for Yorkshire, South Wales and Durham. They were, until rearmament in the late thirties made its impact on the national economy, the years of Great Depression—years characterized by uncovenanted benefits, Public Assistance allowances, the piling up of a massive debt by the Unemployment Insurance Fund, the disorderly collapse of the Labour Government in 1931, and the organization of unemployed workmen's clubs in Durham where skilled miners could be taught to make mats and perform other undignified time-absorbing functions because they had nothing else to do. To get an accurate picture of life in Manchester and Salford during these years it is only necessary to secure a copy of Walter Greenwood's play *Love on the Dole*.

But in spite of this—or because of this—the years of the Great Depression were golden years for adult education tutors, at any rate if their subjects touched upon some aspect of economics, economic history, public administration or political science, as indeed ours did. There was, among thoughtful working-class students, a desperate urgency to answer the question: Why is this happening to us—what should be done about it? I think that only a committed orthodox Marxist would have provided an answer to this question and his answer would have been the wrong one. I certainly could not. Indeed, during these years the W.E.A. lived up to its ideal which was to teach *how* to think rather than *what* to think—which is, of course, the ideal of all good university education.

Another side-benefit of these adult education activities was the close association one achieved with the trade union movement, since most of the class members were keen trade unionists. When the General Strike hit us in 1926 I was tutoring a class at Northwich—a peculiar town, many of whose houses were slowly sinking into the ground owing to the extraction of underground salt deposits by the Brunner Mond chemical works which dominated its economic life. It was difficult to think or talk about general subjects during that crucial period, but the class maintained its morale and its attendance register by the suspension of its normal syllabus in favour of an intensive study of the Coal Commission Report whose findings had indirectly precipitated the crisis.

Incidentally the University Settlement felt the impact of the General Strike since its warden regnant, Miss Rogers, had offered the hospitality of its premises to the local branch of the N.U.R. whose members assembled in its Recreation Room to discuss what to do, and incidentally how to avoid violence or intimidation. When the meeting ended at midnight a headquarters was made in the Settlement's wing of Ancoats Hall for the rest and refreshment of pickets going out in relays through the night. For this participation in an industrial dispute Miss Rogers was sharply censured by the Art Galleries Committee which occupied Ancoats Hall by favour of the railway company which owned it.

John and I were present at the meeting, and as responsible members of the Settlement Council we warmly supported Miss Rogers's imprudent act. After all, what is a settlement for, if its working-class neighbours do not naturally turn to it in a moment of anxiety or stress?

Three other Manchester activities were my own peculiar concern. One was the bench, another was the theatre, and a third was birth-control.

In 1930 I was appointed a J.P. The work of a Magistrates' Court in a large city which contained a dock area, an amusement centre, a vice area, and many areas of primary poverty, needs no description from me. Our contacts with distressed as well as disorderly and disconsolate persons were as varied as the above-defined areas might lead one to suppose. There were, of course, fewer motoring offences because there were fewer motors; no protection rackets, because the multiplication of profitable casinos had yet to come. The gambling racket was limited to street bookmakers' runners. And I was often astonished by the number of wives who appeared to have received black eyes by falling against the elbows of long-suffering husbands who had merely raised their arms to ward off an unprovoked attack.

I doubt if those years on the bench enabled me to make any valuable contribution to Manchester life, but they were certainly valuable to me as throwing light on its stresses and strains, the varied personalities of its streets, and the deplorable gaps in our embryonic social welfare services.

As regards drama, in Settlement ventures John and I worked together. He acted, I wrote. My first attempt at play-writing was a Nativity play called *Everyman of Everystreet*, which brought me the most humiliating criticism I have ever experienced. It was described in next morning's *Manchester Guardian* (I wouldn't have minded if it had been the *Daily Mirror*) as "meritorious in parts". And since it contained passages lifted from William Blake, I could not escape the conclusion that these, and only these, were the meritorious "parts". However, I was not discouraged, and continued to write plays for the Settlement actors, one of which, entitled *Dr Scholefield*, was really interesting. I can say this without conceit because it was lifted scene by scene, almost word for word, from the dusty files of the bi-weekly *Manchester Guardian* during the Chartist troubles of 1842. The play really wrote itself. Its characters, which included Feargus O'Conner, were ready-made. It is a piece of raw history which brings to life events in Ancoats centred on 20 Every Street, the Round House, and the activities of its first incumbent, Dr Scholefield. In due course it was acted in the precise place where those events occurred.

My third particular concern was birth-control. Though Marie Stopes had effectively broken the conspiracy of silence which had shrouded that subject, it was nevertheless still not discussed in polite society and by many people not discussed at all. But by the time we arrived in Manchester two clinics were teaching contraception in London, one under the auspices of Marie Stopes and one working independently at Walworth. In Manchester, unemployment added to the tribulations of mothers under the perpetual strain of unwanted pregnancies and frequent miscarriages. Indeed the poor health of working mothers was beginning to be widely recognized as a reproach to our existing—or rather non-existing medical services. It was imperative to do something about it. A former school friend, Charis Frankenburg, who had married and settled in the Manchester area, after training as a midwife, took the same view. So, too, did a small group of Manchester friends, including Lady Burrows—not very many at that time—who were prepared, with us, to do something about it.

Whatever was done had to be done by voluntary action, partly because public opinion was not ripe for public spending on such a cause. Partly because, even if it had been, local health authorities were still precluded from giving contraceptive advice to mothers even for reasons of health, by a veto imposed by a former Roman Catholic Minister of Health. So we acquired two rooms in a working-class area, found a woman doctor bold enough to officiate, and two nurse-midwives bold enough to assist her, and in 1925 opened what I think was the first provincial birth-control clinic.

Our premises were in one respect fortunately situated; for they were on an upper floor, approached through a shop which sold meat pies. This meant that shy clients were not readily identifiable from the street as visitors to the clinic—they might equally well be regarded as pie purchasers. In another respect we were less fortunately placed, because our clinic was in the near neighbourhood of a large Roman Catholic Church, and officially the Roman

Catholics did not like us at all. Indeed, they did all they could to frustrate our venture; even to the extent of organizing a huge protest meeting at which one speaker accused us of practising abortion. The result of this meeting was not, however, all that its promoters could have wished; because for some time after its occurrence our routine question: "How did you hear of the clinic?" might provoke the answer: "At the Protest."

On one occasion Charis Frankenburg and I found ourselves described in a Roman Catholic publication as "the kind of idle women who visit matinées and sit with cigarettes between their painted lips". This image of ourselves afforded us some pleasure because we were apt to envisage ourselves as rather dowdy social workers. On another occasion the access to our clinic was described as "through a stinking entry". This was a half-truth, because though a potent aroma certainly followed one up its staircase, it was a pleasant and comforting aroma of freshly cooked meat pies.

In view of authoritative Catholic doctrine, the attitude of our local Roman Catholic clergy was easy to understand. Less easy to understand was the non-committal but on the whole hostile aloofness of the Anglican Church. Its attitude was well portrayed in a contemporary play by St John Ervine entitled *Robert's Wife*. In many clerical minds, and indeed many other minds, birth-control was associated with irregular sex relations, as indeed it well may be. It was also, in those far-off days, associated with strange myths which we often encountered and, as time went on, were able to dispel; for instance that it caused cancer, or that once practised, it produced subsequent sterility.

But really very difficult to understand was the attitude, with a few notable exceptions, of the medical profession. Our own young clinic doctor, Olive Gimson, glowed like a kindly light in the encircling gloom of professional non-cooperation. Many doctors were really ignorant of contraceptive technique and chose to turn their backs on its possibilities, though they knew—none better—the effect of repeated unwanted pregnancies and miscarriages on maternal health. They might have been compared with the lawyers, who according to St Luke were accused by Jesus of taking away the key of knowledge because, not wanting to enter themselves, they hindered those who did.

For what can one say of a gynaecologist who, having advised a woman against having more pregnancies, in answer to her question what to do about it, replied: "Best known to yourself!" In the end this particular woman got the advice she needed, but by a roundabout way. Her husband consulted his workmates who informed him of a book by Marie Stopes. He got the book, but the couple found its advice somewhat baffling, so they plucked up courage and wrote to Dr Stopes, who referred them to us and all was well. But suppose we hadn't been there?

In those days our clients were seldom young couples planning their families in the early stages of marriage. They were, for the most part, mothers with over-large families or sad stories of miscarriages, and deplorable health records. Many were surprisingly ignorant of their own physical make-up, and a good husband was often summed up as one "who seldom troubles me" or "only troubles me once a week". Some husbands, in this respect, were not "good"; and for such, our dutch cap contraceptive technique was not easy for wives to operate. Dr Stopes's best-seller *Married Love* had become so closely identified with the advocacy of contraception that those who read it, and indeed those who did not, regarded it from that angle only and forgot that it was primarily a moving plea for recognition of the emotional and spiritual significance of mutually satisfying and reverently conducted sex relations. But in our clinic we had not as yet got beyond ensuring that the weekly, or even more frequent, "troubles" should at any rate have no disastrous consequences.

Nor were we concerned with thoughts of a population problem either national or world-wide. In Great Britain there was no population problem. We envisaged our job as a necessary extension of the maternity service. And thus it was envisaged in 1926, when the House of Lords dared to carry a resolution against the Government demanding a withdrawal of the above-mentioned ministerial veto. Happily, the House of Lords can step out ahead of public opinion when the House of Commons dare not. Happily, as in this case, it sometimes does.

The clinic meant quite a lot of work for the few of us who were running it. Amateurs as we were, we staffed the weekly clinics, undertook the preliminary interrogations, and kept the records. And it meant quite a lot of outside work for me, because the subject was in great demand at women's meetings all over the north-western area and outside it. Eleanor Rathbone accused me of neglecting family allowances for birth-control, so I had to keep a record of meetings addressed to show that I was not. For I always regarded the two subjects as the positive and negative of voluntary parenthood.

It was an inspiriting and rewarding campaign because, in spite of ecclesiastical disapproval and medical non-cooperation, we knew that we were right. Public opinion was on the move; and by the beginning of the thirties it had already moved a long way. Later, it moved like an avalanche which according to Shelley accumulates:

Flake after flake, in heaven defying minds
As thought by thought is piled, till some great truth
Is loosened, and the nations echo round,
Shaken to their roots . . .

Today, under the threat of world over-population, the nations appear to be "echoing round" in a vigorous manner to an inescapable "great truth".

When Charis Frankenburg and I left Manchester at the end of the thirties, I felt rather guilty about the clinic, because it was in the early stage of expansion, and made heavy demands on its faithful voluntary workers. But it was in good hands; and there remained at the helm one of our earliest younger colleagues, Mrs Flora Blumberg, who led it through its subsequent years and left it on its fortieth birthday with outlying branches, a recognized training centre, strong medical backing, and unashamed municipal support.

The reason which called me away from these multifarious Manchester preoccupations, was John's appointment in 1936 as Vice-Chancellor of Liverpool University—a job for which he was supremely well fitted. But there were regrets in leaving Manchester. Years later, when the B.B.C. invited me to do a programme entitled "The Time of my Life", that period in Manchester was the time that I chose. The First World War was a fading memory; the Second, a terrifying menace, but one still hoped against hope that it was an avoidable menace. It had, of course, already produced a German refugee problem in Manchester, which had brought us a delightful guest, Adolf Löwe, a fugitive Jewish professor, who became part of our family at 22 Wilbraham Road until he managed to extract his family from Germany and make a home of his own.

It is surprising how happy ordinary mortals can be when surrounded by social distress or political insecurity, provided their own individual lives are satisfying. In spite of the Great Depression of the twenties and thirties, in spite of the growing menace of Germany and the shameful way in which our government was reacting to it, John and I were very happy in Manchester—with a young family growing up, no financial anxieties, and enough domestic service to open up avenues of interesting outside activities in many of which we could work together.

In his poem *Biography*, Masefield writes: "The days that make us happy make us wise." I hope he is right. I very much hope he is right. But one would have to add: "Provided they don't make us insensitive."

12

Statutory Woman

THANKS TO THE CHANGED climate of opinion with regard to women in public life which followed the First World War, it became a regular ministerial practice for every government committee or Royal Commission to contain at least one woman. In some cases, indeed, it was a statutory requirement. But though the country as a whole teemed with able and public-spirited women, those who sojourned in the "corridors of power" did not know who or where they were, and took little trouble to find out. They knew of the existence of Lady Violet Bonham Carter, Lady Emmott, Margery Fry, Shena Simon—later some others swam into their ken. As a result, the few that they *did* know about were used over and over again. They became a kind of stage army appearing on one government assignment after another. At a later stage somebody—I forget who—described them very aptly as "statutory women".

How and why I came to be a "statutory woman" I do not know, but I am fairly certain that it was due to the influence of my friend Shena Simon, who had herself served on several important inquiries and was a person much respected in more than one ministry. And since my career as a statutory woman began during our time in Manchester and was well under way by the end of it, I will deal with it here and now, though it continued almost unbroken until March 1969, by which time the field of choice had considerably widened.

My first assignment came soon after my appointment as a J.P. and appeared to be wholly relevant to that activity. It was to a Home Office Departmental Committee on Persistent Offenders. It was an interesting experience, involving visits to prisons and Borstal institutions, and my own lasting personal gain from it was the friendship of Alexander Maxwell, then Chief Prison Commissioner at the Home Office. He was at the same time, and indeed till the end of his life, a keen supporter of Leila Rendel. His position at the Home Office, added to his kindness, wisdom, and humanity, were of great value to her Caldecott Community. If all senior civil servants were like Alexander Maxwell there would be less foolish talk about "faceless men" in Whitehall. It was in this connection that I visited Dartmoor prison, and I believe that I was the second female to be admitted behind those gates; the first being, or so I was told, Queen Victoria.

My next assignment as a statutory woman was to the Royal Commission on Betting and Lotteries appointed in 1932. Its work brought me into personal touch with the street-bookmaking confraternity of Manchester and Salford. They seemed to be mostly Irish, and Greenwood's play *Love on the Dole* portrays a fairly convincing specimen. It also brought me into touch with the upper ranks of the horse-racing world. And here one was forcibly struck by the difference between horse-racing and greyhound-racing. Both, of course, attracted corrupt elements and posed social problems. But at the centre of the horse-racing confraternity one encountered gentlemen, and indeed ladies, who were really interested in racing and horse-breeding. They knew and loved their horses, and should not perhaps be blamed for the sins of those who degraded these beautiful creatures by regarding them solely as gambling counters.

With greyhound-racing it was quite otherwise. I will not risk giving offence by recording here my impression of the lords of the greyhound-racing tracks. They included no Lord Astors, no Lord Derbys, certainly no kings and queens. There seemed to be little real love of greyhounds among them. I doubt if many owners knew or habitually met the dogs they raced. Greyhound-racing tracks were aptly summed up by Winston Churchill, when he described them as: "Nothing more than animated roulette boards."

Thereafter government assignments came thick and fast. I was concerned with Unemployment Insurance, the conditions of women in the Services, the relations between the army nursing service and the V.A.D.s, the training of teachers, the training of midwives, the training of dentists, the Post Office, Trade Boards, the B.B.C., the government information services, university grants, and the general practitioner section of the National Health Service.

It is difficult for anybody performing such public services to feel that, however much time and energy one may devote to them, one can emerge with any assurance of creditor status because one gets out of them so much more than one puts in. What I got out of them was, in addition to some interesting journeys at the government's expense, a number of greatly valued personal friendships which outlasted the particular preoccupation with which they had originated.

Most of the assignments here recorded were inquiries. Committees were appointed, they examined witnesses, travelled about to see with their own eyes what their witnesses were talking about, drafted reports, and then dissolved, leaving the government to act, or not to act, on their recommendations. But three assignments were of a more permanent nature and involved administration rather than inquiry. One was the Unemployment Insurance Statutory Committee which managed the insurance side of the 1934 Unemployment Act; a second was the University Grants Committee; and a third was the London Executive Council* of the National Health Service.

The Unemployment Insurance Statutory Committee took over a debt of £105 million, piled up during the early years of the Great Depression. During the worst of those years, Margaret Bondfield, as Minister of Labour in Ramsay MacDonald's precarious Labour Government, had presided over the Insurance Fund's growing insolvency, and I remember her describing its operations as "a rake's progress". She was incapable of window-dressing an unsatisfactory departmental situation: a woman of white-hot integrity, capable of selfless devotion, and withal most lovable. She must have had a discouraging term of office as Great Britain's first woman Cabinet minister.

The Statutory Committee which took over the management of Unemployment Insurance was described by its Chairman, Sir William Beveridge, as "an organ of Government entirely new in type" or "in effect a standing Royal Commission on Unemployment Insurance".† It was designed to put an end to the long

---

* With the passage of the London Government Act it became the Inner London Executive Council.

† *The Unemployment Insurance Statutory Committee*, by Sir William Beveridge, Political Pamphlet No. 1 of a series published by the London School of Economics.

sequence of Acts dealing with unemployment benefits, and provocative of endless changes involving political controversy. Its job was to keep the insurance scheme solvent, report on all draft regulations, and advise the Minister of Labour on any relevant question referred to it. It had, in practice, a very large measure of independence. And of this, its Chairman, Sir William Beveridge, took full advantage. Indeed my impression is that during the ten years of my membership Beveridge transformed the Statutory Committee from an annually reporting watch-dog intended to keep the fund decently in balance, allowing for an annual interest charge and sinking fund designed to extinguish its debt by 1971, into a policymaking body with a long-term plan relating to the whole problem of unemployment in relation to public finance.

The result was that in addition to continuous consideration of detailed administrative orders, and from time to time inquiries into the suggested absorption of other categories of workers into the orbit of national unemployment insurance, we found ourselves thinking in terms of eight-year cyclical trade fluctuations, and the long-term prospect of maintaining the level of benefits through the periodic depressions which experience of the past, and well-informed forecasts of the future, would lead one to expect. But such a long-term policy required new legal powers for the committee regarding debt repayment as well as borrowing: and such was the force of Sir William Beveridge's reasoning in successive annual reports, that these powers were forthcoming.

Fortunately for the insurance fund, but unfortunately for everybody else, these calculations were invalidated first by rearmament and then by war. In fact by 1941 we had paid off the debt. We had started work in 1935 on the upswing from the Great Depression of the early thirties, and almost from the first were able to distribute relatively small surpluses in the form of benefits or conditions for their payment, while at the same time piling up a substantial depression reserve.

Our most important concession to benefits involved a stepping-up of dependants' allowances. This last development enabled us to indicate a dangerous overlap between unemployment benefits and the lower levels of wages. In his 1938 report, Beveridge could point the obvious moral that: "As was urged by the Family Endowment Society, and is obvious from the figures cited above, the problem of dependency needs to be considered as a whole. To consider it only in relation to persons who are unemployed leads to an impasse in one direction or another." It was difficult after that for the Liberal opponents of family allowances to argue that they would endanger individual incentive.

Meanwhile, this long-term attitude to "disposable surpluses" led us into a series of battles with the employers who wanted us to reduce contributions, the trade unions who wanted us to raise benefits, and the Treasury which wanted some diminution of their Exchequer grants. The experience of holding Treasury representatives at bay and accusing them of improvidence was exhilarating.

Seeing Beveridge at work week by week was a memorable experience. As our leading authority on unemployment and the author in 1908 of its first standard textbook* he was the obvious man for the chairmanship of the Statutory Committee. As with the later Inter-departmental Committee on Social Insurance and Allied Services, which gave birth to the famous Beveridge Report in 1942, he could take the bit between his teeth and plunge forward into wider regions than anything foreseen by those who designed his harness. He was impatient and could be testy, and it was not easy to oppose him. In fact I never did, except on one occasion, when I dared to draft a note of dissent to his 1935 report, recommending the equalization of benefits and contributions as between men and women. I held my ground, and my dissent was duly recorded; but he did not conceal his annoyance. Otherwise, working with him was an inspiration and an education. In one respect he resembled Florence Nightingale. He could think in terms of large principles and at the same time envisage the detailed arrangements by which such principles could be carried out. One could see this when it came to evolving administrative machinery for effecting complicated adjustments as between agricultural and industrial insured persons.

I think that he was a vain man with much reason for vanity: and the popular acclaim which greeted his 1942 report on the social services went to his head. He liked admiration, and this I was always able to give him without pretence or hypocrisy because I admired and liked him so much. And, perhaps as a result, I think he liked me. He was certainly capable of warm affection and great personal kindness.

* *Unemployment, a Problem of Industry*, by William Beveridge. Longmans, 1908.

One particularly pleasant interlude brightened the sombre deliberations of his Statutory Committee. In 1936 it was borne in upon us that many share fishermen, who as self-employed persons were not covered by national unemployment insurance, were in fact claiming to be so covered by the simple device of making over their gear and boats to one another, and thus acquiring the appearance of a wage contract. This demanded on-the-spot investigation. One member of the committee undertook the Yorkshire coast. Beveridge and I undertook two journeys. In one we visited Scottish fishing centres from Peterhead to Lossiemouth. In another we explored the whole coast from Brixham to St Ives. We certainly worked hard, interviewing fishermen and local employment officers and on occasion attending fish markets. The Ministry of Labour supplied us with motor transport and paid our hotel bills. Our activities fell in the summer months and the weather was good. My affection for Beveridge grew with my experience of him as a travelling companion.

Three of my more ephemeral assignments as a "statutory woman" involved distant but equally agreeable expeditions. The first arose out of my appointment, during the war, to a committee on the conditions of Service women. Its chairman was Violet Markham. To begin with, this involved visits to A.T.S., W.A.A.F. and W.R.N.S. establishments in this country. Violet Markham had a remarkable capacity for turning a committee into a harmonious and even convivial social unit. Indeed, members of this committee continued to dine together long after the publication of the excellent and very readable report drafted by its chairman.

But an interesting aftermath occurred at the very end of the war, in May 1945. The Government having decided, somewhat late in the day, to send units of the A.T.S. and W.A.A.F. overseas, an ill-informed and surprisingly sentimental clamour, which was reflected in the House of Commons, arose on the suggestion that women were being sent into battle areas where they were subjected to unsuitable conditions. In response to this, Violet Markham and I were sent off by the War Office on a roving commission to France, Belgium, Holland and Germany, to see precisely what was happening to the Service women. We travelled under military auspices, and at one point, when checking in at a Brussels hotel, were required to declare "substantive rank". So Violet assumed that of a brigadier, while I described myself as a colonel. Considering that we had been made free of the generals' mess at Versailles this did not seem unduly arrogant.

The most interesting part of our journey was that which took us into Holland across the Maas to Rotterdam, by improvised ferry, since all the bridges were smashed. There it was possible to see the centre of that great undefended city as the Germans had left it after their savage terrorist carpet-bombing in 1940. All we saw was a dusty area resembling the vast open spaces which have become familiar to citizens of Manchester as temporary rubbish dumps justified by the promise of planned neighbourhood development. As we drove out along the road leading into Germany, we passed marching ranks of depressed and sulky German prisoners, accompanied by British tanks. I must confess to finding it a pleasant sight.

At the time of our visit, the British Army was in process of moving up into occupied Germany; its headquarters had got as far as Süchteln in the Rühr district. There, General Templer was in command during the temporary absence of Field-Marshal Montgomery. And there, it being the end of our journey, we spent a very pleasant evening at dinner in the senior officers' mess, during which meal, news came through that Himmler had disappointed his British captors by swallowing a dose of cyanide which meticulous search of his clothing had not revealed, since it had been concealed in a cavity in his gums.

The highlight of our German visit was a sightseeing flight in a small plane round the Rühr industrial area. To anybody who had stayed in London between 1940 and 1945, scenes of devastation were familiar and I had seen many. But the utter devastation of the Rühr industrial towns blotted out London memories: devastation which was emphasized by the vivid greenness of intervening open country, since our visit was paid in high summer. Here, too, the memory of Rotterdam blunted my finer feelings.

From this it must not be supposed that Viole Markham and I did no work. We earned our convivial dinner and our sightseeing flight by visiting all the A.T.S. and W.A.A.F. units which ministered to the 21st Army Group, and were always careful to give other ranks an opportunity of talking to us without the presence of their officers.

As far as I remember, we encountered few grievances. One was a distaste for improvised lodgings impregnated with pungent insecticide. One was a sense of grievance among certain A.T.S. units because W.A.A.F. units were receiving "Yank rations" while they had to be content with what the British commissariat could supply. A third was a sense of frustration conditioned by the current "no fraternization" rule, which prevented them from making any human response when approached by small German children. On the whole we found that the fears expressed in Great Britain for the safety, both physical and moral, of their daughters overseas were not borne out by what we saw—though Violet was constantly pained by the lack of any attempt to provide education for Service women in addition to light entertainment.

The companionship of Violet Markham on this memorable journey cemented a friendship begun under her earlier chairmanship. I had known of her—and indeed known her—long before that, as a serious social worker. While I was active on the Unemployment Insurance Statutory Committee, she was very much more active as Vice-Chairman of the Unemployment Assistance Board which administered the other half of the 1934 Unemployment Act: It was therefore something of a revelation when, during my researches into betting and lotteries, I attended a race meeting in Manchester and found her recorded on my race-card as the owner of one of the runners. I had not envisaged her in this environment. But I lived and learned.

She was, in fact, at home in any environment. Her marriage, rather late in life, to Colonel Carruthers, brought her into the racing confraternity in which he sojourned. I doubt if their field of common interest was otherwise very wide, but being a wealthy woman, she was in a position to develop this particular bond of interest, and since she adored him beyond measure and was heartbroken when he died in 1936, it was a satisfaction to her that she could indulge and share his taste for race meetings.

It may have been her experience as a Colonel's lady that enabled her to respond so readily to the convivial life of an officers' mess on the many occasions when, in the course of our journeyings, we were hospitably entertained. For all her serious interests and on the whole conventional outlook, she could enjoy a bawdy story. Indeed there seemed very little that she couldn't do or enjoy. She was a good pianist. She liked good food and knew how to cook it. She was an authority on Romanesque architecture and had written a book about it. With the possible exception of Walter Elliot she had the richest mind I have ever encountered. Her reading seemed to cover the whole range of literature; with her, at hand, one had no need to look up a reference in *The Oxford Dictionary of Quotations*.

The second overseas excursion arising from an official assignment arose in connection with the committee appointed by Mr Attlee's Government in 1949, to examine the operations of the B.B.C. whose charter fell due for renewal in 1951, and make recommendations as to the terms of its renewal. The first suggested Chairman had been Lord Radcliffe but his appointment as a Lord of Appeal made it impossible for him to serve, and Lord Beveridge* was appointed in his stead. This gave me great satisfaction as it opened out a new spell of work under Beveridge, though as things turned out the change was in one respect regrettable. However, Beveridge's chairmanship was well up to standard. He subjected the B.B.C. to an intensive investigation which left it gasping, and in spite of a built-in liberal objection to monopoly as such, after hearing the evidence, he came down in favour of the perpetuation of the B.B.C.'s monopoly in the interest of public service broadcasting. In this he was supported by nine out of the ten members of his committee, the one dissident being Mr Selwyn Lloyd, Conservative M.P. for the Wirral Division of Cheshire.

In the course of these deliberations we received much evidence concerning the possibilities of commercial as distinct from public service broadcasting, of which the outstanding example was the American system of broadcasting sponsored and financed by advertisers. It was therefore considered desirable to obtain some first-hand evidence of how it worked; accordingly Selwyn Lloyd and I were sent across the Atlantic to gather information. We visited Montreal, Toronto, Ottawa, New York and Washington. We had a pleasant voyage out by sea, and were booked to return on the Queen Mary; but Selwyn Lloyd had to make a quicker return by air at the summons of an urgent party whip.

Our political views were of course wide apart. I had a built-in addiction to a public service as such. Selwyn Lloyd's addiction was to private enterprise. And my impression is that our approach to the whole problem of broadcasting was rather different. I was primarily interested in programmes, the end product of broadcasting. He was primarily interested in organization. Therefore,

* Sir William became a peer in 1946.

though he tended to take a dim view of the innumerable sponsored programmes which we dutifully sat through, he nevertheless returned to England with a favourable view of some form, though not necessarily the precise form encountered in the U.S.A., of competitive commercial broadcasting.

The outcome of the Beveridge Broadcasting Report is recent history. Mr Attlee's Government which would naturally have supported Beveridge, for some reason shilly-shallied over its implementation and granted a temporary renewal of the B.B.C.'s existing charter. This in effect handed the issue over to the Conservative Party which assumed power in 1951. The result was the Television Act of 1953, which gave us commercial television financed, though not sponsored, by advertisers.

I can excuse the Conservative Party, which in this case acted up to, or down to, its economic philosophy. The same philosophy later gave us betting offices, bingo clubs, and casinos. I cannot however excuse the Labour Party which should have known better. But even in 1953 the issue seemed to hang in the balance because the whole of the educational world, the N.U.T., the W.E.A., and all the university vice-chancellors (with one exception) were solidly opposed to commercial television. So too were a number of leading Conservatives including Lord Radcliffe, Lord Halifax, Lord Brand, Lord Waverley and Lord Hailsham.* Indeed I think that a free vote in both Houses of Parliament might well have produced a different verdict. But it must be admitted that an extremely well-organized and well-endowed pressure group was at work on behalf of commercial television, and its operations have been well and accurately described by H. H. Wilson in his book *Pressure Group. The Campaign for Commercial Television.*†

I thought at the time that this verdict against the B.B.C.'s monopoly was affected by at least one personal factor. This was the substitution of Lord Beveridge for Lord Radcliffe as Chairman of the Broadcasting Committee. The Conservative Government would have thought twice about turning down a conclusion sponsored by Lord Radcliffe. Lord Beveridge was, on the other hand, unpopular in Government circles and the rejection of his advice occasioned no ministerial regrets.

The remaining excursion which accrued as a side benefit of

* Later Mr Quintin Hogg.
† Secker & Warburg, 1961.

these activities was in connection with the 1952 Drogheda Committee on Overseas Information Services. The treatment accorded to this committee was really very odd. Towards the end of its deliberations we were told that our report must be ready by a certain date. As a result we devoted two week-ends of intensive corporate work to finishing it in the luxurious surroundings of "The Node", a country house belonging to Shell-Mex & B.P., where we were hospitably entertained by one of its directors, Mr J. W. Platt, who was a member of the Committee. At about the same time we were informed that all our notes, minutes of evidence and other relevant material must, for reasons of security, be handed over to the Government.

And that, so far as I can remember, was the last we heard of our report; which presumably disappeared into some pigeon-hole, until a brief summary of it was published as a White Paper in 1954. The whole thing seemed to me a great waste of public money—some of which was spent by members of the Committee in connection with visits to various parts of the world for the purpose of finding out what impact, if any, the information services were making.

Happily it fell to me, and my fellow committee-member, Victor Feather of the T.U.C., to visit Eastern Europe. We started with Vienna and covered Greece, Yugoslavia and Turkey. Apart from being a very congenial companion, Vic had the additional advantage of being known, through his international work at the T.U.C., to trade union members in all the centres we visited. On numerous airfields he was warmly welcomed for his own sake apart from the official reason for his coming, and I was able to benefit from many of these personal contacts. Incidentally I have never seen a man so much kissed. At one point, when saying goodbye to trade union colleagues on the frosty airfield at Zagreb, I found myself thinking with Shelley: "What are all these kissings worth, if thou kiss not me?" My initiative in the matter seemed to cause surprise to the Yugoslav trade unionists, but was well received.

I think we both came to the conclusion, which I hope I may now record without risk to security, that where more adequate information services were required was not in centres such as Vienna and Athens, which were already well aware of the advantages of British culture and indeed able to pay for any that they wanted, but in

Belgrade and Ankara which had long been out on the edge of western civilization.

With two other assignments as a "statutory woman" I will deal more fully at a later stage, since they concerned matters requiring a chapter to themselves: The University Grants Committee, and the National Health Service London Executive Council. I have carried my narrative thus far ahead in time, because such extraneous activities continued year by year as a sort of running accompaniment to whatever else I did. It was only in my seventh decade that I realized what I owed to this considerable but apparently useless accumulation of superficial knowledge relating to a large number of unrelated subjects. Only then did I realize that fate had been providing me with the ideal training for an unexpected career as a popular quiz artist on the B.B.C.'s Light Programme.

13

Liverpool and After

LIVERPOOL WAS AS UNLIKE Manchester as any two urban areas speaking the same language and acknowledging the same government could be. Even their climate was different. Liverpool enjoyed a west coast Atlantic climate. Spectacular sunsets had not yet been impregnated and dimmed by travelling through fifty miles of industrial smoke.

Their geographical configuration too was strikingly different. Much the same could be said of Edinburgh and Glasgow; so near together yet so far apart. Manchester, with Salford physically integrated into it, was a compact urban entity, a business centre surrounded by expanding residential areas. Liverpool as an urban entity was cut in half by the Mersey—tunnelled but unbridged. So that ships could steam up into the heart of it, while a short walk in the direction of its estuary brought one into the orbit of great transatlantic liners. Its life was coloured by the sea and those who lived by it. Its commuter activity was coloured by the ferry, which swept continually backwards and forwards from landing-stage to landing-stage, with a scythe-like curve conditioned by the tide.

No less different was the social make-up of the two neighbouring urban communities. The rich were no less benevolently rich than the rich of Manchester—in some ways perhaps even more so, as the variety and magnitude of their charities suggested. But they lived (and I am speaking of the thirties not of today) in large houses round Sefton Park where they entertained with a kind of eighteenth-century grandeur. When guests were invited to lunch in the Town Hall a band played them up the stairs; and when the Lord Mayor went to Sunday service he was carried in a state coach. I cannot remember that such things happened in Manchester.

[177]

And in Liverpool, the Bold Street of those days could be compared with London's Bond Street or the Rue de la Paix in Paris.

If Liverpool riches were more splendid, Liverpool poverty was
more savage. Greenwood, in his play *Love On The Dole,* has
given an accurate picture of Manchester, or rather Salford, poverty
during the Great Depression. In an autobiography called *I, James
Whittaker* by a former member of John Stocks's Rochdale tutorial
class,* the author paints a vivid picture of contemporary conditions in the Scotland Division of Liverpool, which was, as its name
does not suggest, preponderantly Irish. And the religious life of
Liverpool was comparably polarized. Protestants were Protestants
and Catholics were Catholics. But the Protestants had the supreme
advantage of the great Anglican Cathedral whose majestic bulk on
its dominating site was already overtopping surrounding streets,
although its tower was as yet unfinished and its nave and one set
of transepts yet unbuilt. Nevertheless, it was functioning as a very
vital religious centre, already capable of generating in those who
entered it a sense of awe which, now that it is almost completed, I
personally find overwhelming. There is, in its combination of size,
solidity, slowness of growth and traditional architecture, something which in Thomas Hardy's phrase, "gives ballast to a mind
adrift on change, or harassed by the irrepressible new".

In fine, Liverpool was an exciting, dramatic city; and its excitement and drama were intensified for us by the fact that John was
the vice-chancellor of its university. Thus we were provided with
an extremely comfortable official residence, with spacious rooms in
which to entertain, and sufficient cash plus an entertainment allow-
ance to acquire adequate skilled domestic help to enable us to
entertain in a big way.

In spite of their proximity, there was very little social contact
between Manchester and Liverpool. They would *work* together,
economic considerations compelled them to. But they were not
disposed to *play* together. This was clearly illustrated by the railway timetable. During working hours excellent and speedy trains
ran backwards and forwards between the two cities. But after business hours, trains were slow and infrequent. It was easy for a
Liverpudlian to pay a daytime business call in Manchester, but far
from easy to dine with a Manchester friend.

For me, however, a long-standing social contact was already in

* Rich & Cowan Ltd, 1934.

being, since Liverpool was the home of Eleanor Rathbone and I had paid frequent visits to her there, and to members of her family who still inhabited the ancestral Rathbone headquarters at Greenbank. And now we were to become an integral part of it all.

Resettlement of the family presented no great problem. Daughter Ann had already acquired a degree at the London School of Economics and was embarked on an adventurous year as exchange tutor at Mills College, California. Son John, a dedicated engineer from the beginning of his conscious life, having left Rugby, was about to enter Manchester University as an engineering student. Transfer to Liverpool was a simple matter. With daughter Helen it was more difficult. Aged sixteen, and greatly enjoying life at Withington Girls' School in Manchester, Helen resented transplantation to a comparable day school in Liverpool. She was, I think, the most dedicated Mancunian of us all; and would never be brought to admit that anything, but *anything*, in Liverpool could possibly be better than anything in Manchester. No, not even the climate. Educationalists would doubtless agree that sixteen is not the best school age for transplantation.

From the word go, it was obvious that John Stocks was the man for the job and a university vice-chancellorship was the job for John Stocks. His capacity for administration, easy personal relationships, and reforming initiative had full scope, and one measure of reform called aloud for immediate attention. It concerned the position of women members of the university staff, for it appeared that outside academic discussions, they had almost no day-to-day opportunities for social contacts with their male colleagues. There appeared to be no senior common-room life—indeed, as far as I can remember, no senior common-room. This was because members of the university staff achieved such contacts as members of an excellent club not far from the university, at which they mixed with leading civic and business personalities. Such mixing was of great value both to the city and the university. But it was hard on the university women, because club membership was exclusively male. They could not even lunch with their academic colleagues, except possibly as occasional guests.

This then was an immediate problem calling for action. And with the help of Sir Frederick Marquis,* treasurer of the university

---

* At that time head of the great Lewis's provincial department stores. He later became Earl of Woolton.

and an excellent feminist, John set to work on the problem. It involved delicate negotiations, because the vested interest of the club in its university membership had to be considered. However, by the end of his term as vice-chancellor a building scheme including senior common-rooms for both sexes was well under way.

The end of John's term as vice-chancellor came with tragic swiftness after six months of office. He had departed to South Wales to fulfil a W.E.A. speaking engagement. Early on the morning of June 13th, 1937, a policeman appeared at our door with a message to the effect that John Stocks had died suddenly during the night in Swansea. Some of my Liverpool friends were critical of the way in which this news was conveyed. My own view is that if you are going to be knocked out by a violent blow on the head it doesn't much matter whether it is done with a pole-axe or a coke hammer.

Of course I was not "knocked out", merely stunned, because almost immediately there was much to be done: the dismantling of the official residence and the disposal or storage of its furniture: and of course the resettlement of the family; in all of which I was greatly helped. There is really no need to say more of those miserable weeks except to record that they were made memorable by the indescribable and unstinted kindness of so many Liverpool friends. Nor shall I ever forget, though it would perhaps be tactless to describe it in detail, the astonishing ingenuity displayed by Sir Frederick Marquis in proving to me that the university owed me more money than I thought it did, and that my liability for income tax was much less than I supposed it would be.

In one particular respect I was very fortunate. 8 Queen's Gate Terrace was no longer my family headquarters; indeed its street had already moved far along the evolutionary process which led from single family occupation of its tall houses to a region of bridge-clubs, and multiple occupation by a shifting population of flat dwellers. But Campden Hill was still a solid middle-class residential neighbourhood, and in 37 Argyll Road my parents were happily settled. Though smaller than 8 Queen's Gate Terrace and requiring less domestic service, it was big enough to house members of my family when they wanted to go there. Thus I was not homeless when the collapse of our Liverpool régime required me to vacate the vice-chancellor's residence, look for a full-time job, and having found one, set up house wherever the job happened to be and then reintegrate the family. During this restless and uncertain interlude young John remained at Liverpool University in lodgings, Ann returned from her American adventure to work for Civil Service entrance at the London School of Economics, while poor Helen suffered a second transplantation; this time to the house of my sister-in-law, Freda Stocks, who was headmistress of Talbot Heath School in Bournemouth, which Helen was able to attend as a day girl. This second transplantation, precipitated as it was by a family tragedy, occasioned more real distress than the first, and I shall be forever grateful for the kindness and wisdom with which my sister-in-law dealt with it.

However, the closing months of 1937 found us settled in a new pattern of life. London was now our centre. This was not wholly due to my obstinate lifelong attraction to the magnetic south, because I had, at the suggestion of Sir Frederick Marquis, allowed my name to go forward for a post in the Liverpool University Department of Social Science, which in fact I did not get. I should have been glad to remain in Liverpool with so many vivid memories of John Stocks's brief but glorious sojourn there. But with that possibility eliminated, I was glad to return to my native heath as General Secretary of the London Council of Social Service, which occupied a house next door to the National Council of Social Service in Bedford Square.

By which time, young John was in process of completing his engineering degree at Liverpool University, Helen at Talbot Heath was successfully achieving the qualifying exams necessary to allow her to enter as an undergraduate student of Queen Elizabeth College of Domestic Science on Campden Hill, and Ann, having triumphantly survived a highly competitive entrance examination and interview, was a fully-fledged Assistant Principal in the Ministry of Labour. All we needed was a permanent family home, and that we acquired on the fourth floor of a block of flats in Holland Park Gardens. It was a pleasant, spacious flat. One of its amenities was its extreme airy lightness, owing to a long row of passage windows overlooking the back gardens of Addison Road. Thus we settled down, Ann as a civil servant, I as a professional social worker.

This was my first taste of regular office hours. At 10 a.m. I clocked in, preceded by the head clerk who pre-digested my correspondence and had it ready for any replies which I might dictate.

At 5.30 I clocked out, which left time to walk home. A daily domestic worker served us with breakfast, cleaned the flat, and returned in the evening to serve us with supper. Yes, even in the world of the nineteen-thirties we still expected domestic service and got it; though not at vice-chancellorial level. As a Kensington resident and London social worker I was now back where I started, and Bedford Square was familiar ground. No. 13 had been the home of the Ricardos. In its nursery my favourite cousin Esther and I habitually spent Sundays in varied occupations, including the performance of Shakespeare plays. In its Square garden, in company with other young Bedfordians, we played active games which generally took the form of impersonating horses and coachmen. In the basement of No. 13 Harry Ricardo was, during these early years, incarcerated in a small workshop furnished with a lathe, on which he made engines, whose subsequent development was to bring him world-wide fame as an engineer. So that Bedford Square, like Kensington, was home ground.

But, alas, it had suffered the fate of Queen's Gate Terrace. In 1937 it contained only three private residents. At No. 13 my widowed Aunt Kate Ricardo lived alone with the memory of Halsey Ricardo, in the house whose interior decoration he had planned and made beautiful. At No. 44 lived the widowed Countess of Oxford—her blazing personality undimmed, but her mind somewhat inconsequent. The third resident was an elderly architect whose name and number I cannot now recall. For the rest, Bedford Square, apart from the Architectural Association which occupied one side, was almost entirely given over to offices. But its perfect symmetry and the architecture of its terrace houses were so satisfying that no developer had been allowed to destroy it. Even the ever-expanding University of London and the rapacity of the British Museum had been held at bay. And still it stands, while the lovely squares and terraces of surrounding Bloomsbury fall house by house before the marauding predatory armies of Mammon and higher education. Whether, and in what measure, we have to thank the Bedford Estate, the L.C.C. or the relevant minister, for the survival intact of Bedford Square, I do not know. But whoever it is, may God be in their hearts and remain in their understanding.

One small mercy which I owed in 1937 to the Bedford Estate was due to its obstinate and unpublic-spirited refusal to allow any but private residents access to the Square garden. Thus, with my Aunt Kate's key, I could, in fine weather, enjoy lonely picnics while my multitudinous fellow office workers had to eat their lunches under less salubrious conditions elsewhere. It is true that, generously supported by the Countess of Oxford, the London Council of Social Service exerted itself to persuade the Bedford Estate to relax this restrictive policy. But, at any rate during my time there, our agitation was unsuccessful; so I continued to enjoy the privilege with the happy consciousness of having done my best to end it.

Work at the L.C.S.S. was in many ways very agreeable. It was never monotonous, because new developments of social service were continually cropping up and offering scope for initiative. The office was very adequately staffed. All the clerical work, including the accounts, was supervised by the head clerk, Miss Richardson, who had been long in office. She was a delightful colleague, with the additional advantage added to her business competence of a keen sense of humour. I cannot remember that we were ever seriously short of money thanks to the beneficence of the City Parochial Foundation. In this respect life at the L.C.S.S. differed vastly from life at the Manchester University Settlement where one was ever conscious of the snarling of the wolf at the door.

One of the major advantages of the job was the very large number of delightful and intelligent people with whom it brought one into active daily contact. As far as I was concerned perhaps the most interesting and unusual of social service personalities was Sir Wyndham Deedes, Chairman of my Council and a salaried officer of the National Council next door; and in both capacities we were continuously in touch.

He was in fact an old friend, with whom John Stocks had, during our Manchester sojourn, done a lot of work on the organization of Community Centres on new housing estates. The National Council of Social Service ran a special committee for assisting and promoting such ventures all over the country, and Sir Wyndham Deedes had undertaken many journeys on its behalf. In this connection he had stayed with us both in Manchester and Liverpool. A vivid memory of one such visit was of a talk given by him at the Manchester University Settlement. It was concerned not with any aspect of social work, but with his amazing pre-war adventures as organizer of the Turkish police; for which task he had been

seconded from the British Army until it was necessary for him to
resume his military career for service in the Middle East during
the First World War. It was one of the most unusual and enthralling talks I have ever heard, delivered impromptu and at great
speed.

He was of course a most unusual man. Indeed it might be
regarded as unusual for a distinguished and adventurous traveller
and soldier to abandon his career and settle down as a full-time
social worker in East London, for this is what he did. Bethnal
Green is (or was then) a drab and dreary neighbourhood. But the
house in which he embarked on his bachelor existence was not
drab or dreary. It was a beautiful Georgian house, one of a terrace
overlooking the Green. In a map of London dated 1794 it stands
alone in open country; but the urban sprawl of East London had
completely overtaken and surrounded it by the close of the nineteenth century.

Over this establishment Sir Wyndham's widowed mother presided. According to John Stocks, who had on one occasion stayed
there, she had set out to entertain her neighbours with the same
gracious and spacious hospitality that would have been required
of her as a county great lady—which, in fact, I think she had
been. But as time went on, economy had to prevail, and the order-
ing of stores from Fortnum and Mason was abandoned. From
time to time, and with due notice, she visited our London Council
Office; and on such occasions both Miss Richardson and I felt as
though Queen Mary had passed by. Like her son, she was a most
remarkable personality.

One memory of the Bethnal Green scene remains with me and
has coloured all my subsequent reactions to the ever-present problem of working-class housing. Mape Street was in those days
among the dreariest, narrowest, and most ill-built of Bethnal
Green streets. Its two-storey terrace houses viewed from the
front were ripe and over-ripe for demolition—and have in fact
since been demolished. But one evening, when visiting the Oxford
University Settlement which towered over one end of Mape Street,
I had an opportunity of viewing those same houses from the back.
Each had a small back yard in which it seemed that human life and
activity teemed. One saw mechanics, carpentry, horticulture, child
care, ornithology, housecraft, all being pursued at full blast. One
saw washing drying, perambulators standing out, bicycles and

motor bicycles being disintegrated and reintegrated, one saw lilac bushes, pot plants, pigeons, rabbits, cats and dogs—one saw abundant life at the back of Mape Street, while in front, "penury, inertness and grimace, in some strange sort were the land's portion".

When will they ever learn—the architects, the town planners, the housing committees, the ministries—that so much family life is centred on the proprietary back yard and that a spacious communal playground is no real compensation for its absence, especially when viewed from the upper windows of a tower block.

The time schedule mentioned a few pages back might suggest an office-bound existence. In fact, quite a lot of the General Secretary's work was done on location, and some of it in the evening. In fact, I tried to do in the L.C.C. area, what my senior next-door neighbour, the National Council, was doing all over the country in a big way.

Incidentally, my opposite (though senior) number, the General Secretary of the National Council, bore the undescriptive name of Mr Shooten-Sack. It struck me that if I could change my own name by deed poll to Mrs Luton-Byrne, we could together, on paper at least, suggest a more formidable bureaucracy than in fact we were.

I think that though I lacked many qualifications for this job, I had at any rate two which were of value to it. The first was long contact with the North and with working-class activities. Trade Unions and Women's Cooperative Guilds scarcely seemed to exist for us in London.

It is true that London and Birmingham—which last city was at that time supplying us with our prime ministers—had scarcely felt the impact of the Great Depression of the early thirties. The National Council certainly knew there *was* a great depression, and had taken active steps to mitigate its horror by the organization of occupational centres for unemployed workers in the North and North-East. But my fellow-workers in the London Council were —as I had been twenty-five years earlier—London centred.

The other helpful qualification was my vivid memory of the London social service scene at the beginning of the century. This made it possible to see how and in what direction things were moving; nearly always in the right direction. Miss Frere's pioneer work on the acceptance of voluntary workers as agents for the administration of statutory services had made spectacular strides. All over the place public money was flowing through the hands of voluntary bodies with considerable saving of administrative costs to the grant-giving authorities.

This seemed to confront us with the need for a revised vocabulary. At meetings of the various co-ordinating committees which I attended, frequent reference was made to what was described as "the voluntary movement". Indeed the word might be used with a faint but perceptible suggestion that voluntary organizations and those who sustained them were morally superior to statutory bodies and those who served on them.

Now the members of my council and those who sat on its various committees were indeed voluntary workers, doing unpaid work and in fact doing a great deal of it. But I was no more a voluntary worker than was a medical officer of health or an assistant secretary in the Civil Service. I was earning my living for a salary; and so was Miss Richardson. And when we sat round a table at a co-ordinating committee many of those present were in fact salaried officers of voluntary, in the sense of non-statutory, organizations. And I looked forward to the moment, which in fact never occurred, when some hard-working unpaid member of a London Borough Council would rise up and say: *I* am the voluntary worker; most of you are paid officials.

Indeed it seemed that a significant third bureaucracy was evolving as a feature of the social scene. In addition to the Civil Service bureaucracy, and the local government bureaucracy, we now had a third bureaucracy, consisting of the paid officers of non-statutory or, to use the current description, voluntary bodies. And this third bureaucracy had greatly increased in numbers since the beginning of the century. Not that this was a matter for regret. The voluntary bodies were probably more effectively in control of their bureaucrats than were the civil servants of their ministers or the municipal officers of their elected councillors. But they were a significant new feature of the social scene and their evolution seemed to call for a more discriminating use of the word "voluntary".

There was one development which seemed to be generally welcomed and which has since made gigantic strides. This was the multiplication of training schemes for social workers. The universities were already active with the conferment of diplomas by social science departments. These become increasingly active as the years roll by. Good luck to them; but good luck also to the amateur, lest we infringe the Mosaic law and "muzzle the ox when he treadeth out the corn", as we may do if the Third Bureaucracy is allowed to become a trade union "closed shop".

It may be that the word "amateur" like the word "charity" has become tarnished by evil association and misuse: and with the memory of sixty years ago I can see why the Charity Organization Society had to change its name and drop the word "charity" when it changed its outlook. During my reign as General Secretary of the L.C.S.S. it had not as yet changed its name, but it certainly had changed its outlook; and its Secretary, Mr Astbury, was among the most tolerant and progressive members of the Third Bureaucracy with whom the L.C.S.S. was in constant touch.

As we moved week by week nearer to the horror of September 1939 all the social service organizations girded their loins for various forms of war work. The Munich crisis had come and gone, leaving few hopes of permanent peace, only a sense of shame in view of the terms on which we had achieved a momentary relaxation of tension. A programme for co-ordinated social service launched under the title "Plan for Living" could, during those last months, have been more appropriately named "Plan for Dying".

But by the close of 1938 my days as General Secretary of the London Council of Social Service were numbered. Before the end of the year, Eileen Power wrote to say that I was being considered for the Principalship of Westfield College, a small residential women's college in Hampstead, but a constituent part of London University. "Take it if it is offered to you," she wrote. "Do not be bothered about its religious clause,* because none of its heads that I have known have ever been narrowly sectarian nor is that its general tone. What it likes to have is a broad-minded Christian. It is an exceedingly nice little college ... I always liked the place and I feel sure you would." The religious clause *had* bothered me a little, because I am not and never have been a very conforming member of the Church of England; but William Temple seemed to think I was all right, and when offered the new job I accepted it. "Now," wrote Eileen in a congratulatory letter, "if only you can keep your hands off Popery all will be well." In fact that was

* According to the terms of its foundation by devoted evangelicals, both the Principal and the Chairman had to be members of the Church of England.

just what I didn't do because one of my first acts as Principal was to admit, as non-resident Westfield students, six male Jesuits, but that belongs to a later chapter.

My last months as General Secretary of the L.C.S.S. before assuming office as Principal of Westfield in August 1939 were sad ones. All was wrong with the world and all our social work was increasingly bedevilled by the uncertainty of its future and what might be required of it. I was also sad at leaving my office and my colleagues. Before our minds became obsessed by international affairs and fears of the future, it had been an inspiring job presenting ever newly discovered features of the London which I loved. And for a one-time and rather nostalgic member of the Rendel Connection, Bloomsbury was a satisfying location. Lunch hours were always a pleasant interlude—in the Square garden, or with colleagues in the Y.W.C.A. canteen. Or, when tempted to escape from the social service world, at the Arts Theatre Club in Great Newport Street, the way to which led through Seven Dials and the graveyard of St Giles' Church, past the Tomb of "Unparalleled Pendrell", the "Preserver of the Life of Charles II". I doubted whether my new job would offer these freedoms.

But it was a more responsible job, and I felt it a great unlooked-for honour to have been offered it. And did it not take me back to the university world in which I had so long sojourned with John Stocks? There is no doubt that he would have said "go"—as he said it to himself when Liverpool beckoned him away from the Manchester where he had been so happy.

14

Westfield College

WHEN I WALKED INTO Westfield College as its Principal in August 1939, London University, of which it was a constituent college, had already made plans for the dispersal of its colleges in the event of war to various university towns outside London. Westfield was peculiarly fortunate in its allocation. It was destined for evacuation to Oxford, and being wholly residential and small was not threatened with dispersal. Thus it was allotted a compact college building, and the one which finally accommodated it was St Peter's Hall in New Inn Hall Street—in the very centre of Oxford. But until the declaration of war in September all was uncertainty, and I entered Westfield College in Hampstead with the remote possibility of residing there.

I had already spent several nights in the college as guest of the retiring Principal, Miss Chapman, and met members of its staff. Also its Chairman, Sir Thomas Inskip, who was about to become Viscount Caldecote, and, later, Lord Chief Justice. He was at the time of my appointment Minister of Defence in Mr Chamberlain's Government. Up to the last phase of the gathering international storm he shared his Prime Minister's cheerful faith that war was improbable.

As far as my religious suitability for the job was concerned, he seems to have taken me on trust from William Temple, though he himself was a devout evangelical who spoke a somewhat different language from Temple, whose political views he must have disliked. My own would have seemed to him even worse; yet through the period of his chairmanship until his death in 1947 I experienced from him surprising tolerance and unfailing kindness.

The staff of Westfield College was mainly residential and mainly

female. Three male members of it lived out—as did three married
women members. There were in 1939, 156 undergraduate
students, working for honours degrees in history, modern
languages, English, classics, botany and mathematics. There was
one Professor, Canon Sykes of the History Department; other
heads of departments were Readers, and one of them was a man.
Women professors were rare birds in those days, and it was not
until after my departure that we had Professor May McKisack, in
the History Department.

With the exception of Holloway College at Englefield Green in
Surrey, Westfield was the most far-flung of London University's
scattered and variegated colleges. In 1891 its pious founders had
acquired a very attractive country house built by Decimus Burton
for a retired Indian nabob who had presumably made his money
in Kidderpore, since that was the original name of his house and
is still that of the Hampstead street in which it is situated. This
house, which had come to be known as The Old House, and which
contained rooms allotted to the resident principal, had been added
to at various times, and by 1939 three sizeable houses had been
acquired on the opposite side of the road.

One of the most attractive features of the college was its large
garden on both sides of the road—in one corner of which stood the
college chapel, designed, to my mind very satisfactorily, by
Horder, in which it was my duty to officiate every weekday morning at eight o'clock. It had been built as a memorial to the first
Vice-Principal, Miss Ann Richardson, who was a member of the
Society of Friends. This seemed to justify my intention to conduct
the chapel as far as possible on non-denominational lines, which
happily did not preclude me from reading aloud the superb collects
of the Anglican liturgy. With this intention it seemed wise to resist
suggestions for the appointment of a college chaplain. And this I
did successfully during my reign as Principal.

Partly as a result of its physical isolation and partly of certain
very strong traditions implanted by its first Mistress, Miss
Maynard, Westfield had a definite ethos of its own in 1939. Many
members of its staff had been there a long time; at least four were
ex-students. Its students were mainly of the professional class—
the influx of grant-aided entrants had scarcely begun—and very
many, if not the majority, were destined for the teaching profession. Relatively small numbers, physical isolation from other

London colleges, and deeply embedded traditions had made it a peculiarly self-contained community. Academically this meant that students received much individual attention from tutors, and tutors, apart from those non-residents who had family responsibilities and homes of their own, had relatively few outside commitments.

The government of Westfield reflected in some degree its tradition. It was governed by a self-perpetuating council comprising distinguished outsiders both academic and non-academic. The council appointed the Principal, also the College Secretary, who was regarded as the council's officer directly responsible to it for administration and finance.

That this unusual dichotomy of authority as between Principal and Secretary continued to work well was perhaps due to the personality of the council's Secretary, Miss Evelyn Gedge, who had been many years in office at the time of my appointment, and who had already in August 1939 opened negotiatons concerning the financial terms on which we were to occupy an Oxford college should evacuation become necessary. She continued to conduct these negotiations, and it must be admitted that the terms she extracted from Oxford University were exceedingly favourable to Westfield. But I must confess that Miss Gedge's finance at times terrified me. There came to be moments, connected later with food and petrol rationing, when I wondered whether Westfield's responsible agents would find themselves in the dock. Later still, her negotiations with the University Grants Committee on Westfield's behalf proved equally satisfactory for us.

I think that Miss Gedge managed, by a remarkable ingenuity, to combine the ideals of St Francis with the technique of Machiavelli. Anybody who can do this, while managing to live up to (or down to) both philosophies, is indeed a formidable negotiator. Like St Francis, Miss Gedge lived a life of remarkable personal austerity, apart from the enjoyment of war-time rationed petrol which she managed to acquire for journeys to and from Oxford. Her austerity was sweetened by a vein of penetrating, indeed sometimes surprisingly penetrating, humour. When she retired in 1948 St Francis had more scope because she became a whole-time village evangelist, though indeed St Francis had always found expression in her selfless kindness in the service of other people. When she finally retired, the position of the College Secretary as an officer appointed by the Council and directly responsible to it, could be envisaged as a problem, though as yet not a disturbing problem. At any rate I was content to let sleeping dogs lie. It may be that a more perspicacious or less indolent Principal would have awakened and dealt with them instead of leaving the business of doing so to posterity.

If Miss Gedge reads what I have written about her she may not agree with it—in which case she will probably forgive me because she is that sort of person. As Principal I enjoyed unbroken support from her. She did not always agree with what I did—indeed I think she would have liked me to appoint a college chaplain. But having strongly supported my appointment, she was resolved to assume that whatever I did was right. I was always certain of her sympathy and support. And of course it is a delightful experience to work with somebody who is in every way totally unlike anybody else.

The other constitutional feature of Westfield as I first encountered it was, or seemed to me, the poor representation on the council of the academic staff. It was, of course, wholly different from an Oxbridge men's college, whose property is vested in its fellows and whose Principal is elected by them. But it had not moved far from what might be described as the "orphan asylum pattern"—though senior academic staff appointments such as professors or readers were of course made by the university.

The council, and certainly its chairman, had inherited the view that employees interested in their terms of employment should not sit upon the bodies which determined such terms, since they could not be expected to make a wholly unbiased judgement where their own interests were involved. My own superficial observations of university personnel in Manchester had convinced me that such fears were illusory, and I pressed for increased staff representation on the college council—which in due course came about. The University Grants Committee in its early days had been responsive to the same doubts, with the result that for some years nobody in receipt of a university salary could sit as a member. This resulted in a committee of retired academics drawn from a restricted area of selection, and was indeed soon abandoned.

Subsequent experience on our council caused me to think more tolerantly of its traditional distrust of academic disinterest. In the same way observation of student behaviour during the past decade

has caused me to look more tolerantly on the chaperonage rules
which my Westfield predecessors attached to male visits to the
rooms of female students. They seemed to be based on the assumption that male and female students could not be shut up together
without risk of what was then regarded as impropriety. I am beginning to think that this assumption, too, was not wholly baseless.
But, of course, what was then regarded as impropriety, and I must
confess is still so regarded by me, is now generally considered to
be a healthy and natural form of self-expression requiring neither
restrictive rules nor the definition of moral precepts. It is discouraging to find that past generations were not really such fools
as one would have liked to think them.

Of course when we got to Oxford—and by the opening of the
autumn term 1939 we had indeed got to Oxford—our rules concerning hours and visitors were approximated to those of the
Oxford women's colleges. But even if there had been no rules, I
am sure that Westfield students, with two or three exceptions,
would have remained extraordinarily well behaved. The college
had a reputation among London students of being "ladylike".
From what I had observed during my brief pre-war visits, I could
almost sense a kind of softness—excessive concern for minor ail-
ments, over-emphasis on the ordeal of final exams for which
students sat in college, and which seemed to me calculated to
maximize nervous tension in a small community. Indeed, I excised
from the collection of prayers, bequeathed by my predecessor, a
chapel prayer for those about to face this ordeal which I thought
might have an effect quite other than that intended by its com-
poser.

But if this sounds critical of Westfield's ethos, it should be
remembered that its positive side was a tradition of politeness and
consideration for others. Whether this has survived the vast expansion, accompanied by co-education in a "permissive society",
which the college has experienced since my time, I do not know—I
scarcely think it could. But it certainly lasted my time, and doubtless that of my successor, Miss Chesney, who was a more ladylike
Principal than I was. When candidates came up for entrance inter-
views they were invariably impressed by the kindness of the Westfield students who acted as hostesses to them.

Thanks to the efficiency of the bursar and assistant bursar and
to the registrar, who was also my secretary, the beginning of the

autumn term found us all tucked into St Peter's Hall. It was a
tight squeeze, but we managed to fit ourselves in by putting two
students into the sitting-room-plus-bedroom sets designed for the
single occupation of St Peter's male students. The outgoing Principal's house provided a ground-floor senior common-room and
dining-room; its upper rooms were used for lectures. I occupied
an outgoing tutor's study and bedroom in the central block—my
bedroom being available during the day for the coaching of
students by the head of the English Department. A classics
seminar was established on the landing outside my rooms. When
universities today complain of lack of space, I am sometimes
tempted to wonder if they have really made full use of the space
they have, even at the expense of sacrificing a little comfort.

Our own makeshift arrangements in Oxford did not appear to
affect our academic standards, or for that matter our enjoyment of
being in Oxford at the centre of its university life, while at the
same time within easy reach of fields and woods. I have already
remarked on the human capacity for happiness when surrounded
by the distresses of others. One is reminded of the man who
gave up hunting after his wife died, because he felt that he
ought not, after such a loss, to have been as happy as hunting
made him. Perhaps we should have followed his example and
tried not to be as happy as evacuation to Oxford made us. But
there we were; our students joined Oxford undergraduate clubs
and mixed more freely with other students of both sexes than
they had been able to do in Hampstead. And several members of
the staff, being Oxford graduates, felt at home in an Oxford
environment.

It was more difficult for married members of the staff, both male
and female, because they had to transplant their families and
acquire new houses. Indeed, this proved impossible for Mrs
Rutherford of the French Department, because she had a school-
master husband and children in Croydon; so work at Westfield in
Oxford involved an awkward cross-country journey—particularly
awkward during air-raids.

Our six Jesuits mentioned in the preceding chapter, who became
non-resident Westfieldians were equally inconvenienced—or would
have been but for our hospitality. All were embarked on London
arts degree courses at University College. When University College
arts faculties were evacuated to Aberystwyth, the Jesuits could

not follow them because Aberystwyth did not contain a Jesuit House where they could live. Oxford did—at Campion Hall. But in Oxford the only London arts degree courses available were at Westfield in St Peter's Hall. Hence their inclusion as Westfield students. I have always hoped that at some future gathering of old Westfieldians I may meet a Cardinal, or even a Pope; but this has not yet happened.

I think the only member of the Westfield staff to whom our migration to Oxford brought real unhappiness was the Vice-Principal, Miss Martin of the History Department: a brilliant teacher with a special interest in colonial history. She determined that she would not be happy anywhere but at Westfield in Hampstead. Indeed, I think she finally determined not to be happy anywhere; though I am convinced that her academic colleagues did all they could to make her so.

Of course, the war situation being what it was, many of us had personal anxieties. Mrs Rutherford, being French, was, until D-Day brought relief, entirely cut off from her mother in Normandy. Our Senior Student in 1940 was anxious about her parents in the Channel Islands. Another member of the staff was anxious about her sister in Singapore, interned by the Japanese. Alas, she had reason to be. Another had a brother in the Air Force who failed to survive. I was anxious about my son John who, after completing his engineering degree, became an engineer officer in the Royal Navy and was out of view for months on end because, for security reasons, the movements of his ship were shrouded in mystery. And from time to time I was anxious about Ann, who, as a civil servant, had to remain in London through the heaviest bombing raids. Indeed I was sometimes anxious about myself when in London because I didn't at all enjoy air-raids—unlike the lady who took over our local pub in Addison Avenue after her business in Brixton had been put out of action. "Of course, I don't mind bombs," she said. "I'm funny like that."

But I ceased to be anxious about my own parents because we had persuaded them to evacuate 37 Argyll Road and move to West Bay. And this was fortunate; because 37 Argyll Road, though not bombed flat by a direct hit, was at any rate seriously damaged by a bomb in the back garden, and they would probably have been killed or seriously injured if still in residence.

Another member of my family who did not cause personal

day-to-day anxiety, was Helen. When Queen Elizabeth College moved away from Campden Hill to Leicester, instead of following it she abandoned her own educational project in order to devote her time to immediate war service. This led her, since children had to be cared for, to Leila Rendel's Caldecott Community, at its established home near Maidstone. When this became a dangerous military area in the summer of 1940, Westfield students had left St Peter's Hall empty for the vacation and the Caldecott Community found temporary shelter there. But when our students returned it faced an anxious period of dispersal, before achieving a final war-time home in a large untenanted country house on Egdon Heath in Dorset. There, its members gradually evolved a civilized way of life from pioneer conditions, until the coming of peace and the generosity of Lord and Lady Brabourne allowed them to take up permanent residence in the stately home of the Brabourne family at Mersham-le-Hatch in Kent. And there, too, Helen continued to serve for many years.

I have often thought that if, at Helen's christening, a fairy godmother had been present to grant her a future heart's desire, she might have wished on Helen a large family of delinquent or maladjusted boys. She would have been happy with them and they with her. But in the end the business world claimed her and the Welfare State was the loser.

Meanwhile, existence in war-time Oxford was surprisingly serene. German bombers flew over us without dropping anything undesirable on us. The night they destroyed Coventry was particularly noisy. And our immunity was surprising. Many Oxford colleges, set free by the diminution and concentration of their students, were inhabited by government departments; and the gleaming silver thread of the Thames should have given the Germans good guidance to a particularly desirable area of potential destruction.

My own life was diversified by frequent periods in London on university business. There were, too, the inevitable excursions arising from my commitment as a "statutory woman". These involved dealings with Service women, Army nurses, and the rather more relevant McNair Committee on teacher training, all of which took me around and about in London and elsewhere. And during vacations after 1940, a good deal of time was occupied by a tribunal which sat in the Law Courts charged with the job of investigating the dossiers of German internees and deciding which of them to release.

In St Peter's Hall academic life ticked over quietly. We produced some excellent vintages of good honours graduate teachers, several administrative civil servants, and two exceptionally brilliant mathematicians, one of whom was absorbed by the R.A.F. at Farnborough. And in all those six war years there was, so far as I know, only one unwanted pregnancy, and only two cases of emotional disturbance. Being a college principal in those days was child's play compared with what it must be today.

My own family life had its ups and downs. Its ups covered Ann's accession to Bevin's private office in the Ministry of Labour —and in 1940 her marriage to Arthur Patterson, a colleague in the Ministry. A year later there followed the birth of her son Mark.

Another "up" was the safe passage to the U.S.A. of my two old German Jewish friends, Mr and Mrs Heimann. Having chosen to remain in Berlin on the ground that if they kept quiet they would not be murdered, in the summer of 1939 it became obvious to them that such optimism was not justified. They had left their decision rather late, and it was with some difficulty, aided by Nancy Astor's influence with the American Consulate, that I got them over and settled comfortably in Oxford lodgings until they could get a passage, for which they had already paid, to join their sons in America. I think that Mrs Heimann really enjoyed her 1939 autumn in Oxford, or would have done so if her husband had allowed her to. But having all his life been a dispenser of hospitality, he could not bear to be a recipient of it. His wife was therefore required to render a strict account of all expenses down to the last tube of toothpaste. But apart from the beauty of Oxford buildings and good music on the B.B.C., the thing she enjoyed most was being asked to talk German with Westfield modern language students. The thought of being able to do something for somebody gave her real satisfaction. And it was something she did supremely well.

So much for the ups. The downs were mainly concerned with bombing, and excursions to London to deal with its results. At Westfield one of our houses had its top burned off by an incendiary bomb and the rest of it was flooded by the fire hoses which prevented it from being burned down altogether.

Family expansion had necessitated a move from our small

war-time steel and concrete flat, and I bought a large house at 42 Campden Hill Square to accommodate Ann and her family and myself when in London. When flying-bombs began flying over it and exploding round it, Mark and our family nurse came into residence at St Peter's Hall where they were joined by the small niece of Miss Barratt of the Classics Department. The presence of these juniors provided a new age-group for our senior common-room. But soon after that, the south-west corner of Campden Hill Square was well and truly hit by one of those odious gadgets, and a number of houses left in ruins. No. 42 remained standing, though badly cracked and rendered uninhabitable for the next four years. Fortunately the bombing occurred during the afternoon and Ann returned from her Ministry to a scene of ruin—shortly before the birth of her second son, Simon.

But how lucky we were—in view of what was happening to other people. And how lucky Westfield was! Not only because it escaped being bombed to bits, but because it escaped occupation by the Army who were reputed to be no respecters of interior house decoration. Indeed I once saw a country house which had been temporarily occupied by them, and did not want Westfield College to look like that. On the outbreak of war a community of discreet and civilized psychiatrists moved into one of our wings and continued to practise from there until the end of the war. And just in time to avert Army occupation, the main building was commandeered as a training centre for Wrens, who kept the place truly shipshape until we resumed possession of it in 1945. I suspect that the timely appearance of the Wrens owed something of the machinations of Miss Gedge, who continued throughout the war to reside in London and care for our property there.

One of my last memories before the vans rolled back from Oxford to Hampstead was late on the evening of V.E. day. There had been much jollification in the streets of Oxford and some breaking of chairs by exuberant male undergraduates. Female undergraduates, God knows, can be silly enough, but happily they seldom if ever express their silliness by smashing up good property. Later, on returning to my room, I heard a strange chanting from an alley behind our building, where a bonfire seemed to be burning. I went out to see what was afoot. Round the fire a small crowd of Oxford citizens were slowly gyrating. Their chant was an endless

repetition of: "It wasn't the Yanks as won the war. It wasn't the Yanks as won the war. It wasn't. . . ."
Remembering 1940 I chose to agree that it wasn't.

We reassembled in our Hampstead quarters in time for the opening of the autumn term 1945; and the first problem we had to face was domestic. Somehow the bursar had to feed a hungry community of healthy students on rations which, under war conditions, were tolerated as a minor inconvenience compared with the world's greater distresses, but which seemed less tolerable under peace conditions. I don't really think our students suffered from malnutrition, but there were times when some members of the staff feared that they might. At any rate London University life was resumed with gusto on a more convivial basis. Oxford experience had opened up new ambitions regarding student contacts with other colleges and with the London Students' Union in Bloomsbury.

The war years, while holding up an expansion of numbers for Westfield, did at any rate produce one important growing point. This was the establishment of the college library as a separate department in charge of a professional librarian. It had hitherto been a part-time activity for Miss Mackenzie, a lecturer in the English Department. But clearly the moment had come for full-time professional management; and in 1941 Miss D. Moore, F.L.A., was installed as College Librarian. As soon as the college returned to London the library proceeded to grow. Unfortunately the space for its accommodation did not, during my principalship, grow *pari passu* with the increased number of books or the students who wanted to read them; and by the end of my reign in 1951 the expansion of Miss Moore's department was priority number one in the building plans which we were even then beginning to envisage.

Apart from library space it was very soon clear that Westfield did not have to economize on anything, because the golden rain of largesse from the University Grants Committee had begun to fall upon it, as upon other universities. This was accompanied by the increasing readiness of local education authorities to give grants to students who had obtained university places. All of which was wholly desirable because it made university education less of a class privilege. But during my last year at Westfield I did begin to wonder whether it meant that our universities were opening too wide a door to students who, though competent examinees, left school without any very serious interest in academic studies but who naturally regarded with satisfaction the prospect of three years spent in a congenial though not very strenuous social atmosphere at the public expense. The equally natural desire of headmistresses, and presumably headmasters, to record a large number of school-leavers destined for universities could contribute to this risk.

As far as I was concerned it was a scarcely perceptible risk in 1951. In 1969 I am convinced that it is a very real one; and that our universities contain many students who ought not to be there at all. Against this harsh judgement my elder daughter is wont to argue that three years at a university must be good for anybody, whether academically-minded or not, provided they can achieve the minimum standard for entry. This may well be true; but it seems less true if one sees it in terms of priorities. One has to consider the assignment of scarce means to alternative ends in a social structure, some of whose sections are still most meagrely endowed.

But from 1946 to 1951, which comprised the second half of my term as Principal of Westfield, it was not my business to think in terms of social priorities, but rather to get for Westfield a good share of the public money that was flowing into universities, and which in our case flowed through our own London University bureaucracy at the Senate House in Bloomsbury. With more students applying for entry and well up to our academic standards, we needed more staff, and got it. We also needed more living and teaching accommodation both for students and staff. We got that too, in the form of four new houses on the south side of Kidderpore Avenue, two of them facing on to the Finchley Road. They and their gardens were incorporated into the Westfield domain to compose a compact and gracious environment. And our under-graduate numbers grew from 114 when we returned from Oxford, to 225 at the close of my reign.

Any expansion of a teaching institution, certainly one which is residential, is bound to raise the problem of optimum size. Can it become so big as to become impersonal? Can it remain so small as to become inbred? This scarcely troubled us during the years of my residence. We were still a small college, but less self-contained than before the Oxford adventure; and I dare to think that student–staff relationships were excellent. Heads of departments took a personal interest in the work, and indeed the general well-being of their students, and the student–staff ratio allowed for a considerable amount of individual tutorial work. More members of the staff, or rather a larger proportion, since the staff was larger, lived out of college. But even those who did, kept in touch with its social life, which included innumerable college meetings with outside speakers, some organized by the students' political clubs or religious groups, some by particular departments for discussion of their own subjects. One advantage of our London location was that we could call on a wide range of distinguished speakers who were glad to encounter students but would not have been glad to make long journeys to provincial university cities in order to do so.

I attended as many of these various meetings as possible. It was interesting to know something of student reaction to questions discussed in them. Indeed the daily life of the college offered many varied opportunities for student contacts. With the Senior Student regnant the contact was very close, because she visited me every morning to discuss any matter that might crop up. The Deputy Senior Student's business was mainly with the bursar. But I met the members of the Students' Union Committee, I met members of the choir, and the secretaries of societies in connection with their various meetings. I met those students who accepted my open invitations to drink coffee and eat cakes in my room on Wednesday evenings, and those who applied at my office in the morning for late leave in the evening. I met those who were taking a special economic history paper, since that was my subject, and I am sure it is a good thing for a principal to have a finger in the academic pie. And I met the few who from time to time had to be admonished, who had special problems, or who fell sick. But there was always a residue who did none of those things and whom I never met, apart from seeing them from a distance at meals in Hall. I could only assume that their departmental heads succeeded where I failed.

Where I certainly failed with all students was in my inability to remember names. I found it easier when encountering a student to remember where she came from than to remember her name, because a locality has some bearing on personality whereas a name is wholly irrelevant. This defect has since become intensified with advancing age. I can still remember my own name and the names of my children, and even grandchildren. But the names of my great-granddaughter and my great-great-niece are apt to become mixed, since one is called Rebecca and the other Susanna, and remembering that both are connected with the Old Testament is no help.

But to return to Westfield in Hampstead: For me, personally, 1946 was a bad year. It opened with the sudden death of Eleanor Rathbone in the full tide of her activities, which at that moment were centred on concern for the future of Palestine. During the following year I relived my memories of her by writing her life.

Soon after her departure my father died, and a few months later my mother. Mother made it quite clear that she did not really choose to live without him, though we made every effort to lighten the burden of having to do so. But apart from the anxiety and much discomfort of war-time evacuation, their lives had run smoothly; they were both well over eighty, and both reached their end without long or crippling illness. Their departure should have left no reasonable cause for regret. My own regret, though not reasonable, was real. A whole range of early shared memories departed into limbo, and it is sad when one is conscious of getting old to sever contacts with those who still regard one as young. They were greatly loved and sorely missed.

On the other hand, the end of the war, though a matter of regret to John (who had looked forward to being chief engineer of a brand new destroyer destined for active service in the Far East), was a great relief to everybody else. And John found more permanent satisfaction by retiring from the Navy and marrying a Wren. In this he did extremely well for himself, and incidentally for me by providing me with a perfect daughter-in-law and in due course with two more grandchildren. His engineering experience found scope in the service of Shell.

A few years later, 42 Campden Hill Square, being at last fit for human habitation, Ann and Arthur Patterson rounded off their family with a daughter who was christened in Westfield College Chapel. I may add that I did equally well in sons- as in a daughter-in-law.

My impression of these post-war years in Hampstead is that Westfield was becoming increasingly integrated with London University. I say this with some hesitation because I may be comparing a period that I know with an earlier period that I did not know. This was not only true of student activities, it was, I think, also true of the academic sphere where senior members of the staff played an active part on university faculty boards and in intercollegiate teaching. And as Principal of a constituent college of London University I was *ex-officio* a member of its Senate and of its Collegiate Council, as well as of many *ad hoc* appointments committees. All of which involved frequent journeys to and from Bloomsbury at a time when extraneous activities as a "statutory woman" were also involving frequent journeys elsewhere.

It may be that I had too many irons in the fire; but with the support of a very adequate administrative and bursarial staff the temptation to keep them there was considerable; and I would like to think that extraneous interests on the part of a college principal may add something to the abundant life of a college. At any rate I would like to think so, because of the abundant life that Westfield gave me in the form of day-to-day senior common-room contacts with delightful, friendly, and intellectually distinguished colleagues. Meanwhile, the problems of massive building expansion, co-education, and the emergence of a more "permissive" student morale were still below my horizon. It fell to my successor, Miss Chesney, and those who followed her to navigate in those deep waters.

When I retired at the age of 60 in 1951 I received many excellent parting gifts from staff, both academic and domestic, as well as from students. They included an exceedingly comfortable divan bed on which to repose, and a typewriter with which to do the opposite. Both proved to be necessary, for I was soon to learn that retirement was not all that it is sometimes reputed to be.

A number of residual commitments followed me into my approaching dotage. Of these the most time-absorbing were the University Grants Committee, to which I had been appointed in February 1950, and the London Executive Council of the National Health Service, to which I was appointed in April 1951. The first represented my last direct contacts with the university world into which I had married. The second brought me back to where I had started, more than half a century earlier, in the world of general medical practice. Seen together the two raised solemn thoughts concerning priorities: thoughts which very soon began to plague me, and which plague me still.

15

Retirement?

RETIREMENT IN 1951 BROUGHT me back to the Royal Borough in which I had started life sixty years earlier. Not to the house in Campden Hill Square, in which the Patterson family, having expanded, were taking up more room, but to a near-by flat in Aubrey Lodge, within the precincts of Aubrey House, the home of the Alexander family, in which two surviving Miss Alexanders still lived. Aubrey House is a country mansion of great beauty, set in a large garden. Its history from the close of the eighteenth century onward is interesting. In its garden, under an earlier occupancy, Millicent Garratt was introduced to Henry Fawcett. Mazzini had walked in it. Liberals had talked in it. Its later history under Alexander ownership is no less socially significant. The story of Kensington local government and Kensington charity is bound up with the activities of the three Miss Alexanders, Miss Mary, Miss Rachel and Miss Jean, who presided over it when, as a Kensington adolescent, I first became conscious of local social problems. Aubrey House was in fact a power-station of public service, and its garden, as well as its superb picture collection, was ever open to gatherings of aged or infirm persons, or to charitable money-raising activities.

When I returned to inhabit, as a tenant of Miss Rachel Alexander, an adjoining house which she had converted into flats, I felt as though I were stepping back into a familiar childhood environment. I think that Miss Rachel's offer of this tenancy was connected with my and my family's association with social service. Miss Mary had died at a great age shortly after the war. Miss Rachel, by now in her ninth decade, continued to activate and expand the public-spirited ventures for which Alexander philanthropy had long been responsible. Her dynamic activity on behalf of others certainly precluded the possibility of a reposeful background for her more aesthetically minded surviving younger sister, Miss Jean; and her almost obsessive frugality in the matter of food for her own *ménage* caused some members of her family to wonder whether the two old ladies were getting enough to eat. There was no vestige of such frugality in what Miss Rachel was prepared to spend on the old people's homes which she acquired, equipped, sustained and visited, or on the public gatherings which on Saturdays during the summer months enjoyed the hospitality of the Aubrey House garden, with outbuildings specially equipped for large-scale tea-making and washing-up.

Aubrey House itself had suffered little from the flying-bomb which destroyed the south-west corner of Campden Hill Square, the top of Aubrey Road and the west end of Aubrey Walk. But it had lost its outbuildings, which were in due course rebuilt, and the end of the war found its internal structure remodelled into five separate dwellings, the largest of which contained Mr Alexander's valuable picture collection, also Miss Rachel and Miss Jean.

One may continue to hope that Aubrey House, together with its lovely garden, has nothing to fear from a repetition of enemy action. But God alone knows what it may have to fear from the profitable redevelopment of an invaluable urban site by some child of Mammon who might in the future acquire control of it. If such a one ever should be so tempted, he, she, or they, would doubtless have to fight the Kensington Society, the Chelsea Society, the Victorian Society, the Georgian Society, the Fine Arts Council, the Society for the Protection of Ancient Buildings, and—one hopes—whatever local authority and government department may in the future be responsible for such matters.

But alas, such massed legions do not always win. When Mammon sees a good thing, he can "leap to his prey like a tiger chained by cobwebs". Truly, we live in a dangerous world.

Attendance at University Grants Committee meetings during my term of office from 1950 to 1958 covered a period of university expansion and building which looked impressive at the time, but which seems a snail's progress in comparison with the proliferation of new universities which followed the implementation of the Robbins Report.

Before 1958 a number of "red brick" universities had emerged from the tutelage of London University, and were conferring their own degrees; and one completely new university, the University of Keele, in Staffordshire, was embarking on an experimental four-year course involving a first year of general studies inspired by its first Principal, Lord Lindsay of Birker. A significant growing point in this scene was the development of the Manchester Corporation's College of Science and Technology under the principalship of Dr Bowden. This was in the early stages of metamorphosis from municipal ownership, involving the pursuit of vocational techniques such as confectionery and building, into what it is today, the University of Manchester Institute of Science and Technology, still under the principalship of Dr, by now Lord Bowden, and enjoying university status on a vastly expanded site in the heart of Manchester.

Membership of the U.G.C. involved periodic visitations to the various universities and university colleges in receipt of grants. One could thus see with one's own eyes how U.G.C. money was being spent. One could evaluate, or attempt to evaluate, the relative pressures of competing demands for more university places, more building, more science and technology, more student residential accommodation.

This last was a growing pressure, and different ways were being evolved for meeting it. One of the most sought after—though it seems to be less sought after today—was the establishment of more student halls of residence. Some magnificent new halls had been built, and one which sticks in my memory is the luxurious Nightingale Hall for Women on the campus of Nottingham University. But more were demanded, and in 1956 I was put on a U.G.C. sub-committee under the chairmanship of Professor Niblett, to report on Halls of Residence. In the course of it, we considered very carefully the kind of service that the principal or warden of such a hall should perform for its students. I should have liked to have opened our final report with these words: "The recommendations in this report are based on two assumptions: (a) that no British home can be made fit for an undergraduate to live in; and (b) that no university tutor can be regarded as concerned for the personal welfare of his students".

The first of these assumptions seems to arise from the belief that it is always—yes always—a good thing for a young man or woman of university age to leave the home circle. Indeed, during

my sojourn at Westfield I found it to be in very many cases a true
assumption. An increasing number of our students were coming
from homes in which it was difficult to find quiet solitude for
study. And in many such homes university vacations were regarded as over-extended school holidays during which remunerative work should be undertaken; whereas in fact university terms
are based, I suppose as a heritage of the Oxbridge tradition, on the
assumption that vacations exist for the hard reading which students
require as a background for lectures and tutorials.

But I sometimes wonder whether we are overdoing the belief in
student mobility. Is it necessarily desirable that a student who lives
in Devonshire and hopes to be a teacher should go to Newcastle
University and subsequently teach in Essex? Would it be disastrous or dis-educative for him to go to Exeter University and
teach in Devonshire? Is it really true that "travel broadens the
mind"? Is it possibly true that the give and take of home life and
the responsibility of local attachment may deepen the mind?

Or is my doubt due, not merely to the plaguing question of
priorities—since it would doubtless save public money if more
students lived at home and attended their local university—but
also to an aged person's nightmare of a foot-loose generation so
universally mobile that nobody has time to strike roots or think of
anything except how to get somewhere else as quickly as possible?

My second assumption is based on the memory of many university appointments committees, especially those which concerned young lecturers. What post-graduate work has the candidate
done or planned to do? we asked. What, if anything, has he published? These are indeed proper and relevant questions. But how
seldom did we ask candidates whether they were interested in
students and liked the prospect of teaching them, or how they
envisaged the relationship between tutor and student. Thus the
impression grew that advancement in the university world depends
solely on research and publication. Yet there have been, in the
history of learning, great tutors who are remembered as such,
though their published works, if any, were of little or no survival
value. Such, at Oxford, were A. J. Carlyle, A. L. Smith, Sidney
Ball, J. A. Smith. One is left hoping that belief in great tutors may
not perish from the earth.

Meanwhile, as far as I was concerned, while preoccupation with
universities continued to occupy quite a lot of time until 1958—

and incidentally to yield quite a lot of personal pleasure derived from the company of very delightful and intellectually distinguished colleagues—preoccupation with the National Health Service grew. Incidentally, involvement with the latter was the direct result of involvement with the former; because my appointment to the London Executive Council was the result of an encounter with Sir Allen Daley in the course of a U.G.C. visit to the Post-Graduate Medical School at Hammersmith Hospital.

Thus was I brought into the orbit of a service whose progress—and lack of progress—I had followed since 1909, when the Webb-inspired Minority Report of the Poor Law Commission demanded a unified Medical Service in which "neither the promptitude nor the efficiency of the medical treatment must be in any way limited by considerations of whether the patient can or should repay the cost." Lloyd George bedevilled the shape of that vision with his National Health Insurance Act of 1911; but the Labour Government gave it reality in 1946, and the great adventure of a real national health service began—not perhaps as "unified" as the Webbs had envisaged but, on paper at least, available to all, and without the recovery costs for those able to pay which they had conceded.

The London Executive Council was concerned only with the general practitioner section of the service, but that included dentists and opticians as well as medical practitioners. With the hospital service I was concerned only at the receiving end. As a national health patient with pneumonia, I had experienced life in a general ward; so had members of my family. As a road casualty I had been skilfully reintegrated at our local general hospital, St Mary Abbots; but as a member of the Hospital House Committee I was freely accorded the solitary luxury of a side-ward. And it was as a member of that House Committee that I became conscious of the difference between the living accommodation accorded to students in university halls of residence and that accorded to qualified resident housemen on call in hospitals for twenty-four hours a day.

Could we ever bring hospital standards of resident staff accommodation up to those regarded as suitable for university students? I doubt if we ever did. The money wasn't forthcoming.

A few years ago I visited the University of Manchester Institute of Science and Technology in the month of August. "Dull would he be of soul who could pass by a sight so touching in its majesty": over-passes, under-passes, engineering, science, and physics blocks, lecture theatres, common-rooms, acres and acres of it. And yet—"Ne'er saw I, never felt, a calm so deep!" because it was vacation time. It may not have been that much deep in some of those buildings, research projects were doubtless going on, but there was little sign of activity. And then I thought of all the other great university buildings up and down the country with their massively expensive new engineering and science equipment, their lecture theatres and common-rooms and assembly halls, all at minimal use for perhaps five months of university vacation. And I thought of the university staffs during these months—and indeed of myself in days gone by, with freedom to plan my own hours of work, and use, or not use, vacations for writing what interested me, or might be likely to advance my professional status.

And then I thought of the hospitals, with their equipment and space occupied for twenty-four hours a day, and three hundred and sixty-five days a year—in many cases with insufficient equipment and space to do the work they could do if the money were forthcoming.

At which point I began to wonder whether the time has come for our universities to think seriously of a revolutionary recasting of terms and vacations aimed at more economical use of these valuable capital resources conferred on them by the taxpayer. It may be, also, that the time has come for the taxpayer to reflect on whether too many young people are regarding three or even four years of university life, broken by prolonged vacations, as the only alternative to making fuller use of the many opportunities now existing for part-time or evening pursuit of intellectual interests, while at the same time earning their living.

I am inclined to think that sociology presents a tempting field of study for such persons. Unlike science, mathematics, or classics, it demands no severe or concentrated effort of intellectual discipline, and none of the subjects comprised in it appears to be studied in depth. Moreover, much of its subject-matter is so relevant to passing contemporary events as to offer its students a disproportionate opportunity for talking about them on radio or television.

However, it must be admitted that there is today a tendency to regard a university degree, wherever or however acquired, as necessary for salvation. Every institution pursuing higher or vocational education must so adjust its syllabus as to acquire recognition as a university degree-giving body. If one doesn't, others will. Only, as W. S. Gilbert has remarked:

> When everyone is somebodee,
> Then no one's anybody!

On the London Executive Council we were not concerned with hospitals, we were mainly concerned with the general medical practitioners who were in contract with the council and appointed by it to national health practices. It was composed of professional representatives of medicine, dentistry and pharmacology, and lay representatives of the local authorities and the ministry. It worked through committees, of which the most hard-worked was the Dental Service Committee, and the most interesting, the Medical Service Committee, both of which considered complaints by the public. But one which I also found interesting was the Joint Committee on Vacancies, which dealt with the appointment of general practitioners to vacant national health practices. It was interesting because it presented a general picture of the doctors in the contemporary field, and showed the enormous proportion of applicants from overseas. It also demonstrated the existence on the medical register of a relatively small proportion of applicants whom we would never under any circumstances appoint to a responsible job but who repeatedly applied for one.

The Dental Service Committee was hard worked, partly because of the inability of so many elderly persons to come to terms with their false teeth, partly because so many dentists failed to make clear to their patients precisely what they were prepared to do or not to do under the National Health Service.

This, of course, did not arise on the Medical Service Committee, since all treatment by practitioners in contract with the council was, with negligible exceptions, "on the health service". It was to me the most interesting committee, because in the course of eighteen years' membership of it, certain conclusions seemed to be taking shape concerning the working of this branch of the service.

The first is that the permitted practitioner's case-load of 3,500 list patients is far too high to enable him to give the kind of service a good family doctor would like to give. It is indeed surprising how many of them in fact do. Admittedly the average case-load is well below this figure, but still too high. The remedy would be lower case-loads, and this would mean more doctors, who at present are not available, and more money which the government seems not disposed to give. The actual earnings of national health doctors today, together with additional benefits conceded during the last few years, seem not unreasonable, but the work they are expected to do, if really done properly, surely is unreasonable.

A second conclusion is that national health patients require education in what they can expect of doctors and what they demand of them. In some cases, being unaccustomed to the services of a family doctor, they expect too little. A doctor is a doctor—any doctor will do provided a bottle of medicine is forthcoming. This means that they are ready to accept whatever deputizing arrangements may suit their own doctor's convenience. The doctor is therefore encouraged to make an office-hour job of general practice and live far away from his patients, secure from night or weekend calls. On the other hand, many patients expect far too much, which conduces to the same result. When my father worked a singlehanded private practice, night calls were few and far between and were well remunerated when they occurred. In a working-class national health practice they are neither. They often concern trivial discomforts and one is apt to encounter the view: the doctor is paid to attend me, and must come when I call him; an attitude which does not conduce to friendly relations. Under such circumstances a singlehanded practice requires some form of deputizing service, because no doctor can be on call for twenty-four hours a day. The remedy seems to lie with the organization of group practices, such as the one in Kensington comprising four doctors, to which I and all my family are attached as national health patients. There is always one of the four on call.

Whether the private deputizing services, as they have evolved to meet this genuine need, offer the best solution is another matter. The deputizing services at present operating, grew up, as far at any rate as London is concerned, without preliminary discussion by the Executive Council or, I presume, with the Ministry of Health. We suddenly awoke to the fact that one such service was functioning, in connection with a medical service case where a deputy doctor (or "emergency doctor" as they came to be called) had, for some reason which I forget, not been able to notify the doctor for whom he was deputizing of the treatment he had prescribed. As a result the patient did not get the right follow-up treatment from his own doctor, and a complaint was lodged. Thus we became for the first time aware of the existence of such services.

They are operated by individuals or companies, which establish a centre with a manned telephone perpetually on call. The service employs a panel of qualified doctors equipped with radio cars and in communication with the centre, and these can be directed to any call as deputy for the national health doctor who subscribes to the service and who has arranged for his own calls to be transferred to the centre. The subscribing national health doctor can arrange for his calls to be thus taken on certain nights, at weekends, or half-holidays—and can be sure that at such times a qualified doctor will be available for his patients. What he cannot be sure of is the quality of the deputy. He may be a general practitioner with a very small list and able to do private work in his spare time. He may be a newly arrived immigrant doctor with imperfect English. He may be a hospital doctor anxious for a little extra money and doubtless needing it. Some of the deputies are of very high quality; some, I suspect, are not. The deputizing services may be, and I think are, careful who they employ on their panels, but the turn-over of their employees is rapid and the deputy, in addition to knowing nothing about the patient, may also know very little about the district and how to find his way about in it—hence delays.

When I left the Executive Council there were four such services operating in the London area and more than fifty per cent of the national health practitioners were subscribing to them. I believe the system is now spreading in most large urban centres. The curious thing is that very few people know of the existence of these services, and it was only in 1962 that the Ministry of Health took sufficient notice of them to issue an order requiring national health practitioners to obtain the consent of their Executive Councils before making use of them. Since then, in the teeth of some opposition from the medical members, who regarded any such questioning as inquisitorial, my own Executive Council has required national health practitioners to indicate not only the fact that they use a deputizing service, but the exact extent of their use. This might be expected to act as a brake on over-use by those doctors who are anxious to make an office-hour job of medical practice, but I am not convinced that it has succeeded in doing so.

As far as ministerial attention is concerned, the whole question of deputizing seems up to now to have been swept under the carpet. Its existence was mentioned in the Gillie Report on *The Field Work of the Family Doctor* in 1963, and it was referred to in the Annual Report for 1969 of my own Executive Council. In no other official publication have I seen it mentioned—unless one can include *Hansard's Parliamentary Debates*, Feb. 25, 1969, when I raised the question in the House of Lords. Yet quite a considerable sum of public money which is paid to national health service practitioners, is in fact flowing through them into the pockets of practitioners operating privately on behalf of commercial deputizing services. We seem to have moved some way from the ideal of a free national practitioner service giving to all something of the doctor–patient relationship which the well-to-do are able to pay for and can still get. It is time the whole question of deputizing, since deputizing there must be, were dragged out from under the carpet, seriously discussed, systemized, and, I hope, brought right inside the national health service as an essential part of it.

Another aspect of our national health service which troubles me is the relationship between national and private medicine. There is still one law for the rich and another for the poor, though the area of the law's operation is negligible compared with what it was in the days when the rich had all the medical attention they needed and the poor had almost none. But it is still perceptible. The private doctor visits more readily and gives more time to his patient than it is possible to give in a surgery with an impatient crowd assembling on the other side of the door. Or, when it comes to the need for a consultant, it is often a question of tomorrow in my consulting room in Wimpole Street, instead of Tuesday week at 9.30 in the hospital—and 9.30 may well prove to be 11.30 or 1.30. If it is a question of an emergency operation or the result of an accident I doubt if there is much to gain from private practice. If it is a question of an operation or a treatment that is not an emergency, the private paying patient has the advantage of not having to face an interminable uncertain delay.

Now it would doubtless be an infringement of personal liberty to prohibit private practice. If some people have larger incomes, they must have freedom to secure thereby a more agreeable existence. The Labour Party is anxious that they shall not have this option by using their larger incomes to buy superior education for

[213]

their young; but has so far not thought fit to restrict their freedom to buy larger houses in pleasanter places, first-class travel or more convenient theatre seats. It may, perhaps, be unethical to allow the rich to spend their money on superior medical attention resulting in better health. But to prevent them from doing so would doubtless precipitate a revolt of the medical profession which is probably the most powerful trade union in the country.

I fear that a severe, though perhaps less insistent, revolt might be precipitated by prohibiting, not private medical practice, but the mixture of private and national health practice by the same general practitioner or consultant, and to my mind there is a lot to be said for prohibiting this mixture. I know doctors who serve both private paying patients and non-paying national health patients, and manage to do this without provoking the slightest vestige of suspicion that they give better attention to their private, at the expense of time given to their national health patients. It may require a supercharge of integrity to do this, and many doctors have this supercharge, but some have not. Therefore, where a partnership or an assistantship is concerned, mixed practice may result in the principal turning over as many as possible of his national health patients to his junior partner or assistant, while leaving himself more time for attention to his private patients. And since one man's time is limited to twenty-four hours a day, it may well happen that extra time given to paying patients, especially if the doctor has a heavy case-load, may involve curtailment of time for non-paying patients.

Do I appear critical of the national health service? I am; and I shall continue to be, if not on an Executive Council, then in "another place". It is the greatest, most imaginative, most widely beneficent of all our social services. We are already a healthier nation than we were before its advent. But in some respects it is imperfect. What public service is not?

Do I appear critical of the medical profession? I sometimes have reason to be; especially on an Executive Council, when they obstinately dig in their toes to resist any attempt to question or control deputizing arrangements, which enable their colleagues to sub-contract obligations to patients who live in insalubrious neighbourhoods such as East London. Or on a Medical Service Committee when a medical member of the panel assumes the role of counsel for the defence of a colleague faced by an ignorant uneducated complainant, thus precipitating me unwillingly into the invidious role of counsel for the prosecution.

Yet when we emerge from such fights, and always without any aftermath of rancour, I see my medical colleagues as delightful and friendly members of the profession under whose auspices I was born and lived: the greatest profession in the world, with a larger proportion of saints to sinners than any other—perhaps because it offers more insistent opportunity for sainthood. Why, oh why, should I, who can account for three children and five grand-children, have produced not a single doctor to follow in the foot-steps of Roland Brinton, M.D., F.R.C.P.?

This activity on the Executive Council, centred on Insurance House in Islington, was one among a number of less insistent or more ephemeral activities which followed me into so-called retire-ment. One, nearly related to it, was the Chairmanship of the High Coombe Residential College for the training of midwife teachers. This was an aftermath of the Departmental Committee—or Work-ing Party as such efforts had come to be called—on the training of midwives, on which I had sat in 1949. During the operations of that Working Party I think I learned everything about midwifery except how to do it. As later, being invited to write the history of district nursing'* I learned everything about district nursing except how to do it.

Meanwhile, three incidental activities carried me right outside both the medical and university worlds: one was concerned with the Press, a second with the theatre, a third with broadcasting.

Contact with the Press began in 1949 with an invitation from Viscount Astor to become a member of *The Observer* Trust which he and his son David had created in 1945 to take over their shares in that paper, in order, as he said, "to try an experiment in journalism". He indicated the outlook of the trust as demonstrated by that of the existing trustees. "You will see," he wrote, "that the Trustees do not all hold the same political views. But none are extreme—all are sensible and willing to co-operate. We should not invite an M.P.—or a parliamentary candidate—or anyone who held an important position in any party such as would make it difficult for him to be independent at election time. We believe you are leftish but not intolerant and would fit into the team." I was

* *A Hundred Years of District Nursing,* by Mary Stocks. Allen & Unwin, 1960.

certainly uncommitted in these respects, since, though formerly a member of the Labour Party, I had allowed membership to lapse on becoming Principal of Westfield and had indeed unsuccessfully contested two university parliamentary seats as an independent candidate. I hope that I fulfilled the other condition of being "sensible". I was certainly "willing to co-operate", and felt deeply honoured at being asked to do so.

A final paragraph in Lord Astor's letter of invitation contained what might be regarded as a word of warning. "By the way I ought to tell you that my wife does not approve of the paper being independent—she believes it should be strictly Tory—but I still hope to convince her that our policy is worthy of support." I doubt if he ever did; and it was with some trepidation that I confessed to Lady Astor that I had accepted this invitation. My initial castigation was followed by absolution, and the closing paragraph of Chapter 10 may suggest that the absolution was plenary.

It was, for me, an altogether agreeable, inspiriting and at one moment, exciting assignment. The excitement occurred in 1956 when Dingle Foot, then chairman of the Trust in succession to Lord Astor, was adopted as a Labour Parliamentary candidate and had, in accordance with the conditions mentioned above, to resign both from the chairmanship and the Trust. The selection of a suitable successor required much deliberation. Therefore, as the oldest member of the trust, I was required to act as chairman for a year pending the very happy outcome of such deliberation in the appointment of Sir Ifor Evans,* Provost of University College, London. It was during that year that the Suez crisis erupted, and David Astor, as Editor of *The Observer* took a strong uncompromising line against the Government's handling of it. His views came later to be widely shared, but *The Observer* was early in the field, and no punches were pulled by its Editor. As a result three trustees resigned, and their resignation caused a flutter in Fleet Street which produced numerous telephone calls.

These calls were, however, exceeded by the number of letters which poured in from disgruntled readers protesting that they had cancelled their orders for the paper. It is true that temporarily we lost circulation; but I choose to think that we gained repute, because the Editor, in addition to showing notable courage, was,

* Now Lord Evans of Hungershall.

as subsequent events showed, absolutely right. So I regard November 1956 as *The Observer*'s finest hour.

I retired from the *Observer* Trust in 1961, having passed the age at which trustees were normally required to resign. During those years I enjoyed many contacts with the editorial staff and learned a lot about the goings-on of the Press world. And my year as Chairman made me *pro tem Observer* representative on the Commonwealth Press Union, on one of whose sub-committees I continued to serve and serve to this day. So the thread which ties me to Fleet Street, though tenuous, has not been completely severed.

Contact with the theatre came with an invitation in 1950 to serve on the governing body of the Central School of Speech and Drama, then occupying one wing of the Albert Hall and a house not very far away at Hyde Park Gate. Its Principal, Gwynneth Thurburn, had inherited it from Elsie Fogerty, and maintained intact the standard of superb voice production with which Miss Fogerty had endowed it. I remained a member of that body longer than anyone should remain on any committee, and am about to tear myself away from it. It was a great school of drama and voice training, and the stage today reflects its excellence in the work of its old students, among whom it can count Vanessa Redgrave and Peggy Ashcroft.

At one point financial stringency brought it to the brink of disaster and the loss of its Albert Hall tenancy threatened it with exile. But Heaven put it into the head of John Davis of the Rank Organization to step into its chairmanship and apply his financial genius to restoring its fortunes, acquiring the Embassy Theatre at Swiss Cottage, and erecting a teaching block on an adjoining site. He himself once accused Miss Thurburn and me of putting this adventure into his head by deliberately deceiving him into thinking that the chairmanship would not involve much work. If this is so I still choose to believe that Heaven was at work, in which case we were its divine instruments; and our deception even if deliberate, was sanctified by its result.

Among the many debts I owe to the Central School was the fact that it involved contacts with Lewis Casson who was an active member of its governing body. And one day—though in what year I cannot remember but it seems a long time ago—I received a letter written from the Haymarket Theatre which said: "Dear

Mrs Stocks, Lewis says I must know you! and I want to! Can you come and lunch at 98 Swan Court . . . Yours very sincerely, Sybil Thorndike Casson." Thus began the second of the two corporate loves of my life, the first being Lawrence and Barbara Hammond.

Contact with broadcasting began in 1951. In fact I suppose it began earlier because between the wars I had done a few odd broadcasts from Manchester or Savoy Hill, and produced scripts of one or two historical plays for children under the auspices of Rhoda Power. In one adventure at Savoy Hill I became aware of the influence and personality of Sir John Reith,* the B.B.C.'s first Director-General—that humourless, monolithic, and to my mind, very great man, whose dictatorship endowed the B.B.C. with a built-in integrity of which I dare to hope its work still bears traces.

It was not, however, until 1951 that I became a fairly regular broadcaster, beginning with my inclusion in an *Any Questions?* team under the Chairmanship of Freddy Grisewood. Thereafter I think I must have performed on every possible kind of talks programme. I lifted up hearts, interviewed bishops, educated the young, reviewed books, selected discs for a desert island, gambolled with Renée Houston on "Petticoat Line", and from Bush House expounded British ways of life to listeners—if indeed there were any listeners to such programmes—in the Far East. I even flowed over on rare occasions into television.

In the course of these agreeable and remunerative activities I encountered so many eminent, interesting and intellectually distinguished persons, that were I to mention them all, the result would resemble a digest of *Who's Who*. But one name glows with especial warmth: that of Freddy Grisewood, who for nearly twenty years acted as chairman of *Any Questions?* Few performers in the broadcasting world have been so greatly loved by so many people.

It was not only contact with fellow performers, programme producers and script editors, that helped to enlarge and diversify my personal circle, but unseen listeners. All broadcasters are doubtless the recipients of letters—some friendly, some argumentative, some insolent and on rare occasions obscene, some anonymous, many more signed. Of the anonymous letters, some are inspired by the writers' imaginative consideration for the recipient who might

* Now Lord Reith.

otherwise feel bound to reply. Some however come from writers who take delight in writing offensive comments which they would not dare to make in person. Many indicate the prevalence of what might be described as "half-listening". The listener hears a word which for him or her has an emotional association. This sets up a train of thought which leads to the belief that the broadcaster has in fact said what the listener is accustomed to hear said in connection with that particular word, whether the broadcaster has said it or not.

But most of the letters I have received through the years testify to the existence of a large circle of listeners, many of them lonely, elderly, or both, who find in the voices of regular sound broadcasters a circle of familiar personal friends whose personalities seem to become part of their lives. Letters from such persons deserve an answer; and as far as I am concerned, they get it.

One other feature of such correspondence is the very wide class, age and educational distribution of the listening public—yes, even for "Petticoat Line"—from the House of Lords and university senior common-rooms to the ranks of unskilled labour. The moral of which is: may sound radio never grow less!

This unexpected, incongruous, fortuitous, and unsought eruption of an ageing superannuated academic into the entertainment world shows that the unexpected may be always round the corner. In an earlier chapter entitled "Statutory Woman" I have indicated how fate had indeed schooled me for it. In a final epilogue I will indicate how it led, in due course, to something even more unexpected: membership of the House of Lords.

16

Middle Eastern Interlude

RETIREMENT DID, HOWEVER, LEAVE time for travel, of which I had until 1951 singularly little experience, unlike my grandchildren who go everywhere with rucksacks on their backs and adventurous wonder in their eyes. Visits to Germany with John Stocks, and even before his advent, had produced emotional links with that country which did not survive the Second World War. A journey to Russia with him and a group of young people (including daughter Ann) in 1932 left us critical of communism in action. Our stay occurred during what W. H. Chamberlin has described as "Russia's Iron Age". This has been so frequently and, by some visitors, so accurately described that there is no need for me to say more here, except that we visited the Tolstoy home and village in high summer. Lack of amenities in the house provided for visitors caused me to carry my blanket and pillow outside into the long dewy grass of Tolstoy's orchard. As a night it was unrestful; but regarded as a vigil it was unforgettable: a night of circling stars followed by slow, grey dawn, and the distant sounds of a Russian village waking up. John did not share this pleasure. As an experienced soldier he adhered to the view that "the worst billet is superior to the best bivouac". And indeed I think he slept soundly.

Our impressions of Russia were quite other than those of Mrs Sidney Webb as recorded in a letter to me dated May 27, 1936. Referring to opponents of Soviet Communism she writes: "They will no doubt soon discover that the U.S.S.R. has reverted to Liberalism in its growing tolerance of free discussion and religious services." I hope, and indeed believe, that Beatrice Webb died with this comforting belief intact.

[220]

Our only other major joint excursion was to the West Indies in 1934, when John, having been given a term's sick-leave, was there and I was able to join him halfway through his holiday. This involved, as far as I was concerned, careful and (as I believed) satisfactory arrangements for parking out the family, since No 22 Wilbraham Road was shut up during our absence. Together, John and I moved from island to island, swimming in warm seas and enjoying unfamiliar convivial contacts with the administrators of our overseas Empire.

We loved those islands, and indeed I was so happy there with John, apparently recovering his health, that I do not really wish to revisit them alone.

Travel during later years of so-called retirement did however generate a permanent emotional commitment: to Cyprus and the Middle East.

My son-in-law, Arthur Patterson—"Pat" to all who know him —did not share the fate of most senior civil servants in being tied to the bureaucracy of Whitehall. Having grown up with social insurance, he became an expert administrator of it. This expertise took him all over the world and on both sides of the Iron Curtain, often in connection with conferences or the elaboration of reciprocal social insurance agreements with other nations, and on occasion to areas of the British Commonwealth where social insurance schemes had to be initiated. Such areas were Malta, Jamaica and Cyprus. And in Cyprus the whole Patterson family set up house temporarily in 1952 while the framework of such a scheme was being planned by my son-in-law.

To the Patterson family in Cyprus, in the spring of 1953, Helen and I paid a long visit. Still under colonial rule by a surprisingly unimaginative colonial administration, the demand for Enosis, or union with Greece, was becoming urgent on the part of the Greek-speaking majority. Whence came that demand? Not I think from the common people who, when they emigrated, went not to Athens but to Islington and Finsbury. In fact, innumerable families in Cyprus were London-centred, and it was to London they went for holidays and for medical treatment. In a letter received from Ann before our arrival she recorded a conversation on the subject with a Nicosia shoemaker. "He, like all Greeks," she wrote, "was for Enosis. But he added reflectively, 'Greece is a poor country' . . . It is all very odd. Sometimes it seems rather like the way children ask to be allowed to do something dangerous counting on the parents to say 'no'."

In this case the parents did say "no", which was about all they did say. In England the Colonial Secretary used the provocative word "never". In Cyprus the Governor attempted to enforce a Sedition Act and to prohibit the unauthorized use of loudspeakers. The trade unions were unrepresented on the Governor's Executive Council. Nobody under eighteen might join one. Their status was thus seen to be inferior to that enjoyed at the time by their fellow unionists in Athens. It was not surprising that communist as well as Enosis propaganda was well received in trade union circles.

Meanwhile, with the Cyprus broadcasting system at the disposal of the Government, no attempt was made to promote discussion of the pros and cons of Enosis as it would affect the common people. No comparison was made between the social and economic amenities of life in Cyprus and those prevailing in the Greek islands of Rhodes and Crete. No attempt was made to point out the effect on conditions of emigration to England if Cypriots became Greek instead of British citizens. Even within the framework of our niggardly expenditure on foreign information services, as criticized by the Drogheda Committee, there should have been resources available for a little intelligent propaganda involving the selection and presentation of facts and figures. But no—it was not attempted. Crude but, in fact, ineffective suppression was the answer.

The root of the trouble lies some way back in the history of Cyprus when, following its liberation from Turkish rule, secondary education for the Greek-speaking majority was left in the hands of the Greek Church. It may be that Mr Gladstone shared the Emperor Nero's belief that all culture came from the Greeks. At any rate by 1953 the Greek Church had a firm hand on the educational tiller. London University, which had laid many fertile university eggs all over the Commonwealth, had never, it seems, been encouraged to lay one in Cyprus, which remained without a university. The majority of its secondary school teachers were trained and appointed in Athens, and in many cases looked to Athens for their pensions. The Colonial Government, which had done so much for welfare, afforestation, roadmaking, and agricultural research, seemed to be unaware of the importance of secondary or higher education.

These reflections were set in train by the fact that Helen and I arrived in Cyprus on the eve of Greek Independence Day. A great procession had been organized in Nicosia for its celebration. We stood and watched it from a vantage point in Metaxas Square. Observing that we were English, a friendly Greek-speaking crowd pushed us forward so that we could see everything, and explained to us what we saw. Rank on rank of secondary school children marched past us, marshalled by their teachers. There were also groups of trade unionists, and doubtless others, but I cannot remember what they represented. My impression was of a great marching concourse of teenage children—marching with Greek national flags to Archbishop Makarios's palace, to be addressed by him on the greatness of their Greek national heritage.

It is not perhaps surprising that the Greek Government should have looked with covetous eyes on a rich island. If the word "imperialism" were still usable in its dictionary sense, one might indicate the Enosis movement as an example of Greek imperialism.

My remaining impression of that visit was a happy friendly island in which Greek and Turkish-speaking Cypriots lived peaceably together under this top-dressing of political discontent and colonial misrule. There seemed to be Turkish quarters in the larger towns but these were no more defined and isolated than, let us say, the Italian quarter in Saffron Hill or the Jewish quarter in Whitechapel. And in Nicosia, the municipal market, though in a mainly Turkish quarter, was shared by Greek and Turkish stall-holders. Greeks employed Turks and Turks Greeks. The Greeks were on the whole better educated, and staffed offices and the Civil Service; the Turks made helpful and efficient policemen. The Postmaster-General and Miss Aziz, the matron of the big general hospital, were Turkish. The leading business men were largely Greek.

It was during this first visit that I fell in love with Cyprus: its people, its coastline, its villages, its streets, its cafés—one could run on—and I found I could not keep away from it.

In the autumn of 1955 Helen and I returned after a visit to Israel and Jordan. By which time the Enosis movement had become savage and young gunmen were enrolled in a resistance movement known as Eoka. We arrived a day after the burning of the British Institute Library in Metaxas Square by a Greek mob. It appeared that the police had failed to function, and the mob was unchecked for some two hours until the Army was called in, too late to save the library. Recriminations were flying next day—how many of those responsible for law and order were busy celebrating the anniversary of the Battle of Britain at cocktail parties? There was a growing demand for military rule.

Meanwhile a British policeman had been shot in Ledra Street, the main Nicosia shopping centre, by a young Greek called Cariolis—he was a clerk in the Inland Revenue Office, aged twenty-one. I attended his preliminary hearing in a Nicosia Court, the approaches to which were cordoned off by barbed wire and military patrols. There was no doubt of his guilt, and in due course he was hanged. But I found myself plagued by a line from Browning's *The Ring and the Book*. "Who taught the dog those tricks they hanged him for?" He had, of course, been emotionally conditioned by the Greek Church since the age of eleven.

It was during this visit that the Governor, Sir Robert Armitage, was summarily dismissed by the Colonial Office at five days' notice. He had been a first-rate and efficient Finance Officer on the Gold Coast, and after his ordeal in Cyprus was sent to govern Nyasaland, then in a state of potentially disturbing political unrest. The Colonial Office at that time, like God, "moved in a mysterious way". But, unlike God, failed "His wonders to perform".

Sir Robert Armitage was succeeded by Sir John Harding,* an appointment which represented military rule and a stiffening of policy against Eoka. Cyprus was no longer a happy island; but still Turks and Greeks continued to live peaceably together, and one still walked about the streets taking very little notice of Eoka slogans chalked on walls.

By this time the Patterson family, having returned to England, my point of vantage for observing events was the household of Harold Chudleigh, Commissioner for Labour, who had worked with Pat on his social insurance scheme. Both Harold and Mrs Chudleigh had become more closely integrated with the life of the island at all levels than any of the British administrators I encountered; and I think that Mrs Chudleigh was the only one of the colonial ladies who had taken the trouble to learn modern Greek. This enabled her to achieve friendly contact with the villages; indeed, at the Chudleigh home one was conscious of being in touch with a complete cross-section of Cypriot society.

* Now Lord Harding of Petherton.

My next visit was in the autumn of 1958, and much had happened since 1955. Greeks and Turks were now at one another's throats and there had been a lot of mutual killing. Who, and what, had started it? My own belief is that the Turks started it, possibly with encouragement from Ankara, in the belief that the Turkish case was receiving scant attention from Great Britain. But Greeks and Turks had now drawn apart; Greeks were leaving Turkish firms. Turks were leaving Greek firms. Makarios had been deported and the Eoka gunmen were playing hide and seek with the British Army in the hills. In the towns and villages peaceful Greek citizens were faced with a dilemma. If they were suspected of co-operating with the Eoka gunmen, their houses were ransacked by British soldiers, exasperated past bearing by the harassment of brutal but elusive gunmen, and if guns were found they stood a chance of incarceration in a concentration camp. But if they were suspected by the Eoka gunmen of co-operating with the British, they were likely to be shot. It was therefore on balance safer to co-operate with Eoka, though it was not really very safe to do anything—or even nothing.

Three days before my arrival the wife of a British N.C.O. had been shot in the streets of Famagusta by an unknown gunman, and Famagusta had, in consequence, suffered a very "roughhouse" from the British Army. I visited Famagusta in company with *The Observer* correspondent, Rawle Knox. Military discipline had been restored, but the atmosphere was highly charged. It was indeed highly charged almost everywhere, certainly in Nicosia. Barbed wire was much in evidence. At the house of the British Commissioner for Labour we were advised not to sit on the lighted veranda of an evening for fear of possible shots from a near-by office; though I do not think that anyone would have wanted to shoot either of the Chudleighs. It was not unusual to hear shots in the night.

Meanwhile, Harold Macmillan's Government was turning this way and that to find a solution of the Cyprus question. Military rule under Sir John Harding had been softened in 1957 by the appointment of the notably liberal-minded Sir Hugh Foot*— whose first act was to walk unarmed down Ledra Street, as a gesture of goodwill to the Greeks. It was an extremely courageous gesture because Ledra Street had come to be known as "the

* Now Lord Caradon.

murder mile". But life at Government House was lived as in a beleaguered fortress, and a vivid account of it can be found in Lady Foot's book, *Emergency Exit*.* Sir Hugh Foot was nevertheless optimistic, or so it seemed to me when I visited him behind his barbed wire, that a "partnership plan" promulgated by Harold Macmillan would work, given time. From what I had seen and heard, I did not share that optimism; and I left Cyprus in 1958 feeling very sad.

When I returned in the summer of 1959 all, on the surface, was sweetness and light. The intervention of the NATO powers had been precipitated by considerations of more world-wide importance than the destiny of Cyprus. Greco–Turkish relations must not, it was felt by the Great Powers, be bedevilled by the Cyprus issue. The Zurich Agreements had been signed, involving abandonment by the Greek Government of insistence on Enosis, and a guarantee to the Turkish minority of various complicated privileges built in to the constitution of an independent Cyprus. Makarios had returned from exile to form a Cyprus Government, the Eoka gunmen had come down from the hills, and one of them, a highly experienced killer and escaper, had been appointed by Makarios as Minister for Labour. He was busily mastering the intricacies of Pat's social insurance scheme which, in spite of military rule, Sir John Harding had rescued from its pigeon-hole and actually implemented. The barbed wire had been dismantled and rolled up. The British Army was in occupation of the two very salubrious sovereign bases accorded to it by the Zurich Agreement. All was set for the celebration of the birth of an independent Cyprus within the Commonwealth, and the evacuation of Government House by the former representative of the British Raj.

I was able to attend these celebrations. First came a last British military parade to celebrate the Queen's birthday. Sir Hugh Foot, on horseback in full-dress uniform, took the salute. He must have been very hot. In the evening a "party to end all parties" was held at Government House—there were fairy lights in the trees, bands, dancing, food and drink—everybody who was anybody was there, Greek or Turkish. It was a lovely party, thanks largely to Lady Foot who could be counted on to handle a delicate situation with superb tact.

Two further celebrations followed. Greek Cypriots gathered in

* Chatto & Windus, 1960.

force in the Nicosia stadium to watch a display by Greek athletes and hear an address by President Archbishop Makarios and a relayed message from the Eoka leader, General Grivas. Greek nationalism was its keynote. Turkish Cypriots held a similar display in the Nicosia Moat, of which the star-turn was a spectacular march-past by the Janissaries' band from Ankara. Turkish nationalism was its keynote. I could detect no evidence of enthusiasm for Cypriot independence, nor was there any renewed mingling of Greek and Turkish personnel. The complicated terms of the Zurich Agreements rather accentuated the separation.

An English visitor could no longer count on the old friendliness —at any rate from the young. Children in the villages and youths in buses could be mildly insolent. Had they not beaten the British Army? But at any rate the killing had stopped; and in connection with the killing, I was able, with the help of the British Information Service, to compile an analysis of who was killed and by whom during "the troubles" of 1957. The result was as follows: Of a total of 691 killed, 84 were Turkish, 142 were British and 461 were Greek. Of 457 Greek Cypriots who were killed (I cannot account for four of the 461), 56 were killed by Turks, 182 by the British and 219 by fellow Greeks. I can only account for these figures by assuming the existence of a considerable element of terrorism in the Eoka movement.

So from a political point of view this visit was not encouraging. Nor was I encouraged when I returned to Cyprus in 1965. There was still no sign of integration. I visited President Makarios in the place where Sir Hugh Foot had sat. He was friendly and courteous, and looked much less formidable without the tall black hat and veil which he habitually wears out of doors. I was so bold as to suggest that what Cyprus needed was to rebuild from the top downwards by means of a bilingual university; but he did not encourage the idea. Most of the British had departed, but Pat's social insurance scheme seemed to be working well. That, at any rate, was a positive and enduring result of British rule.

My last visit to Cyprus was with Helen in October 1967. The Zurich Agreements had not worked and I doubt if anybody had ever thought they would. They had temporarily stopped the killing which had, however, been resumed shortly before our visit, and a United Nations force had been brought in to keep the peace. In and round Nicosia, Greek and Turkish areas were demarcated by road blocks and barbed wire entanglements. In Limassol and Paphos conditions were easier and Helen and I, being English, were free of these barriers. But in the old city of Nicosia the Turks were penned in a sort of ghetto where we visited our old friend, Miss Aziz, the former matron of the Nicosia General Hospital, who had improvised a makeshift Turkish hospital surrounded by scenes of desolation comparable with a North Kensington housing development area.

At the present time, to judge from what I read of Cyprus, things are on the mend; and if the Turks remain in their ghettos it is because for political reasons they choose to do so.

I have described this as my last visit to Cyprus, but I hope that it will not prove to be so, because I am still in love with it. And should Venus be tempted once again to descend from Olympus and come among us, I would advise her to come ashore where she came ashore long ago: in the shadow of a great rock on the south coast of Cyprus. She would find her beach still unencumbered by holiday huts and ice-cream barrows, and modern usage would not require her to don the voluminous bath robe which Botticelli's nymphs had ready for her when she landed before.

It is, as a glance at the map will show, difficult to visit Cyprus without being tempted to visit Israel, as I did in 1953, and have done on several occasions since. But so many people have visited Israel and described it from various angles that I will not indulge in vain repetition, except to say that one cannot visit Israel without being impressed and encouraged by the dynamic quality of its citizens, and their extraordinary capacity for integrating different races and widely different cultural standards. I was, however, sometimes tempted to wish that they could display more sensitive imagination in their attitude to Palestinian Arabs who had suffered a raw deal as a result, not of their own, but of Western Europe's vicious anti-semitism. But the origin of these troubles lies far back in human history, further indeed than the Balfour Declaration which foreshadowed a Jewish homeland—right back to a covenant negotiated between Abraham and God which conferred upon Abraham's descendants the title to land already occupied by others.

Only in the course of one of these visits with Helen in 1955 did we equip ourselves with the necessary separate passports and Arab

visas to cross that patch of no-man's-land known as the Mandel-
baum Gate, in order to sojourn in the Hashemite Kingdom of
Jordan. We were kindly received, and even accorded the honour of
a visit to the Queen in her Palace at Amman. She did not give us
the impression of a happy queen, nor had she reason to be so,
because Hashemite tradition prohibited her from doing anything
which a modern queen might wish to do in the service of her
country. And as a Cambridge graduate formerly domiciled in
Egypt, where women's education is taken seriously, she could have
done so much. The presence of two formidable ladies-in-waiting
and the natural reserve of a frustrated queen did not, on this
occasion, help conversation; and I was glad, later, to learn that she
had been set free from that marriage. Yet she had for a short time
shared the personal companionship, if not the public life, of a very
brave man, whose life I should not have wished to insure.

That visit to Jordan ended, for Helen and me, with a traumatic
experience at Dera'a—less physically distressing doubtless than the
one which T. E. Lawrence had, or thought he had, or said he had,
in that ill-fated spot on the border of Jordan and Syria. It did not
in our case engender a life-long neurosis; but it did, in my case at
any rate, engender a built-in hostility to Syria and Syrians.

Our intention had been to proceed from Jordan to the Lebanon,
spending a night at Damascus, which was familiar to Helen but
unfamiliar to me. We had been instructed by Thomas Cook, by
whom our journey had been planned, that those who entered Arab
territory from Israel might not re-enter Israel but must leave
through an Arab state. This we arranged to do, having our passports duly provided with visas to enable us to travel from Amman
through Syria to Beirut there to catch a plane to Cyprus. The
Syrian Consulate in London knew precisely what we intended to
do and I seem to remember that we paid them a fee for the privilege of doing it.

Great, therefore, was our surprise on arriving at the frontier
post at Dera'a to find ourselves forced to abandon the car which
was taking us, and other passengers, to Damascus, and be informed
that we could go no farther. Why? We were not told. As night fell
on this bleak and hostile spot, we pressed our question. Why? Our
question was met by blank smirking insolence. With growing
realization of our lonely helplessness and our increasing inability to
control our tempers, we rejected the suggestion that a Syrian might

for a large sum of money drive us back to Amman. We did not want to be driven anywhere by any Syrian.

The Holy Land is a land of miracles, and at this point of our desperation, one happened. A Morris estate car containing an English headmistress accompanied by her school secretary, returning to Jordan from a holiday in the Lebanon, appeared on the scene, took us on board, and drove us safely back to Amman. From there next day we were flown out by friendly Jordanians to catch our plane at Beirut. On returning to London I wrote to the Syrian Consulate to demand an explanation of our monstrous treatment by their minions on the Syrian frontier. No answer was forthcoming. I visited them to press the point. I was met by the same smirking insolence and the same refusal to supply any explanation. I suggested to Thomas Cook that they might in future warn travellers to Syria of the treatment they might expect, however meticulously they had kept the international rules. They, too, had no explanation. They said it hadn't happened before. So that was that.

I had wanted to visit Damascus, and still hope that some day I may do so—but not before it is occupied and administered by Israel.

Epilogue

IF I ASSOCIATE MY elevation to the Peerage in 1966 with my activities as a broadcaster, it must not be supposed that Mr Harold Wilson recommended the conferment of this honour upon me in recognition of such activities; because of course he didn't. If any female person had been ennobled for such a reason, it certainly would not have been me. It would have been either Anona Winn or Isobel Barnett. On the other hand, if ennoblement were envisaged as a reward for public and political services it certainly would not have been me either; because any public services that I have been able to perform are insignificant compared with what others have done without achieving peerages. And though, before and after my reign as Principal of Westfield, I was a paid-up member of the Labour Party, I have never been an active member in the field; and anyway at the age of seventy-five I might be regarded as unlikely to play a very useful part in sustaining the day-to-day vitality of the Labour minority in the Upper House.

What the B.B.C. did was to force me into the public eye—or rather ear—and focus a lot of personal publicity on any other activities that I might pursue. Without this advertisement I should have lapsed into a decent obscurity; though it must not be assumed that I sought advertisement with this ulterior motive. I liked broadcasting, and the rest just happened. I therefore persist in the belief that the B.B.C. had a lot to do with my life peerage. I am therefore grateful to it, because the House of Lords is a perfect eventide home. It keeps one in touch with what is going on in the corridors of power, it provides one with a platform on which the bees in one's bonnet can sometimes be given a chance to buzz—in my case, such matters as the defects of the national health service or the pollution of beaches by sewage, and it brings one into daily contact with interesting and delightful fellow-peers in an atmosphere wholly devoid of class consciousness, party rancour, or sex-discrimination.

It also offers agreeable side benefits. Among these are the use of a beautiful library with windows overlooking the river and within sound of barges and steamers swishing up and down outside, the aesthetic delight of walking through Westminster Hall on the way to and from the London Underground, the opportunity of being able to entertain guests to lunch or tea in surroundings which many of them find unfamiliar and even exciting, and of being able to introduce such guests as are female to the engaging "period piece" of Early Victorian plumbing known as the peeresses' lavatory. Many amenities in Barry's Palace of Westminster have been modernized; but I am sure that any proposal to modernize the amenity indicated above would encounter the united opposition of our growing body of women peers. Baroness Wootton of Abinger has already indicated her sympathy with this view.*

It is fashionable among those who do not sit in the House of Lords, and indeed in the case of one or two who do, to decry it as a useless, expensive, undemocratic, time-wasting, out-dated, absurd relic of historical lumber. But even before I sat in it I listened from its gallery to three debates which did it credit and seemed to typify its virtues. The first, described in an earlier chapter, was in 1918 when the fate of women's suffrage seemed to hang precariously on the Lords' attitude to the vital clause of the Representation of the People Bill. In those days, apart from the Law Lords, the Upper House was wholly hereditary and exclusively male.† The course of the debate made it clear that a majority of its members regarded even a limited measure of women's suffrage with distaste, amounting to horror. But in view of the movement of public opinion outside, as demonstrated by an overwhelming vote in the House of Commons, the House of Lords was not prepared to flout democratically expressed public opinion. The anti-suffrage peers abstained from voting in sufficient numbers, thus enabling the vital clause to go through. In fact the Upper House was not in 1918 prepared to frustrate the clearly expressed will of the people. Nor should it be so prepared.

* *A World I Never Made*, by Barbara Wootton. Allen & Unwin, 1967.
† See Chapter 5.

Epilogue

The second occasion on which I was able to observe it in action was in 1926,* when Lord Buckmaster introduced his resolution demanding the abrogation of an official veto which precluded local health authorities from giving contraceptive advice to mothers for reasons of health. This resolution was carried in the teeth of Government opposition. An earlier attempt had been made, without success, to raise the question in the House of Commons. The House of Lords dared in 1926 to take a step ahead of public opinion. It has since shown comparable independence in dealing with such matters as homosexuality and abortion. And I still hope that it may lead the way to legalized voluntary euthanasia.

The third occasion—and indeed the last before I myself sat on its red benches—was the debate in which Lord Simon of Wythenshawe urged the Government to undertake a full-scale review of higher education. A galaxy of highly expert university experience was brought to bear on the subject, since vice-chancellors, professors, and members of the University Grants Committee even at that time proliferated in the Upper House. The debate achieved a quality which can seldom, if ever, be reached in the Commons. It carried great weight, and its immediate result was the appointment of the Robbins Committee.

I have since observed that debates of similar quality often occur when foreign or commonwealth affairs are under discussion, since membership of the House includes a significant proportion of experienced ex-administrators or diplomats who know what they are talking about, whatever may be the sometimes deplorable political angle from which they talk.

It must, however, be conceded that many speeches are too long. I suspect that the widespread, though not universal, habit of reading one's speech conduces to prolixity. If one has taken the trouble to compose a speech in advance of the debate, and written or typed it with some care, the temptation not to waste such portions of it as may have been covered by earlier speakers is difficult to resist and sometimes not resisted. The compilers of *Hansard* doubtless benefit from this habit. Strictly speaking, according to a Resolution of the House dated June 17th, 1936, it is "declared to be alien to the custom of the House and injurious to the traditional conduct of its debates that speeches should be read". But it seems now to have become traditional that they should be.

* See Chapter 11.

[233]

If sometimes tedious or repetitive, speakers in the House of Lords are never rude or disorderly. A standing order first recorded in 1626 continues to govern our behaviour. It requires that:

> To prevent misunderstanding, and for avoiding of offensive speeches, when matters are debating, either in the House or at Committees, it is for honour sake thought fit and so ordered, That all personal, sharp, or taxing speeches be forborne, and whosoever answereth another man's speech shall apply his answer to the matter without wrong to the person: and as nothing offensive is to be spoken, so nothing is to be ill taken. . . .

Is, there another legislative chamber in the world whose personnel conform to such a standard of good manners? I doubt if there is.

In this rarefied atmosphere it is difficult not to contemplate with a tolerance, amounting to affection, the quaint forms and ceremonies which clearly waste time, sometimes border on absurdity, and may indeed occasion inconvenience. The introduction of a heavily robed peer with his solemn perambulation round the chamber is delightful but could perhaps be equally impressive without the concluding threefold repetition of "rise, bow, sit" conducted by the Garter King of Arms from a back bench kept clear for the purpose. And without this addition the Garter King of Arms could still conduct the perambulation in the resplendent colourful garment which he clearly enjoys wearing and the rest of us enjoy seeing.

The customary method of recording a division is certainly time-consuming and would be so regarded by members of those chambers which record votes more swiftly, and perhaps more accurately, by pressing electric buttons. But there is a certain time-honoured charm in the slow march through the division lobbies and in the use, prescribed by a standing order dated 1865, of a "four-minute sand glass" by the Clerk at the Table, to measure the time between the clearing of the Bar and the repetition of the question by the Lord on the Woolsack before the slow march begins.

And what finer and more colourful historical pageant could be staged than the State Opening of Parliament by the Queen; and how many directors of pageants or ballets could attain the perfect precision and timing achieved year after year by the Earl Marshal and his experienced minions, with a leading lady who never puts a foot wrong!

Thus comfortably settled in my eventide home, and with the good excuse of advanced age for indulging in the pleasures of idleness, I should now be able to sing the *nunc dimittis* with a clear conscience. Indeed my eyes have seen a good deal of the salvation which I envisaged as a castle in the air sixty years ago. I am no longer a member of a privileged class, and I have never thought there should be one. I am no longer a member of an unprivileged sex, and I have never thought there should be one.

Two beneficent causes have conditioned the fusing of Disraeli's "two nations". The first is the spread of effective purchasing power brought about by the paring down of top incomes by taxation, and the shoring up of low incomes by welfare services. There are still pockets of near-destitution, and these are manageable and should be managed. At any rate I can now walk round Saffron Hill without seeing ill-shod undernourished children. Nor is there any further need for Miss Canney's Factory Girls' Country Holiday Fund. Those formerly dependent on it now enjoy package tours to the French Riviera, Majorca or the Costa del Sol. Those of us who abhor the companionship of our fellow nationals when encountered abroad, have to peep about to find ourselves less popular resorts; and as the years roll by we have to peep increasingly further afield. And when we, the one-time privileged, grapple with our domestic chores, at least our consciences are at rest, with the thought that our female fellow-citizens are no longer dependent on serving us, because more satisfying and remunerative occupations are now open to them. Domestic work is, after all, both tedious and repetitive, and it is not surprising that most women and all men avoid as much of it as possible.

The other great conditioning cause which has undermined our class structure is the spread of educational opportunity. Admittedly it is still difficult for a child with a poverty-stricken, ignorant, or disorderly home background to take full advantage of the education now freely available to all. But many can and do, and we no longer have an education system which inexorably perpetuates inequality of income and public esteem. The formerly privileged classes are slowly, in some cases reluctantly, bringing themselves to share in the educational ministrations of the welfare state. They have already accepted those of the national health service. All of which, like the imposition of domestic work on the formerly privileged minority, tends to minimize class-consciousness and maximize the area of shared human experience.

So much for salvation. But I do not find it altogether easy to "depart in peace" because there is menace in the salvation. Widely distributed affluence combined with a perfected technique of mass communication has put new power into the hands of the advertising industry which, armed with massive financial resources, can tell us to do what is bad for us, such as smoking cigarettes, as well as what is good for us, such as washing whiter. Its total message seems to be: "Use more things, want more things, other people have more things so why not you, because on the multiplicity of your material wants and your success in satisfying them depends your happiness and the greatness of your nation." But does it?

Meanwhile, powerful business interests are now reaping substantial profit from the exploitation of our lower instincts: a thing which even John Stuart Mill, that passionate exponent of liberty, reluctantly agreed that they should not be allowed to do. Gambling is profitable. The titillation of sex is profitable. The dramatization of violence is profitable. The more salacious the newspaper, the greater its circulation and its advertising revenue—and that, too, seems to be profitable; at least many newspaper proprietors think it can be made so.

And all these pressures bear with concentrated force on the young. Why do so many of their elders and no-betters say that the young are frustrated? Never, surely, have they been less so. The passing years have put enough money in their pockets to constitute an economically significant "teenage market"; the decline of reticence and the loosening of sex restraints have liberated them from conventional moral precepts; they are healthier and more mobile; their opinions are recorded and taken seriously by the Press, and their more foolish actions are displayed on television. At the same time, they are subjected to a bombardment of flattery by elders who are anxious to be "with it". How is it that so many young people still manage to remain decent, compassionate, thoughtful, and, within limits, self-controlled, under these inexorable unremitting pressures?

But they do—and may their resistance never grow less. Meanwhile, there is nothing I can do to help them. I am too old and too square.

[236]

Epilogue

Thus my record of activity may be concluded. It cannot be called a career, because on looking up the word "career" in Chambers Twentieth Century Dictionary I find it described as "a progress through life" which might conceivably serve my purpose, but "esp. advancement in profession" which could not. I have never advanced in any profession, merely marked time in one or two. With the possible exception of deciding to enter the School of Economics in 1910 and helping to start a birth-control clinic in 1925, I have never taken positive steps to initiate or open up any opportunity. Opportunities have come my way, to which I have responded, and a disjointed mish-mash of activities has been the result. I did not even seek the opportunity to record them on paper, since they seemed to me to be scarcely worth recording. But Peter Davies Ltd urged me to write an autobiography, and from time to time inquired whether I was getting on with it, so I responded to that, as to other unsought opportunities.

The finest opportunity that ever came my way was the opportunity to marry John Stocks. It was presented with arresting suddenness at the close of my first visit to Oxford. It left me momentarily stunned, and I hesitated. Thank God I did not hesitate long.

Index

Agrarian Problem in the Sixteenth Century (Tawney), 90
Alexander, the Misses, 204–5
Alexander, Samuel, 139, 151–2; bust by Epstein, 151
Angell (Sir) Norman, 89, 97
Anstey, Percy, 92
Anstey, Vera (*née* Powell), 87, 88, 92, 96
Any Questions?, B.B.C. programme, 218
Arch, Joseph, 112
Armitage, Sir Robert, 224
Arts Theatre Club, 188
Ashcroft Dame Peggy, 26, 217
Ashley, W. J., 83
Asquith, H. H. (Earl of Oxford and Asquith), 42, 52, 138: and women's suffrage, 63, 65, 67, 68; Chairman of Royal Commission on Oxford and Cambridge Universities, 128
Asquith, Margot (Countess of Oxford and Asquith), 127, 182, 183
Asquith of Yarnbury, Baroness, 64, 65, 165
Astbury, B. E., 187
Astor family, 143–7, 215–16
Astor, David, 147, 215, 216
Astor, Michael, 146 and n.
Astor, Nancy (Viscountess Astor), 143–7, 197, 216
Astor, Viscount, 144, 147, 215, 216
A.T.S. units, 170–2
Attlee, C. R. (Earl Attlee), 68, 82, 173, 174
Austen, Jane, 9, 131
Avebury, Lord, 91
Ayer, A. J., 110

Baird, Dorothea (Dolly), 18–19
Baldwin, Stanley (Earl Baldwin of of Bewdley), 78
Balfour Declaration, 228

Balfour Education Act (1902), 6, 52
Balfour, Lady Frances, 73
Ball, Sidney, 94, 95, 108, 113, 127 207
Ball, Mrs Sidney, 94, 95
Barker, Sir Ernest, 6
Barnett, Isobel (Lady Barnett), 231
Barry, Sir Charles, 232
B.B.C., 173–4, 176, 218, 231; Beveridge Committee on, 173–4
Bebel, August, 131
Bedford Square, 181–3
Beggar's Opera, original acting version, 16
Belloc, Hilaire, 87
Bell's British Theatre, 16
Benson, Sir Frank, 19
Benson, Rev. R. H. 87
Bentinck, Lord Henry, 138
Besant, Anne, 101
Bethnal Green, 184–5: Sir Wyndham Deedes' house, 184
Beveridge, Sir William (Lord Beveridge), 53, 119, 155, 167–70: Chairman of Unemployment Statutory Committee, 167–70; Beveridge Report (1942), 169; Committee on B.B.C., 173–4
Bevin, Ernest, 197
Biography (Masefield), 164
Birth control, 160–3
Blair, Sir Robert, 59
Blake, William, 159
Blumberg, Flora, 163
Board Schools, 6–7, 59–60
Boer War, the, 3
Bondfield, Margaret, 167
Bonham-Carter, Lady Violet, *see* Asquith of Yarnbury
Bottomley, Horatio, 144–5
Bowden, Dr B. V. (Lord Bowden), 206

Index

Elizabeth II, 234-5
Elliot, Walter, 172
Embassy Theatre, Swiss Cottage, 217
Emergency Exit (Foot), 226 and n.
Eminent Victorians (Strachey), 15
Emmott, Lady, 165
Engels, Friedrich, 131, 153
Epstein, (Sir) Jacob, 151
Equal Pay and the Family, 121
Ervine, St John, 161
Evans, Sir Ifor (Lord Evans of Hungershall), 216
Everyman of Everystreet (Stocks), 159

Factory Girls' Country Holiday Fund, 50, 235
Fallowfield, Manchester, 148, 149, 154, 163
Family allowances, 120-2
Farnell, Dr Lewis R., 134-7
Fawcett, Henry, 204
Fawcett, Mrs Henry (Dame Millicent), 63-5, 67, 73, 75-7, 79, 87, 121, 204: and London School of Economics, 91; characteristics, 71-2
Feather, Victor, 175
Field Work of the Family Doctor, The (Gillie Report), 213
Fifty Years in Every Street (Stocks), 154 n.
Fisher, H. A. L., 118 n.
Fisher, Mrs H. A. L., 143
Fletcher family, 117, 149-50
Fletcher, Kitty (*née* Stocks), 117, 149-50
Fletcher, Leonard, 149, 150
Fogerty, Elsie, 217
Foot, (Sir) Dingle, 147, 216
Foot, Sir Hugh (Lord Caradon), 225-7
Foot, Lady (Lady Caradon), 226
Frankenburg, Charis, 160, 161, 163
Frere, Margaret, 57-8, 185
Fry, Margery, 165
Fry, Roger, 92
Fulford, Roger, 65
Furniss, Mr and Mrs Sanderson, 111

Garrett Anderson, Dr Elizabeth, 70
Gaskell, Mrs, 148
Gedge, Evelyn, 191-2, 198
Geldart, Professor, 80, 106
George, Mrs M. D., 59
Georgian London (Summerson), 43 and n.
Gielgud, (Sir) John, 128
Gilbert, W. S., 7, 210
Gimson, Olive, 161
Girls' Public Day School Trust, 8
Gladstone, W. E., 23, 25, 222

Goodhart-Rendel, H. S. (Hal), 25
Gould, Gerald, 113
Granville-Barker, Harley, 19
Gray, Frances, 9
Greenwood, Walter, 158, 166, 178
Gregory, Lady, 19
Grenfell, Joyce, 145
Grisewood, Freddy, 218
Grivas, General, 227
Growth of English Industry and Commerce (Cunningham), 90
Gugenheim, Theo (Sir Theodore Gregory), 80, 87-9, 92, 96, 114
Guild Socialist movement, 114
Guthrie, (Sir) Tyrone, 128

Hailsham, Viscount (Quintin Hogg), 174
Haldane, R. B. (Viscount Haldane), 81
Halifax, Earl of, 174
Hambledon, Viscountess, *see* Smith, Mrs W. H.
Hammond, J. L. and Barbara, 83, 84, 90, 138, 141-3, 151, 218
Hardie, James Keir, 73
Harding, Sir John (Lord Harding of Petherton) 224-6
Hardy, Miss R. J., 134-5
Hardy, Thomas, quoted, 178
Harrison, Jane, 104
Harvey, Ethel, 37-9
Hatchlands, near Dorking, 23,26
Heberden, C. B., 106, 107
Heimann family, 131-2, 197
Heimann, Hugo, 131
Heimann, Peter, 131
Henderson, Arthur, 80
High Coombe residential college for training of midwife teachers, 215
Hill, Miranda, 56
Hill, Octavia, 53-8: and C.O.S., 53, 54; and National Trust, 56; and Poor Law Commission, 53, 54; housing work, 55-6
Himmler, Heinrich, 171
History of Trade Unionism (S. and B. Webb), 96
Hitler, Adolf, 70, 146
Hobhouse, L. T. 85, 94
Hobson, Polly (Aunt Polly), 26-7, 110
Holroyd, Michael, 13, 15
Holtby, Winifred, 128
Home Office Departmental Committee on Persistent Offenders, 165
Horder, Morley, 190
Horniman repertory company, 19, 105
House of Lords, 231-5
Houston, Renée, 218

Index

Hubback, Eva, 76, 79
Hundred Years of District Nursing, A (Stocks), 215

I, James Whittaker, 178 and n.
Imperial Institute, 3
Industrial Democracy (S. and B. Webb), 96
Inskip, Sir Thomas (Viscount Caldecote), 189
Inter-Departmental Committee on Social Insurance and Allied Services, 169
Iremonger, F. A., 156 and n.
Irving, H. B., 18
Irving, Sir Henry, 18
Irving, Laurence, 18
Israel, 228–9

James, Dr H. A., 108–9, 127
John Bull, 144
Jordan, Hashemite Kingdom of, 229–30

Keele, University of, 206
Kenny, Annie, 64
Kensington: Argyll Road, 180, 195; Aubrey House and Aubrey Lodge, 204–5; Board of Guardians, 49; Campden Hill Square, 198, 202, 204, 205; Holland Park Gardens, 181; Kensington Gardens, 9; Queen's Gate Terrace, 1–2, 4, 9–12, 93, 95, 115, 123, 124, 126, 180; St Mary Abbotts Hospital, 49, 208
Keynes, Maynard (Lord Keynes), 133
Knight, Margaret, 110
Knowles, Lilian, 84, 85, 88–90, 96
Knox, Rawle, 225
Krassin and Mme Krassin, visit to Oxford, 134
Krönert, Professor, 132
Kruger, President Paul, 3–4

Labour Exchange Act (1909), 53
Lancaster Gate, 11, 13, 22
Lansbury, George, 80
Larkin, Jim, 101
Last of the Radicals, The (Wedgwood), 16 n.
Lawrence, T. E., 101, 229
Leno, Dan, 4
Lindsay, A. D. (Lord Lindsay of Birker), 138, 206
Lindsay, Kenneth, 136
Liverpool in the thirties, 177–8
Liverpool University, 179–81
Lloyd, Selwyn, 173–4

Lloyd George, David (Earl Lloyd George), 53, 119, 129, 208: and Ireland, 138–9
London Council of Social Service (L.C.S.S.), 181–8
London School of Economics, 60, 79, 80, Chapter 6 *passim*, 99, 108, 114, 179, 181: first-year degree course, 82–4; social science diploma, 82; Clare Market Parliament, 87–8; economic history department, 88–90; Query Club, 92; present position, 97
Love on the Dole (Greenwood), 158, 166, 178
Löwe, Adolf, 163
Lytton Strachey (Holroyd), 13 n.

MacArthur, Mary, 96
Macaulay, Dame Rose, 103–5
MacDonald, Ramsay, 167
Mackinder, H. J. (Sir Halford), 81
McKisack, Professor May, 190
Macmillan, Harold, 147, 225, 226
McNair Committee on teacher training, 196
Mactaggart, Miss, 60, 81
Major Barbara (Shaw), 101
Makarios, Archbishop, 223, 225–7
Malthus, 133
Manchester College (Institute) of Science and Technology, 206, 208–9
Manchester Free Trade Hall, suffragette incident (1905), 64, 65
Manchester Guardian, 117, 138, 142, 150–3, 159, 160
Manchester University Settlement, 150, 153–5, 158–60, 183: Ancoats Hall, 153, 154, 158–60; 20 Every Street, 153–4, 160; Round House Theatre, 154, 160; Wilbraham Association, 155
Markham, Violet (Mrs Carruthers), 170–3
Marquis, Sir Frederick (Earl of Woolton), 179–81
Married Love (Stopes), 124, 162
Marshall, Alfred, 83
Martin, Kingsley, 150, 154
Marx, Karl and Marxism, 129, 131, 133
Mary Barton (Mrs Gaskell), 148
Masefield, John, 130, 164
Masters, The (Snow), 94 and n.
Maternity (Women's Co-operative Guild), 123, 124
Matheson, Hilda, 144
Maxton, James, 16
Maxwell, (Sir, Alexander, 166
May, Phil, 43

Index

Mazzini, Giuseppe, 204
Memories and Machines: The Pattern of My Life (Ricardo), 29 and n.
Mersham-le-Hatch, 196
Midwives, training of, 215
Mill, John Stuart, 63, 76, 83, 90, 236
Millicent Garrett Fawcett (Strachey), 68 n.
Mills College, California, 179
Milner, Alfred (Viscount Milner), 50
Moberly, (Sir) Walter, 138
Moberly Bell, Miss E., 55 and n.
Monteagle, Lord, 138
Montessori, Maria, 101
Montgomery of Alamein, Field Marshal Viscount, 171
Moore, Miss D., 199
Muggeridge, Malcolm, 150
Murray, Agnes, 114
Murray, Gilbert, 19, 80, 95, 101–6, 114, 130, 133
Murray, Lady Mary, 101–3, 108, 109, 130, 133

Nansen, Fridtjof, 101
National Association of Housing Managers, 55
National Council of Social Service, 155, 181, 183, 185
National Health Insurance Act (1911), 53, 208
National Health Service, 208, 210–15: London (now Inner London) Executive Council, 167, 176, 203, 208, 210–15: deputizing services, 211–13; group practices, 211; national and private medicine, 213–14; practitioners' high case-load, 210–11
National Trust, 56
National Union of Societies for Equal Citizenship, 75, 78, 121
National Union of Women's Suffrage Societies (N.U.W.S.S.), 63–5, 67, 68, 72–7: and W.S.P.U., 67; democratically controlled, 68, 76–7; processions, 73–4; and Labour Party, 76; expansion of objects, 76–8; change of name, 76, 78
Neilson, Julia, 19
Nettleship, family, 17
Nettleship, Ethel, 39
Niblett, Professor W. R., 206
1917 Club, 121
Nix, Miss, 4, 5, 43–4
Noble, Sir Andrew, 23

Observer, The and *Observer* Trust, 147, 215–17, 225
Ochs, Siegfried, 131

Octavia Hill (Moberly Bell), 55 n.
Odlum, Doris, 111
O'Hea, Father Leo, 133
Old Age Pensions Act (1908), 53
Olivia (Olivia) (Mme Bussy), 7 and n.
Omdurman, Battle of, 3
Oxford, Chapters 7 and 9 *passim*: St Michael's Street, 102, 108, 113, 115; campaign for women's degrees, 106–7, 128; St John's College, 108–9, 113, 126–8; in First World War, 127; St John's House, 126, 127, 130, 133, 138; Playhouse, 128; Royal Commission, 128; Modern Greats school instituted, 129; Austrian refugees, 130–1; German visitors, 133; University Labour Club, 134–6; Dr Farnell's Vice-Chancellorship, 134–7; and the Irish question, 137–9; St Peters, Hall, 189, 194–8; in Second World War, 196–7
Oxford, Countess of, *see* Asquith, Margot

Pankhurst, Christabel, 64, 69, 78 and n., 87
Pankhurst, Mrs Emmeline, 64–73, 78–9, 124: founds W.S.P.U., 64; imprisoned, 64, 70; and N.U.W.S.S., 67; ruthlessness, 68–9; characteristics, 70, 78; supports war effort, 78
Parliament Act (1911), 42
Patterson, Ann, *see* Stocks, Ann
Patterson, Arthur, 197, 202, 221, 224, 226, 227
Patterson, Mark, 197, 198
Patterson, Simon, 198
Paul, Kegan, 28
Peacock Pie (de la Mare), 113
Penlee House, Devonport, 26–7
Penrose, Miss, 106, 114
Pethick-Lawrence, Emmeline, 68–9, 87
Pethick-Lawrence, Fred (Lord Pethick-Lawrence), 68–70, 87
Piercy, William (Lord Piercy), 87, 88, 90, 96, 114
Pioneer cars, 30–1, 49
Pirbright Camp, 115: educational programmes, 126
Platt, J. W., 175
Playfair, Sir Nigel, 16
Plunket, Sir Horace, 101, 138
Poor Law, the, 43, 49, 86: Royal Commission on, 52–4, 208
Potter, Beatrice, *see* Webb, Beatrice
Potter, Phyllis, 45–6
Powell, Vera, *see* Anstey, Vera

[243]

Index

Power, Beryl, 93
Power, Eileen, 90, 93–4, 187
Power, Rhoda, 93, 218
Pressure Group, The Campaign for Commercial Television (Wilson), 174 and n.

Queen Elizabeth College of Domestic Science, 115, 181, 196

Rackham, Mrs C. D., 77
Radcliffe, Lord, 173, 174
Rathbone, Eleanor, 47, 75, 77–9, 119–23, 142, 162, 179, 202: analysis of casual labour in Liverpool docks, 119; and economics of motherhood, 120–1; and family allowances, 120–2; characteristics, 122–3
Redgrave, Vanessa, 217
Reeves, Pember, 81, 84
Reith, Sir John (Lord Reith), 218
Relf, Mrs, 34–7, 40
Rendel family (and Rendel Connection), 12–13, 15–17, 19–21, Chapter 3 *passim*, 42–50, 53, 54, 63, 72, 90, 94, 119, 149, 188: entrance qualification for prospective fiancés, 20–1
Rendel, Sir Alexander, 11, 22–4, 30–1, 33–4: engineering achievements, 22–3
Rendel, Anne (Mrs Herbert Rendel), 27–8
Rendel, Arthur, 28, 29
Rendel, Hon. Clare, 25–6
Rendel, Dick, 73
Rendel, Edith, 18, 24, 27, 28, 40, 47–50, 72, 73: and the Daley family, 32; Poor Law Guardian, 31, 43; work in St Pancras, 31, 43–5, 47–8
Rendel, Elinor (*née* Strachey), 48
Rendel, Elinor (Ellie), 29, 39, 40, 73
Rendel, Elsie (*née* Blair), 29
Rendel, George, 23
Rendel, Sir George, 23 and n.
Rendel, Hamilton, 23
Rendel, Harry, 27
Rendel, Herbert, 13–14, 27–8, 30, 49–50
Rendel, James (Uncle Jim), 13, 28, 39, 48–50, 73
Rendel, James Meadows, 22
Rendel, Jane, 29
Rendel, Lady (*née* Hobson), 11, 22, 24, 39–40
Rendel, Leila, 28–30, 54, 72, 166, 196: work in St Pancras, 44–7
Rendel, Hon. Maud, 25
Rendel, Ruth (*née* Paul), 28
Rendel, Stuart (Lord Rendel), 23–5: his houses, 23, 75

Rendel, William, 28
Ricardo, Beatrice (*née* Hale), 39, 72
Ricardo, David, 97
Ricardo, Esther, 40, 41
Ricardo, Halsey, 15–16, 28, 40, 41, 182
Ricardo, Harry, 29, 30, 34, 39, 49, 72: making of engines, 29, 47, 182
Ricardo, Kate (*née* Rudd), 15, 40, 182–3
Ricardo, Ralph, 39
Richardson, Ann, 190
Richardson, Miss, head clerk of L.C.S.S., 183–4, 186
Rickettswood, Charlwood, 11, 16, 22, 24, 28, 30–40, 42–4, 73, 113, 119: household staff and domestic personalities, 32–9
Robbins Committee and Report, 205, 233
Robert's Wife (Ervine), 161
Rogers, Annie, 106 and n., 107
Royal Commission on Betting and Lotteries (1932), 166
Royal Commission on Oxford and Cambridge Universities (1919), 128
Royden, Dame Maude, 71, 121, 136–7
Rugby School, 149, 179
Ruskin College, Oxford, 111, 133
Russell, Bertrand, 134, 136
Russell Square, 11, 22, 40

Saffron Hill Elementary School, 58–60
Saint Joan (Shaw), 154
St Pancras: Board of Guardians, 49; Caldecott Community, 46–7; crèche, 45, 47; Girls' Club, 43–5, 47, 50; Poor Law school, Leavesden, 48
St Paul's Girls' School, 8, 54, 57, 112
Sargent, J. S., 17, 56
Sayers, Dorothy, 85, 109, 128
Schreiner, Olive, 118
Schreiner, W. P., 118
Science and Health (Eddy), 145
Scott, C. P., 80, 117, 138–9, 150–1: bust by Epstein, 151
Selbie, Dr W. B., 137
Service women's conditions, inquiry into, 170–2
Sex Disqualification (Removal) Act (1919), 128
Shaftesbury, Lord, 72
Shaw, Bernard, 2, 5, 18 19, 87, 101, 105, 154
Shaw, Charlotte (Mrs Bernard Shaw), 93
Shelley, quoted, 163, 175

Index

Simon, Ernest (Lord Simon of Wythenshawe), 152 and n., 165, 233
Simon, Sir John (Viscount Simon), 80, 138
Simon, Shena (Lady Simon of Wythenshawe), 152, 165
Smallhythe, Ellen Terry museum, 17
Smiles, Samuel, 83
Smith, A. L., 207
Smith, J. A., 207
Smith, W. H., 7, 11
Smith, Mrs W. H. (Viscountess Hambleden) (Aunt Emily), 11
Snow, C. P., 94 and n.
Snowden, Philip (Viscount Snowden), 80
Soddy, Professor F., 137
Souvestre, Marie, 7
Spencer, Herbert, 110
Stalin, 134
Steinermayer, 130–1
Stevenson, Mr, Librarian of St John's College, Oxford, 127, 139–40
Stocks, Ann (daughter of Mary Stocks), 116, 124, 126, 143, 179, 181, 195, 198, 202, 220, 221: marriage to Arthur Patterson, 197
Stocks, Freda (sister of John Stocks), 181
Stocks, Helen (daughter of Mary Stocks), 126, 139, 179, 181, 196, 221, 223, 227–9
Stocks, Helen (sister of John Stocks), 95, 96, 109
Stocks, John, 19–20, 24, 47, 66, 69, 80, 89, 91, 96, 100–2, 104–7, 126–9, 132, 137, 143, 146, 164, 178, 181, 183, 184, 188, 220, 221, 237: engagement to Mary Brinton, 94–5; Junior Proctor, 105–6; and women's degrees, 106–7; marriage, 107; war service, 107–8, 115, 116, 124, 125; wounded, 115; awarded D.S.O., 115; religious views, 109–10; and W.E.A., 111; ardent games player, 112–13; Senior Treasurer of Oxford University Labour Club, 134, 136; Professor of Philosophy at Manchester, 139; in Manchester, 148–52; and Manchester University Settlement, 153–5, 159; and adult education, 155–7; Vice-Chancellor of Liverpool University, 163, 179–80; death, 180
Stocks, John, junior, 116, 124, 179, 181, 195, 202
Stocks, Mary: early memories, 3, 9–10; at St Paul's Girls' School, 8, 53–4, 57, 112; at Rickettswood,

40–1; and Octavia Hill, 56; and Saffron Hill School Care Committee, 58–60; at London School of Economics, 60, 81–98; and women's suffrage campaign, 66–7, 69, 72–4, 79; on Executive of N.U.W.S.S., 74; engagement to John Stocks, 94–5; marriage, 107; on staff of L.S.E., 108, 115; religious views, 110–11; tutoring at Oxford, 111; and W.E.A., 111–12, 157–8; economics lecturer at King's College, 115; and First World War, 117–19, 124–5; work for family allowances, 120–1; visits to Germany, 131–3; University Extension lecturer, 139; appointed J.P., 159, 165; playwriting, 159–60; establishes birth-control clinic, 160–3; membership of committees and commissions, 165–76, 205–15; her husband's death, 181; General Secretary of London Council of Social Service, 181–8; Principal of Westfield College, 187–203; and *Observer* Trust, 147, 215–17; and Central School of Speech and Drama, 217; broadcasting activities, 163, 218–19, 231; visit to Russia, 220; visits to Cyprus and Middle East, 221–30; elevated to Peerage, 231; in House of Lords, 231–5
Stopes, Marie, 124, 133, 160, 162
Strachey, family, 13–15, 63, 72–3
Strachey, Dorothy, *see* Bussy, Madame
Strachey, Eleanor (Mrs James Rendel), 13
Strachey, James, 13
Strachey, Lady, 13–15, 73
Strachey, Lytton, 13–15: *Spectator* reviews, 14; literary fame, 15
Strachey, Marjorie, 14, 39
Strachey, Oliver, 39
Strachey, Pernel, 14
Strachey, Philippa (Pippa), 13, 14, 39, 73, 75
Strachey, Ray (*née* Costello), 39, 68 n., 73, 75, 76, 79, 144
Strachey, Sir Richard, 13–14
Strachey, St Loe, 14
Successors, The (Irving), 18 and n.
Summerson, Sir John, 43
Sword and the Olive, The (Rendel), 23 n.
Sykes, Canon Norman, 190

Talbot Heath School, Bournemouth, 181
Tawney, R. H. 90, 95, 96, 155–7

Index